Epiduralized Birth and

Nurse-Midwifery:

Childbirth

in the

United States.

A Medical Ethnography

By

Maureen May CNM, PhD

Cover Design by Bill Krumperman, Barcelona Spain

Printed by CreateSpace.
Available from Amazon.com and other retail outlets.

This book is dedicated to my two men:
my husband, Kurt Krumperman,
and our son, Bill Sampson Krumperman.

I also wish to give remembrance to Doris Haire,
our mother of childbirth activism.

Contents

List of Figures

The Centrality of the Epidural

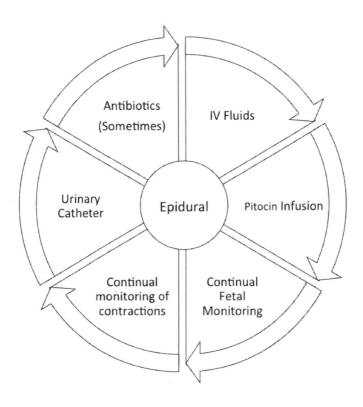

Graphic by Bill Krumperman; Barcelona, Spain

Preface

> *"Anthropologists of reproduction can help inform birthing women and clinicians, and work to improve the quality of care in childbirth, through systematic ethnographic research into local cultures of obstetric practice. ... Ethnographers are uniquely positioned with tools to access the gap between formal quality assessment measures and how work actually takes place by observing social interactions; indeed, we have long been doing this in other work settings (Christine Morton 2009, 10)."*

This book is an edited version of my 2014 doctoral dissertation: a medical ethnography of the clinical practice of nurse-midwifery in one American hospital maternity unit. Research stretched between the years 2010 and 2011 after which I received a PhD in Social Science from Syracuse University in 2014. The research was initially intended to focus on the clinical activities of American nurse-midwifery, as well as the professional culture and organization that form the basis for those clinical activities. It soon became clear, however, that I could not begin to understand American nurse-midwifery without also scrutinizing their clinical activity within the context of the overall maternity care system of the United States.

There are 11,000+ Certified Nurse-Midwives (CNM) in the United States, all of whom are licensed by the states. Most have a degree in nursing and a master's degree of midwifery. An increasing number also have a doctorate. They are credentialed by the American Midwifery Certification Board (AMCB). The AMCB also credentials 100+ Certified Midwifes (CM) in the several states that license these midwives; they do not have a nursing degree but do hold a master's of midwifery. In addition to CNMs, there are other classifications of midwives that have emerged from the homebirth movement—Certified Professional Midwives (CM); Licensed Midwives (LM); Direct-Entry Midwife (DEM), to name a few. Some of these midwives are licensed; others are not. This book is about nurse-midwifery. I do not pass judgment on the credibility on any other midwifery credential.

The reader may assume, based on the title of this book, that I am anti-epidural. An honest, careful reading will correct such an assumption. What I describe in this book is a system of childbirth where the normative use of the epidural has created an integrated, fused system of interventions, all of which have become commonplace in American maternity units. There are, of course, situations where the benefits of an epidural, and the interventions which inevitably accompany it, far outweigh its risks. For the vast majority of births in the United States, however, the benefits of an epidural do not outweigh the risks.

I am concerned about the intensive use of technology in childbirth as a routine clinical practice in the United States. At the same time I am concerned about the worldwide disparity with regards to access to lifesaving technology. Technology has its place and saves the lives of mothers and babies. The very technology that is so often used unnecessarily in US maternity units, to the detriment of mothers and babies, is inaccessible to the many mothers and babies worldwide who suffer from the lack of this same technology.

When used judiciously, modern medicine saves lives. For example, in the case of fatal hemorrhage, the life of a mother in Africa can often be saved when her provider has access to a single 1 cc vial of pitocin. When a cesarean is needed to save the life of a mother or baby, access to a medical clinic where the mother is able to have a safe, medically necessary cesarean becomes a matter of life or death. These medical interventions are all too often unavailable for women in so many parts of the world. Yet in the United States we have a cesarean rate greater than 30%, many of which are totally unnecessary. This occurs as women throughout the world die on a daily basis for lack of access to life-saving technology. I was all too aware of this as I watched pitocin flowing through the veins of most mothers—the need for pitocin caused by birth technology itself.

****

For years I have had one foot in women's health and midwifery, the other foot in social science/anthropology. Long before this, I was involved in the second-wave feminist movement. Part of that involvement included an advocacy for change in the area of women's health. I ultimately trained as both a women's health nurse practitioner (WHNP) and as a certified nurse-midwife (CNM). During these years, I also worked on my doctoral studies, first in anthropology and finally in social science.

A dramatic transformation in the American way of birth has existed as a backdrop to my life experience. My mother was born at home in 1914. Her mother was attended by a general practitioner (GP). At the time, an understanding of aseptic technique, as well as advances in the use of instruments during labor, had greatly decreased the scourge of puerperal (childbed) fever and maternal death from obstructed labor. My grandmother's family was far from wealthy but the extended family was stable. Laboring in the privacy and comfort of her home, my grandmother was likely surrounded by female relatives, who in turn would have carefully watched over the actions of the GP.

So childbirth for my maternal grandmother would have felt relatively safe compared to the past, though still entailing some risk. I do not suggest a romantic view of birth during this era. For poor women, and for women without social support, childbirth represented a circumstance of potentially dire consequences. For my grandmother, as with other women, childbirth still posed a danger of death and morbidity, although to a much lesser extent than in earlier years. My maternal grandmother, however, with her comparative comfort and support would have likely viewed childbirth more as something to be endured and she ultimately gave birth to five children.

By 1945, the year my mother delivered her first child, the situation had changed drastically. The Industrial Era had already disrupted communities and traditional support networks. Intermittent and deep social changes reinforced the upending of traditional communities. The assault on midwives by the medical profession had rapidly decreased the availability of midwives in the United States.

The era before and during World War II was a transformative moment for birth systems in Western countries. These years became a major historical moment in defining how midwifery and childbirth are today culturally and structurally crafted throughout the Western world. The decade long deprivation of the Great Depression, followed by another five years of World War II, accelerated the reorganization of childbirth practices. Hospital birth became a necessity for many families.

Later, in the years following the two world wars, social change occurred at an increasingly rapid pace. World War II had accelerated the trend toward hospital birth in the United States. Physicians were scarce and allied hospital staffing inadequate. Each Western country arrived at culturally and socially specific public policies to deal with the demands placed on health care systems during this time. Subsequently, most industrialized countries experienced a reshaping of birth practices.

My mother gave birth to her first child in a hospital ward while my father was in the military. By her account it was a highly unpleasant experience. She never described the details of the birth itself. Even when asked outright, she refused to go into the "gory" details. What she described to me was a dehumanizing, routinized care.

> I was in a hospital ward for a week. We were not allowed out of bed the entire time. What I remember most was the pain of a full bladder in the morning. The pain was unbearable. I can still hear the sound of the bedpan cart rolling down the hall, the sound of clanging bedpans. The sound meant relief. It was just awful.

Thirteen years later, with her tenth (and last) birth, the country had seen an expansion of hospitals as a result of federal money in the form of Hill-Barton grants. So with her last birth, my mother had a private room. "It was heaven," she said to me years later. She spent almost a week in the hospital, leaving behind at home her nine other children—what must have felt a like a vacation for a woman having her tenth baby. My grandmother came by train to be with her and to care for our family in her absence. This had been the case in all of her births.

And so birth has been a fact of life for me. I look at family pictures and know what year it is by the number of children in the picture, who is the youngest sibling, where I fit in the picture, and whether my mother is pregnant. For my own pregnancy, I took a very pragmatic, no-nonsense approach. Birth was a healthy state and it never occurred to me that anything could go wrong.

****

It was 1980 and I was pregnant. The sharing of birth stories was common among my friends. I heard of a thing called Friedman's Curve,[1] frequent cervix checks, and the use of a drug called pitocin. Doctors and nurses ramped up the administration of the drug to move labor along. Without IV pumps, pitocin was titrated by counting drips of the fluid. The result was often excruciating pain.[2] It seemed that an unusual number of my pregnant friends were having cesarean sections. This was peculiar to what I had known of childbirth. No one in my family had ever birthed with a cesarean, at least as far I was aware. It is no wonder then that with my anxiety I got "stuck at five", laboring against the clock as determined by Friedman's Curve. I did, however, eventually have a vaginal delivery despite these hurdles.

What I experienced was an unexpected, life-altering event. No one had told me about the moment when this baby to whom you have given birth looks into your eyes. I fell in love. I would not describe it as a spiritual moment. It was simply the relationship: pure love. My experience was so profound I wished for other women to have the opportunity to experience the same. It is also why so many nurse-midwives I have interviewed were called to midwifery. My desire was to give every woman the experience that I had: every birth is special; every baby is special, deserving of love, deserving of a mother who has fallen in love with her baby. It is a value I share with the nurse-midwives I have studied. However, so many women come from circumstances that make such an experience difficult, or impossible, to obtain.

Like so many nurse-midwives, I am not overly ideological. I am a realist. Birth is physiologic [3] and works best when undisturbed. I *respect* birth but I do not *trust* birth (a term recently taken up by some birth activists). I am all too aware of the curve balls that birth can send our way to have complete trust in birth.

5

While this book criticizes the intensification of technology as an essential element of American childbirth, it is not meant to convey that I am anti-technology. Technology saves lives when used appropriately. At the same time, I believe that the process of birth needs to be respected and mothers treated with dignity.

****

The role of informed consent, choice, and decision-making in birth is discussed throughout this book. Informed consent has become a key element of modern health care, systematized in the codes of ethics for health care professions. My perspective on this essential element of nurse-midwifery care was influenced by a personal experience that occurred while I was in the process of writing my dissertation. In late 2013/early 2014, I came upon medical records revealing that major surgery I underwent in 2009 had been performed with significant medical information concealed from me. The lobectomy, as I discovered much later, had been quite avoidable. I am still experiencing the consequences of going through a potentially fatal surgery with relevant information having been kept from me. This betrayal by my surgeon, the lack of informed consent, and concealment of significant information, led me to reassess my data. The resulting rewrite of the dissertation gives greater consideration to the role of informed consent, or the lack therein, at the labor and delivery research site.

I have had doubts throughout this research, my dissertation, and now the publication of this book. The process has been quite a journey. First-generation students often face hindrances unfamiliar to other students. I had the same doubts that many other first-generation PhD students' experience. There were times when I felt that I had overstepped my place in life, resulting in periods of personal paralysis.

Some obstacles include the bias of professors and administrators, both overt and covert. Other obstacles are a continuation of systemic institutional traditions while others come from personal feelings of inadequacy. Some obstacles are simply ignorance on the part of the student regarding the formal, and informal, rules of the game. Only individuals who have faced these limitations can fully understand the urge to pull away. I too encountered these limitations from time to time. With my self-doubt, I considered settling for ABD (all but dissertation). However, I remained aware of the importance of my project, and was fortunate to have the support of several professors who honored me with their encouragement and advice. They know who they are. I will forever hold dear the memory of their kindness and support.

****

This research falls firmly within the tradition of ethnography. Participatory observation is fundamental to how anthropology defines itself in relation to other disciplines, even as we make use of a variety of research methods, both qualitative and quantative (Frankel and Devers 2000). At the same time, my research is quite transdisciplinary, drawing on medical research, public policy, history, sociology, as well as anthropology. Within which discipline does this research reside? Can we place it within the boundaries of a single academic discipline? I will let the reader choose to place my work where they will.

After receiving numerous rejections from publishers, I decided to publish through Amazon's CreateSpace. It was a decision not easily made. For new authors this has become a viable option as publishers increasingly cut back on their portfolio of titles. I also chose, as a result, to format this book myself. I faced a steep learning curve. However, I encourage other authors to do the same. It gave me a sense of control over my work, which I cherish. It also gave me a sense of ownership as well as an intimate relationship with my work that is sometimes lost when an author hands over a book to a publisher for editing and book design.

A short note on this book's format: Endnotes can be found at the end of each section. They are substantive; I encourage the reader to look at them. Several unorthodox decisions have been made with regard to punctuation. I have chosen to place two spaces, as opposed to one, at the end of a sentence. (The Chicago Manual of Style 16th edition accepts this as an option.) In my opinion, one space following end of sentence punctuation does not create the strong, visual pause needed for clarity. One space results in an optic where sentences tend to run into each other. The book was formatted using Microsoft Word. Word does not provide the option of a 1.5 spacing between sentences and so I continue to use two spaces.

With regards to the relationship of quotation marks and punctuation, I have chosen to adapt a commingling of American and British rules of punctuation. My own rules are as follows: when a quotation mark clearly signifies the end of a complete quote, the quotation mark follows punctuation. When quotation marks are used to emphasize a term, or a collective quote, I have placed punctuation after the quotation mark. In the end, I place punctuation where I hope it will provide clarity of meaning for the reader—choosing to avoid a fixed rule. In general, I find the British rules to be more commonsensical than the American rule, that a comma or period must always be placed before a quotation mark, whether for quotation or emphasis.

With regards to transcription from midwife interviews, I have utilized conventions common to ethnographers. "MAM" refers to the researcher (myself). When text has been left out in a quotation, I have utilized ellipses to reveal to the reader the omission. I have used italics to reflect the emphasis of a word or phrase in the voice of the interviewee. Where I have added words for clarity's sake, those words have been placed in brackets.

---

[1] Friedman's Curve refers to a graph developed by the obstetrician Emanuel Friedman, which provided a visual representation for what is considered to be a normal

[2] This was before IV pumps. Nurses counted drips in order to titrate infusion rates. I had one friend who told a story of a doctor coming in saying, "We need to speed things up here," and he proceeded to just open up the IV.

[3] One definition of physiologic birth: "A normal physiologic labor and birth is one that is powered by the innate human capacity of the woman and fetus (Consensus Statement by ACNM, MANA, and NACPM 2112a; 529)." Characteristics of physiologic birth include, "spontaneous onset and progress of labor", and the "biologic and psychologic conditions that promote effective labor."

Introduction
The Centrality of the Epidural

"Anthropology can benefit from viewing reproduction itself as a key site for understanding the ways in which people re-conceptualize and re-organize the world in which they live (Cecilia Van Hollen 2003, 5)."

"Every life has only one beginning. You owe it to yourself and your baby to make it the very best possible (Doris Haire 1994)."

This medical ethnography provides rich, thick description of the clinical practice of nurse-midwives at a Community Hospital—a small hospital in a medium-sized American city. The names of the nurse-midwives, as well as the name of the hospital, remain anonymous. These midwives graciously brought me into their circle, allowing me to observe them as they practiced their art and science of midwifery. They did so out of love and commitment to their patients and profession, as well as to further their mission to provide quality, humane care to mothers and babies. I was continually amazed by their dedication and service even as they faced a highly technological system of birth, a system in which they found it necessary to negotiate their own beliefs and actions against the demands of the American system of birth.

When choosing to carry out ethnographic research in a hospital setting, I was acutely aware of the paucity of such research. The anthropologist Christine Morton (2009) has pointed out this very fact—the lack of research in the arena of mainstream obstetrical institutional practices—and has challenged reproduction social scientists to attend to this deficiency in academic research.

> Much social science research on US childbirth has largely focused on the 1% of women choosing homebirth and their midwives ... Focusing on edge cases leaves mainstream obstetrics and everyday practices in hospital birth unexamined. There have been very few ethnographic studies of more prevalent maternity care roles, such as doulas, childbirth educators, labor and delivery nurses and obstetricians.

> Improving childbirth outcomes in the US will require
> thick description and earnest efforts to understand the
> cultures that have created current obstetric practices and
> the variation that exists within and between them.
> Unfortunately, reproductive scholars often dismiss
> conducting research on obstetric practices in hospitals as
> too difficult (in terms of access) or uninteresting
> (because they are mainstream). However, approximately
> 99% of women are giving birth in hospital settings;
> without systematic ethnographic research findings,
> these women will not be fully informed on how obstetric
> care is delivered, in all its variation (Morton 2009, 10).

This ethnography analyzes the hospital-based clinical practice
of American nurse-midwives through the lens of one nurse-
midwifery service. The research made no claim as to the
generalizability of one clinical practice to that of all nurse-
midwives. However, having interviewed many nurse-midwives
over the past ten years (along with field observations) I am
convinced the ethnographic evidence suggests that the
epiduralized[4] births I witnessed at Community Hospital are
indeed the rule rather than the exception.[5]

It is difficult for ethnographers to carry out our unique
methodology within modern institutions. This is particularly true
in health care settings. IRB (Institutional Review Board) criteria
make observation-based research in health care settings difficult
to carry out in a way that protects the rights of subjects, while at
the same time obtaining enough data to give ethnographic
research a degree of validity. This is especially true in the world
of obstetrics. Beyond ethical considerations, many obstetricians
are leery of the inclusion of the ethnographer's gaze on the
maternity setting.

Three key areas of interest are woven throughout this book:
(1) The role of nurse-midwifery at Community Hospital,
particularly the ways in which nurse-midwives navigate care,
attempting to maintain their value system while at the same time
conforming to an obstetrical system of care at odds with those
values. (2) An analysis of a maternity system of care that has
increasingly utilized technology to replace one-on-one care. (3)
Description of the interactions between providers and mothers.

Unlike some academics, I observed and describe women to be active agents: self-aware and demanding technological interventions.

Nurse-midwives face a paradox in today's labor and delivery units. Physiologic, undisturbed birth (a value that nurse-midwives hold dear) must often be negotiated with obstetrical care processes that are in opposition to the process of midwifery care. The demands of mothers, staff, obstetricians, and the overall needs of the hospital contribute to this paradox. Nurse-midwifery's professional history, including long-held values of pragmatism and an incremental approach to change, helps to explain how nurse-midwives survive in this discordant environment.

Midwives at Community Hospital consistently talked up physiologic birth during prenatal care, discouraged elective induction of labor, and encouraged vaginal birth after cesarean (VBAC). They were proud of what they claimed was an 18% cesarean rate as compared to a national rate of approximately 33%. (As will be seen later in this book, their understanding of the hospital's cesarean rate was inaccurate.) Despite the philosophical beliefs and clinical opinions of the nurse-midwives, the vast majority of mothers chose to avail themselves of highly technical births, demanding induction and epidurals. Within the modern notion of individual choice, nurse-midwives find it difficult to sway mothers away from the intensive birth technology that has come to be expected by mothers and physicians alike.

A central element of this ethnography is the description of an extreme, intensified use of technology in American childbirth. In wealthy, developed countries, the social and cultural aspects of childbirth are quite different than from thirty to forty years ago. Wealthy countries have embraced technology and most have adopted centralization and regionalization of maternity services in normal birth. The technology of modern birth, however, is particularly intensive in the United States as compared to European countries.

Another significant characteristic of the American way of birth includes the fact that birth falls under the professional control of the obstetrical profession as opposed to midwifery. American birth is also entrenched within a privatized, two-tiered health care system. Childbirth costs in the U.S. are three times that of other wealthy countries (Perkins 2004; IFHP 2012). Despite these excessive expenditures for childbirth and newborn care, we see in the United States a perinatal death rate that in some communities mirrors that of poor, developing nations (MacDorman et al. 2013; OECD 2013).

Increased use of nurse-midwives has long been identified as a key reform for improving health care outcomes of mothers and babies in the United States (Gabay and Wolfe 1995a, 1995b; Pew Health Professions Commission 1999). Studies have shown that clinical outcomes of nurse-midwives are equal or superior to that of obstetricians (MacDorman and Singh 1998; Rosenblatt et al. 1997). Furthermore, significant cost savings are associated with nurse-midwifery care (Rosenblatt et at. 1997; Gabay and Wolfe 1987, 1995b).

While these outcome studies show a difference in obstetrical and nurse-midwife care, they do not explain this phenomenon. Much of nurse-midwifery clinical practice intersects that of obstetrical practice and yet is quite different. What is it about the way that nurse-midwives provide care that results in better outcomes, even when nurse-midwives and obstetricians work in the same clinical setting? I believe that the significant differences revealed by these outcome studies result from factors that are intangible and difficult to quantify. An imbedded, qualitative approach unique to ethnographic methodology, as carried out in my research, is well-suited to better understand the care provided by nurse-midwives.

As is common in ethnographic studies, my focus shifted during fieldwork. There have been numerous books by academics and activists alike analyzing and critiquing the American way of birth. I did not set out to add to this abundance of work. However, I found it difficult to study nurse-midwives out of the context of the system of birth in which they negotiate clinical practice. I also discovered that critical research in the area of American childbirth is outdated. My research provides further understanding of the extent to which the birth process in the

United States has been distorted through the progressive intensification of technology.

What I observed during fieldwork is a profound change in our system of childbirth, a change of immense consequence that has rapidly occurred over several decades. The overwhelming use of epidurals for pain relief, and the inevitable augmentation of labor with pitocin that accompanies it, has cemented a mechanized and routinized system of childbirth that is now conceived of as normal.

Epiduralized birth is the end result of a progressive use of technology and interventions in the process of birth. For at least three decades, academics and social critics of interventionist obstetrics have used the term *cascade of interventions* to describe a phenomenon where one intervention leads to another. The term was accurate in the 1970s and 1980s with the advent of the increased practice of augmentation of labor and external fetal monitoring—a response to the routine adoption of Friedman's Curve by the obstetrical profession. However, we have moved beyond a cascade of interventions; it is an outdated term. What I observed at Community Hospital was an entirety of interventions with the epidural at its core—what I call the centrality of the epidural.

The cascade of interventions has been standardized into a complex entirety of interventions, all of which work in alignment with the other, making up a complete whole—a Gleichschaltung [6] of birth, if you will. Interventions are enmeshed in the process of epiduralized birth, operating in tandem, with each performing an essential, inseparable role in relation to the other. This uniform, totalistic way of birth occurs as a complete procedure. If we view normality as a hegemony of practices that have come to be taken for granted in the context of power relations (Van Hollen 2003), then the system of epiduralized birth can be viewed as occurring within a hegemonic medical system that has redefined the very meaning of human birth.

I use several terms to describe this system of birth. *Epiduralized birth* is the term I use to describe an inseparable entirety of interventions made inevitable with the centrality of the epidural. Odent (2002) uses the term *industrialized birth*, referring to the intensification of technology seen in birth throughout the developed world. Walsh (2006b) refers to *assembly-line birth* and *Fordism* to describe highly technical birth. These terms are close in meaning yet are also distinct. Industrialized birth, in the sense used by Odent, refers to the manipulation of the ecology of birth in the industrial age. Assembly-line birth describes the factory-like conditions of maternity care where birth is routinized, standardized and managed. Epiduralized birth, as I use the term, encompasses both industrialized birth and assembly-line birth.

How do we explain the appeal of epiduralized birth? Given the active decision-making by women, as described in this book, the appeal cannot be attributed simply to patriarchy or the male take-over of birth. Nor is it merely the movement of the place of birth from home to hospital. Nor can it alone be explained as the transformation of birth into a medical case rather than a social event. We are not dealing simply with authoritative knowledge where women acquiesce and give up decision-making to those in power. The industrialization of birth has not been merely the result of organizational rationalization. Nor can cultural hegemony in the Gramscian sense completely explain the compelling attraction of epiduralized birth. Nor are we merely dealing with obstetrical monopoly; I have seen too many women walk away from the option of a non-medicalized birth: So it is all of these and yet more.

The term *cascade of interventions* continues to be used to such an extent that its true meaning has become obscured and its origin unclear. The term is often attributed to Suzanne Arms' (1981[1975]) book *Immaculate Deception,* an early theoretical critique of obstetrics. However, Arms did not use the precise term *cascade of interventions.* Instead, she described a *merry-go-round of interventions.*

> Of course not every doctor nor every hospital is so technologically dependent as to subject all normal births to all interferences. The point is that generally one intervention leads to another in a kind of merry-go-round that not only increases risk to the baby, but also strips the birth mother of control of her own birth (Arms 1981[1975], 109).

This *merry-go-round of interventions,* as described by Arms, has become a complex of interventions that fit together as a unitary whole as opposed to a cascade. I doubt if Arms' assertion that women are "deceived" and "coerced" into a way of giving birth would ring true for the many women today who are demanding the very interventions that she saw as a reflection of patriarchy and male control over birth—"an autonomous world of authoritarian rule to which *all* [italics original] patients must conform if they are to regain their health and return to society (Arms 1981[1975], 63)."

This view of birth as rooted in patriarchy and male domination, has been echoed in academic literature. An analysis of epiduralized birth that emphasizes patriarchy camouflages the extent to which mothers are involved in the decision-making within today's labor and delivery units. The patients at Community Hospital were women with vivid memories of being denied epidurals while women of means have had ready access. I can only imagine what access to inductions and epidurals must represent for the women who received care at Community Hospital, ninety-five percent of whom were African American and on Medicaid. The hegemony of modern obstetrics can look quite different through the eyes of poor women who have historical memories of crushing health care disparities.

Given the reality of daily life for many mothers, including those at Community Hospital, the desire for interventions such as inductions can be quite rational. It is an irony that the physiologic birth advocated for by midwives has become a privilege for many mothers. Work, transportation, and the lack of social support are real factors that play into the decision-making of today's mothers, many of whom adamantly demand induction of labor and epidurals.

With most pregnancies, ultrasounds are anticipated with excitement: the more the better. Each and every ultrasound represents proof that a baby is healthy and alive. The tragedy is that the proof of a baby's health, traditionally found in the mother-baby-connection, is lost—the feel of the baby's rhythms, knowing when it is asleep, feeling its vigorous kicking when it is awake, having the awareness that the baby responds to noises around it, placing one's hand over your belly and feeling the baby move in response. These mother/fetus interactions no longer represent proof that a baby is alive and well. We no longer trust our own body to tell us that the baby in fact exists. For this we rely on an ultrasound picture.

Epiduralized birth represents a crisis in our relationship to the self and the transcendental aspects of life, a modern crisis in the very meaning of life: a conflict described by Charles Taylor in *A Secular Life*. Taylor describes this crisis of self as a lack of "fullness" in the secular world that we all struggle to rediscover. "We have moved," says Taylor, "from a world in which the place of fullness was understood as unproblematically outside of or 'beyond' human life, to a conflicted age in which this construal is challenged by others which place it (in a wide range of different ways) 'within' human life (Taylor 2007, 15)." Life was simpler when construed through the certainty of religious doctrine. Birth was God's will and we bowed to it.

The question for us now is this: How do we as modern humans understand life? What is our understanding, our perception, of the emergence of new life into this world? For some romanticists, birth is a moment when a baby is born coming "into vibes full of crystal clear life force (Gaskin 1975, 252)." For others, it is a Kodak or, more recently, a Twitter or iPhone moment. Birth no longer resembles the type of social event it once was, a time of joy and an event to share with those to whom we are close. Rather, it has become a time to feel special as an individual in this isolating world. It is a brief time to escape from our generic life. Instant messaging and twitter has taken over the moment of birth. It is a time to stand out from the crowd at the expense of taking in the beauty of the moment.

When it comes to choosing a technological birth, for most mothers the choice is simple: the technology is available; why not use it? As one midwife confided to me, "Both my daughters had epidurals with their birth. Their attitude was, 'Why would *anyone* want to feel pain?' " The problem lies in the fact that even as women embrace birth technology, mothers who are engaged in decision-making are not provided complete information. The very technology they see as representing modernity, convenience, and equality has not been proven to be safe in scientific studies. In fact, evidence points to the possibility that the interventions inherent to epiduralized birth may in fact be dangerous for both the mother and baby.

I doubt that the many mothers who avail themselves of every birth intervention possible are aware of the philosophical foundations and justification for epiduralized birth. How many mothers recognize that their embrace of birth technology, a birth that need not be felt nor experienced in any way that is remotely natural or existential, was articulated by radical feminist theorists like Shulamith Firestone? Firestone, in her treatise *The Dialectic of Sex. The Case for Feminist Revolution* presented the case for reproduction as the basis for women's oppression. Natural birth was in and of itself oppressive for women, "oppressive power structures set up by nature and reinforced by man (Firestone 1970, 23)." In the world of epiduralized birth, the philosophy of the radical feminist Shulamith Firestone has become mainstream.

One nurse-midwife, who was involved early on in the alternative childbirth movement, said to me, "The fundamental problem is that [obstetrics took] what is a 24/7 human process and ... tried to turn it into a nine to five business." Cohen and Esner (1983) said essentially the same thing decades ago.

> Problems arise ... when we interfere with Nature's plan, when we egotistically believe that we have a design that surpasses the original, and when we believe that our technology can produce a birth process superior to Nature's own. When we become so confident as to believe that we can reproduce and redesign such a complex event as birth, we are assuming that we can, indeed, play God ... We believe that birth requires teamwork among mother, uterus, and baby, and that all three know instinctively how to work together to complete the process . (1983, 1-3).

Decades have passed since these words were written. During that time modern obstetrics has continued its march to an ever more intensive use of technology and has wrought an "epidemic" of cesarean sections (a word used by numerous writers). Despite research and activism, the pace in the use of birth technology has continued unabated. It is very possible that we have engaged in an enormous human scientific experiment, and the stakes are quite high. As prophetically stated by Cohen and Esner (1983:3), "We see a fascination with technology that may someday actually destroy the blueprints for natural birth."

Thoughts on Research

I have previously presented my thoughts on the nature of ethnographic research. This basic approach to ethnographic research, one that I wrote in 2006, continues to be reflected in my work.

> Ethnography is both a framework and a method of research. As a framework, ethnography holds as a core value the concept that there are real parts of the world and the human experience that cannot be quantified. Ethnographic research involves back-and-forth dialogue and close relationships between researchers and informants. Through this process, the ethnographer is able to access information unobtainable through other methodologies. ... Ethnography recognizes that "facts" are not only contested, but are reflected in the richness and details of the informant's own words, and thus requires that the voices of the individuals under study be heard to the greatest extent possible (May and Davis-Floyd 2006, 84).

I place high value on providing extensive quotes from informants, in this case from midwives. I do so not only that their voices will be heard but also to illuminate the facts as I have observed them. As with all ethnographers, the words of informants, as well as my observations, are the hard-core data that I work with. Statistics enhances my observations and interviews.

The initial research question was to look at how nurse-midwifery care results in positive outcomes along with cost efficiency. From that research question flowed a research design and Institutional Review Board (IRB) protocols. Finding a site and working through two IRB committees (my university and the hospital) created more than a fair share of obstacles. The research design included data collection, clinical observations, interviews, as well as the use of archival information and observation at professional meetings. Prior to writing my dissertation proposal, I gathered survey data from 600 respondents. (The survey had been randomly sent to 1,000 CNMs.) A further source of data, which became significant, was a review of medical research. This came about as a result of questions regarding the safety of the epiduralized births that I observed.

During my observations, I took note of common characteristics among the midwives—the care and concern provided to clients; the intimacy and emotional connection between the mother and individual nurse-midwifes; the time given for education and individualized care; the fight by midwives to provide the patience and time needed for patients to successfully give birth vaginally. These professional characteristics are discussed in later chapters. They all go to the heart of the culture of nurse-midwifery. I had expected that many mothers would express satisfaction with the care given to them but was surprised by what I can only describe as overwhelming satisfaction with nurse-midwifery care.

As previously described, I ultimately strayed away from my original proposal and while doing so had to be conscious of my activities so as to stay within the confines set by two IRBs. The modern ritual of ethnography involves an initial development of an elaborate research design. This is often an expectation of the IRB even before the ethnographer has stepped into the research site. I soon learned that it was necessary to move beyond the initial research design. Ethnographic research requires flexibility and adaptability to the realities of the environment in question.

Ethnography is increasingly a family of approaches. Ethnographic methodology faces an academic world where research involves the crossing of traditional academic boundaries, what Horlick-Jones and Sime (2004) refer to as "border-work" or "transdisciplinarity". Cross-disciplinary work, both in research design as well as teamwork among researchers from various academic disciplines, is increasingly recognized as necessary to address progressively complicated problems presented by the modern world. The process of crossing borders, drawing from various disciplines and methodologies, has become a necessary development in the production of knowledge as well as meeting the need "to develop such cross-disciplinary understandings so as to embody the active ways in which people make sense of their worlds... (Horlick-Jones and Sime 2004, 442)."

The design of an ethnographic research project is a "process" as opposed to a static protocol, as Marcus (2009) has pointed out. Marcus describes the ethnographic project as employing artistic methods, similar to that of art and design. Ethnography, in Marcus' vision, should be "rethought as a design process"... that would "encompass and preserve classic fieldwork perhaps still as a core modality (2009,26-27)." The modern world, with components varied and in constant motion, cannot be studied with a fixed protocol as one would in a laboratory. I have never agreed with Geertz (1973) that there is no true reality to be discovered through the interpretive process. However, I have come to see that the ethnographic process does indeed involve a great deal of interpretation.

The reader of this ethnography will feel my passion. I felt in the core of my being the frustration of nurse-midwives as they engaged in births contrary to their values. At the same time, I have strived to make my observations as neutral as possible and am comfortable with the fact that I have incorporated objectivity with my passion. As Rosaldo (1993[1989], 168) asks in his discussion of the "myth of detachment", can there truly be such a thing as value free inquiry in social science? A firm answer to this question eludes us. As ethnographers, the best we can do is to attempt to keep an open eye and an open mind, while recognizing our own biases. We also cannot sit by merely observing. Advocacy has become an essential element of the ethnographic process.

Ethnography is confronting a global village. All ethnographers grapple with the methodological issue of insider research. Self-reflexivity has become an essential element of ethnographic research for precisely the purpose of bringing to light the inevitable biases of the researcher. The questions for me as a nurse-midwife were these: Am I too close to the subject of my research? Can I get this story right? Ironically, it was my desire to get the story right, my very passion and concern about maternity care, that helped drive this research. Perhaps the entire concept of insider researcher, the concern surrounding bias, is itself an invention. In the end, isn't it probable that all ethnographers ultimately become an insider, even if they begin their research as an outsider?

My place as both a midwife and an ethnographer places me in the position of "virtual anthropologist" (Weston (2000). In both realms, that of midwife and ethnographer, I am in a sense "the other". I do not completely belong to either discipline. However, I have come to believe that it is my very place as a hybrid, somehow always "the other" even when inside my profession, that has made it possible for me to write what I believe is a credible, persuasive description of maternity care at Community Hospital.

---

[4] The epidural is a form of spinal anesthesia that involves the administration of a local anesthetic (usually bupivacaine) and a low-dose opiate (often fentanyl) via a catheter that is placed into the epidural space of the spinal column, resulting in the blockage of nerve impulses to the uterus and pelvic region.

[5] There are no reliable estimates of the rate of epidural use during labor and delivery in the United States. I estimate that approximately 80% of mothers at Community Hospital received an epidural. Osterman and Martin (2011) estimate the epidural rate to be about 60% nationwide. They state that there is wide variation based on region and ethnicity.

[6] It is difficult to provide a transliteration for the word Gleichschaltung. In the German language, its original meaning refers to a state where all elements of a mechanical system work in concert with the other so that the whole operates as one. According to Evans (2004), the closest translation for the word is "co-ordination", a mechanical state where all elements must work in unison for a system to function. The source of the term lies in electrical mechanics, where an electrical system only functions when all circuits are in sync and interconnected. The word took on political meaning as a cultural metaphor during Fascist Germany. The term's political-cultural meaning refers to the totalistic nature of the social system within the Third Reich. As will be discussed, this is similar to the state of epiduralized birth, with each intervention serving to create a uniform, standardized system of birth.

Chapter One
Theoretical Discussion: The Social Science
of American Childbirth

"The natural childbirth movement of the 1970s and 1980s highlighted a growing recognition of the intimate relationship between the physiological aspects of parturition and their social and organizational management. ... There is no known society where birth is treated ... as a merely physiological function. ... it is everywhere socially marked and shaped. ... To speak of birth as a biosocial event, then, suggests and recognizes at the same time this universal biological function and the culture-specific matrix within which human biology is embedded (Brigitte Jordon 1993[1978], 3)."

Over the last forty to fifty years, there has been a proliferation of popular and academic literature on childbirth and midwifery—both cross-cultural analysis of childbirth systems as well as research that specifically discusses the American system of childbirth. Social scientists studying American midwifery and the American system of childbirth, anthropologists and sociologists alike, have been drawn to study direct-entry midwifery and homebirth. Numerous works have been written (both published and unpublished) describing direct-entry midwives[7] and the homebirth movement. There has been a proliferation of personal narratives by direct-entry midwives [8] as well as oral histories of traditional southern African American midwives.

The study of nurse-midwifery and hospital birth, by comparison, has been ignored. Direct-entry midwifery and homebirth practice are exotic. Perhaps just as important to the researcher, homebirth is more easily accessible for study, lacking the obstacles that come with carrying out research within health care institutions.

The disinterest in nurse-midwifery may also come from a larger bias. In the past, nurse-midwives have been dismissed by direct-entry midwives, and some academics, as sell-outs for their accommodation to obstetrics. The logic is thus: because nurse-midwives must negotiate their everyday clinical practice to accommodate modern obstetrics, what they do cannot be "true" midwifery (Arms 1981; Simonds, Rothman and Norman 2006) nor "authentic" midwives (Odent 2002).

On the other hand, nurse-midwives are feared by the obstetrical profession, even as obstetricians have come to rely ever more on the nurse-midwife—under their supervision of course. Obstetricians fear, at their core, that nurse-midwives threaten their monopoly over normal childbirth. Perinatologists, a subspecialty of obstetrics, have become the expert in high-risk pregnancy. If midwives are recognized as independent experts in normal birth, what is left for obstetricians?

As Jordan (1993[1978]) pointed out, it is very difficult for researchers studying the American system of childbirth to gain access to hospitals as research sites. The American medical establishment has little to gain from having the gaze of critical researchers placed upon them. As a result, the voices of nurse-midwives have remained unheard, for the most part, by non-medical academics. This is a significant gap in our academic study of American childbirth.

Origins of Academic Interest in Childbirth and Midwifery

The interconnection between academic interest in childbirth, also discussed as reproduction, and popular movements predate the latest literature. Prior to postmodernism, academic interest in childbirth was heavily influenced by a materialist and structural outlook. Engels (1884) placed reproduction on par with, and in a dialectical relationship with, the means of production, with both determining the course of human history. Reflective of the strong influence of structuralism on the discipline of anthropology, early anthropologists "tended to focus on how reproductive practices and beliefs reflected social and cultural systems (Van Hollen 2003, 5)."

Margaret Mead was perhaps the singular social scientist to first look upon childbirth from the standpoint of women, both as individuals and as a group, as opposed to regarding mothers as unaware agents of the historical march of society and its structural elements. She was also influenced by the social movements of her time. Her work on maternal-infant attachment in the 1960s reflected a growing interest in childbirth, not only as a social process, but also as an interaction between physiological, social, and cultural factors. The popular movements of the time influenced her academic interests—the movement for legalization of birth control and abortion, as well as the La Leche League movement (Grimm 1967).

Popular writings emergent from the Women Rights Movement, and soon afterward the Alternative Childbirth Movement, captured the attention of a generation of young women, activists and academics alike, beginning in the late 1960s. Firestone (1970) in *The Dialectic of Sex* argued that for women to gain equality they need to free themselves from the binds of biology; that their reproductive capacity forms the basis for their oppression as women (see Introduction).

Firestone's theoretical critique of human birth was broader than the notion that pain during birth is inhumane. Firestone's critique extended to an advocacy of technological birth as liberating for women. She stated that "natural is not necessarily a 'human value' (1970, 18)," and eschewed the very physicality of birth. "Artificial reproduction" presented the possibility of true equality of the sexes. Through technology, it would be possible for men to carry the "burden" of childbirth. It was through technology that women would be liberated from the fundamental oppression created by their biological status as breeders. "Pregnancy is barbaric," Firestone asserted. "Pregnancy is the temporary deformation of the body of the individual for the sake of the species (1970, 18)." I wonder if Firestone, in later years, ever considered that the very technology she advocated as liberating had brought about the "age of the fetus" (Bridges 2011). This alienating, mechanized separation of the maternal-fetal unit, a characteristic of a highly technological approach to birth, is profoundly disempowering of women.

Within this same women's movement, a very different, antithetical, philosophy towards childbirth was developing: a nascent critique of the modern obstetrical profession. This critique held that childbirth had become medicalized and lacked a respect for normal childbirth. Modern obstetrics, with its mechanistic, patriarchal notions, as well as its corresponding clinical practices, had turned childbirth into an assembly-line activity. This philosophical wing of the second-wave women's rights movement viewed the struggle over control of childbirth as a form of self-empowerment.

Firestone's work was quickly followed by *Our Bodies, Ourselves* (Boston Women's Health Book Collective 1971), a book that presented a very different take on biology. Women could empower themselves by coming to know their bodies. In many ways, these two works set up an oppositional duality within the second wave feminist movement—a contradiction between those who rejected childbirth as a fundamental part of what it means to be female and those who embraced, and to some extent romanticized, childbirth, as is reflected in Ina May Gaskin's (1975) *Spiritual Midwifery*.

Mainstream feminist organizations, in the meantime, focused on a limited vision of women's reproductive rights, fighting for an equal rights amendment and the right to contraception and abortion. At the same time, some childbirth activists, most notably midwives at The Farm,[9] opposed abortion rights. It was only in the past fifteen to twenty years that the National Organization of Women, finally bridging this biology impasse, passed a resolution stating that the right of each woman to decide where and with whom to give birth is a fundamental aspect of reproductive freedom.

In 1973, Ehrenreich and English published a political treatise, *Witches, Midwives and Nurses*, which claimed a historical connection between midwifery and the persecution of witches in medieval Europe. While slim on historical documentation, their work was a bridge between the world of academia and the popular women's movement. Their book inspired interest within academia for the study of the social science of childbirth and midwifery, even as childbirth was becoming increasingly technical and managed.

During this developmental period of a fledging homebirth movement, the American College of Nurse-Midwives (ACNM) did not support homebirth. (This has since changed.) At the very moment in time when the homebirth movement was gaining momentum, the ACNM, in 1973, took an official position against homebirth, stating that hospital was the safest and "preferred site for childbirth" (Rooks 1997, 67). The ACNM's rejection of homebirth was a factor in the rise of direct-entry midwifery. ACNM's leadership failed to recognize the possibilities for American nurse-midwifery in the alternative childbirth movement. At the same time, direct-entry midwives painted a broad brush in dismissing nurse-midwives as "med-wives". Women who were alienated from the rise of assembly-line birth became determined to have their babies at home. Completely on their own, marginalized by the obstetrical profession, they set about learning by doing, whatever the costs; nurse-midwifery, itself a marginalized profession at the time, did not stand with them. A divide was created within American midwifery, a divide that is only now beginning to be reconciled.[10]

The debate, conflict, and dialogue between nurse-midwives and direct-entry midwives went on for years. The debate was both public and private. The private debate between these two American threads of midwifery took on the form of what Scott (1985, 1990) calls the "hidden transcripts" of political subordinates. These hidden transcripts centered on the issues of safety, professional competence, credentialing, and education. The following is a prototype of such debates.

> Nurse-Midwife: You have copped out.
> Direct-Entry Midwife: No I haven't. I've opted out.
>
> Direct-Entry Midwife: You have sold out.
> Nurse-Midwife: No I haven't. I'm holding out.
>
> (May and Davis Floyd 2006, 121)

Also significant for the developing alternative childbirth movement at the time were two highly charged critiques of the American obstetrical system. Suzanne Arms (1981) in *Immaculate Deception* was the first to describe the "wheel of interventions" that characterized the growing medicalization of birth. Her critique of our system of childbirth was not restricted to obstetricians. She criticized the role of nurse-midwives for their involvement in hospital birth, essentially characterizing the profession as having sold out—a characterization that has stuck even as the nurse-midwifery profession has evolved.

The voice of a generation of women facing the alienation of medicalized birth, including the growing trend of unnecessary cesarean sections, was also reflected in Cohen and Esner's *Silent Knife* (1983). Their criticism of the cavalier attitude of the obstetrical profession toward rising cesarean rates, along with a passionate comparison of unnecessary cesarean to rape, was compelling. Their voice represented a growing popular movement of resistance to cesarean sections. *The American Way of Birth* by the influential author Jessica Mitford (1992), while appearing later than other popular works, added to the social commentary of American childbirth because of its documentation and measured tone.

These popular books heavily influenced an entire generation of women, giving voice to a (mostly) white, middle class, alternative childbirth movement. It is probable that female academics, taking up the study of childbirth and midwifery starting in the 1970s, were strongly influenced by these works. Their subsequent academic works have been advocacy driven. The early characterization of nurse-midwifery, in popular works, as having sold out to the medical profession can perhaps partially explain the lack of interest among these academics regarding the nurse-midwifery profession.

Childbirth and Midwifery in the Social Sciences

Within academia, historians led the study of American childbirth starting in the early 1970s; their works are numerous.[11] The academic discourse on childbirth and midwifery has also been influenced by several theoretical orientations. First, the theoretical concepts of medicalization (along with the conception of the body as machine), hegemony, authoritative knowledge, and the relationship of biology to culture have permeated these works. These concepts are distinct but at the same time are not easily separated. All involve the question of how normal childbirth has come to be seen as a medical event and how the power to define childbirth is expressed. Secondly, while most modern theoreticians mention, or give lip service to, the concept of biology, few place the reality of childbirth as a biological and evolutionary event as central to their analysis.

Childbirth has long been of interest to anthropologists who recognized that reproduction was a central element to human organization. However, early anthropologists did not study childbirth "for its own sake" but rather as a means to study analytical concepts of traditional interest to anthropology, i.e. ritual, indigenous forms of medicine, or kinship systems (Davis-Floyd and Sargent 1997, 1-2). Rapp (1997, xi) comments that the study of childbirth perhaps remained on the margins of theory and praxis because it was considered a "women's subject". Despite this marginalization, Davis-Floyd and Sargent (1997), in their summary of the history of the anthropology of childbirth, document how quite a few anthropologists, despite their lonely position within the discipline, endured in making the cross-cultural analysis of childbirth central to the study of social life.

A turning point in anthropology, for what has become a dynamic and prolific sub-discipline in its own right, was Brigitte Jordan's "seminal" work (Van Hollen 2003, 14). Jordon's work initiated an "explosion" in the study of childbirth by anthropologists (Davis-Floyd and Sargent 1997, 5). Van Hollen (2003, 5) sums up this development:

> Whereas earlier anthropological approaches to reproduction tended to focus on how reproductive practices and beliefs reflected social and cultural systems, scholars now argue that anthropology can benefit from viewing reproduction itself as a key site for understanding the ways in which people re-conceptualize and re-organize the world in which they live.

Sociologists have also made childbirth a focus of study, most notably Barbara Katz Rothman, Ann Oakley, and Raymond DeVries. Their works have been parallel to that of anthropologists over the past several decades. What these sociologists tend to share with anthropologists is a qualitative approach to research and a blending of academic disciplines. The sociologist Raymond DeVries (2004b) asserts that the theoretical boundaries of academia have stifled academic discourse and has created a false dichotomy between social structure and culture; in real life, social structure and culture are interrelated and inseparable. This is particularly true for childbirth.

The more recent trend towards critical analysis has begun to transcend these arbitrary boundaries, focusing on how "reproduction is structured across social and cultural boundaries, particularly at local/global intersections ... (Ginsburg and Rapp 1995, 3)." Ginsburg and Rapp have led in criticizing the "erasure" and "exclusion" of women in discourse and policy-making by institutions and the inherent inequalities revealed within that discourse. They have emphasized the need to focus on and recognize "women's centrality to reproduction in all its complexity ... documenting, empowering and theorizing about female experience (Ginsburg and Rapp 1995, 4)."

Medicalization as a theoretical construct comes directly from Ivan Illich's (1976) analysis of the impact of biomedicine on modern society. The origins of the term hegemony in the social sciences of heath care flows from the influence of Antonio Gramsci on modern intellectual thought. The term has come to be used in a variety of ways in academic discourse and its meaning has evolved. The original meaning of hegemony as used by Gramsci is far more complicated and encompassing than is reflected in its frequent use. The concept of authoritative knowledge coined by Brigitte Jordan (1993[1978]), while related to the concept of hegemony, has gone beyond a Gramscian analysis.

Gramsci is particularly relevant to the discussion of modern childbirth. Gramsci essentially argued against a mechanical, economic deterministic view of how social norms change. His concept was that the subordinate classes take on the belief systems of the dominant class, internalizing that belief system and coming to see it as their own. Essential to any analysis of childbirth systems is the notion that culture does not automatically flow from economic structure, that there is a degree of intentionality in cultural changes. This goes directly to my description of our childbirth system as being one of Gleichschaltung. The nurse-midwives I observed know that the system they work with is dysfunctional. However, because the machine works so well with each piece dependent on the next, they find it difficult to change the system, to disassemble it. There is a sense of inevitability and frustration that I heard in the words of nurse-midwives. Within a Gleichschaltung system, people may *question* the acceptable norms. However, *acting* against the norms, *resisting* those norms, can result in grave consequences (for example losing a job, losing ones reputation, facing ostracism).

Prior to discussing these key concepts, I wish to ground this discussion on a theoretical focus shared by most theoreticians: the domination of childbirth in the United States by the obstetrical profession. A story told by the sociologist Raymond DeVries (2004a) describes this phenomenon.

In his study of childbirth in the Netherlands, DeVries was able to interview the Dutch physician, Geerrit-Jan Kloosterman, prior to his death. Professor Kloosterman, the author of a Dutch midwifery text, became renowned, both in the Netherlands and throughout the international alternative childbirth community, for his support of midwifery and homebirth. It is no exaggeration to suggest that the support given to homebirth and midwifery by Kloosterman during his lifetime was a significant factor in the continuation of a dynamic Dutch midwifery in the latter twentieth century.

As told by Raymond Devries (2004a), Professor Kloosterman was invited to London to give a lecture to an international meeting of obstetricians and gynecologists. Kloosterman, Chair of Obstetrics at the University of Amsterdam at the time, was well-respected and well-known for his support of the Dutch practice of midwife-assisted births at home. He was in the middle of his lecture—an analysis of the Dutch system, which showed that the continued use of midwife-attended home birth was safe for mothers and babies—when there was, to him, a strange occurrence. While he was talking, members of the audience, led by American obstetricians, noisily got up from their chairs, leaving the room in an obvious display of displeasure with his presentation.

After finishing the lecture, Kloosterman and the organizer of the meeting discussed the small protest. They asked themselves, "Why doesn't this happen in other specialties?" They agreed it would be unheard of for physicians to walk out in the middle of a lecture about cardiology, even if they thought the data was suspect. Informal professional rules in medicine dictate that disagreements about data are hashed out in collegial exchanges; one does not protest against data, one challenges the data on the basis of evidence. Kloosterman concluded that obstetrics does not really belong in the field of medicine. Perhaps, he conjectured, obstetrics would be better located in the field of physiology. After all, it is the only discipline in medicine where something happens by itself, and, in most cases, everything ends well with no intervention (DeVries 2004a, 13-14).

Our "outlook on life", as stated by Kloosterman, goes to the heart of this discussion on the academic discourse surrounding childbirth. Kloosterman has been quoted as stating, "Obstetrics is wider and broader than pure medicine. It has to do with the whole of life, the way you look at life, making objective discussion difficult. You are almost unable to split the problem off into pure science, always your outlook on life is involved (DeVries 2004a, 14)."

Medicalization

Ivan Illich put forth the analytic concept of medicalization, along with the associated concept of iatrogenesis, in his influential 1976 book *Medical Nemesis. The Expropriation of Health.* This critique of biomedicine as "diagnostic imperialism" proposed that the "medical monopoly" had an iatrogenic impact on society at the clinical, social and cultural level. Modern medicine, with its singular clinical emphasis on technology, fails in its attempts to solve the modern epidemics associated with culture (i.e. hypertension and obesity) and often actually causes more harm than benefit. On a social level, modern medicine has turned individuals into consumers, expropriating health and creating "a morbid society in which social control of the population by the medical system turns into a principal economic activity (Illich 1976, 43)." Medicine's asserted right to define health and illness, as well as to create medical conditions out of normal life processes, creates a social paralysis: taking health out of the realm of individual responsibility into one of institutional responsibility.

On a cultural level, medicalization replaces the traditional forms in society of coping with suffering and pain through self-care.

Perhaps more than any other analytic concept, medicalization has influenced the recent academic discourse on childbirth. In order to illustrate the varied ways in which medicalization is understood, I have chosen to compare the initial works of five social scientists who are well recognized for their work in the field of childbirth—the anthropologists Brigitte Jordon, Robbie Davis-Floyd, and Emily Martin, along with the sociologists Barbara Katz Rothman and Ann Oakley. Their works are written as if they are speaking to each other, an academic conversation if you will. This makes sense when one considers that they are of the same generation; the initial research of each academic was carried out in the late 1970s and 1980s. As academics they were aware of each other's work, and their writings were carried out in the context of the alternative childbirth movement and the drive for an independent midwifery. A survey of the initial works of these five researchers reveals that each reflects the training of her discipline, while at the same time defying disciplinary boundaries.

Brigitte Jordan pursued a cross-cultural study of childbirth during the 1970s, carrying out ethnographic research of childbirth practices in four countries—Mexico, the United States, the Netherlands, and Sweden. Jordan's research was particularly focused on Mexico where she lived for extended periods of time, establishing a relationship with an indigenous midwife. She ultimately was allowed to accompany the midwife to births where she was able to observe and participate.

In the preface of the fourth edition of her 1978 book, Jordan comments that when she first began her research "there were no analytic concepts that would handle my material (1993, xi)." She drew inspiration from Margaret Mead as one of the few social scientists to have written on childbirth as a significant social event.

Key elements of Jordan's analysis include:

- Childbirth practices are not isolated practices on the part of individuals but are socially patterned systems with cultural internal consistency. Birth is a universal biological event that is socially regulated and consensually shaped with "the particular pattern depending on local history, ecology, social structure, technological development, and the like (1993, 4)."

- A concern for the impact on indigenous systems of childbirth by highly technological childbirth systems. Local systems of childbirth are transformed, often not for the better, as they interact with and incorporate western knowledge, technology, and ideology.

Ann Oakley's (1980) initial research was contemporaneous to Jordan. Like Jordan, she described how, when she was beginning her research, there existed little in the way of research in the area of childbirth. Her focus has been on the "social character" of childbirth—"an understanding of what happens, why and with what consequences to women having babies in any culture (1980, 2)." Not surprisingly, as a sociologist Oakley looked to structural relationships in her analysis of childbirth.

The fundamental characteristic of childbirth in British society, according to Oakley, is the transformation of childbirth into a medical "case", with control and power in the hands of the physician and medical institutions, as opposed to a social event with support coming from a woman's immediate community.

> Obstetrics, like midwifery, in its original meaning describes a female province. The management of reproduction has been, throughout most of history and in most cultures, a female concern; what is characteristic about childbirth in the industrial world is, conversely, its control by men. The conversion of female-controlled community management to male-controlled medical management alone would suggest that the propagation of particular paradigms of women as maternity cases has been central to the whole development of medically dominated maternity care (Oakley 1980, 11).

The progressive role of prenatal care brought with it the fundamental element of the "monitoring of maternal behavior", a social phenomenon with mixed implications for the health of mothers (Oakley 1986[1984], 42). Prior to this monitoring of maternal behavior by health care professionals, "medical practitioners in the eighteenth and nineteenth centuries had to place some reliance on women's own opinions as to whether or not they were pregnant (Oakley 1986[1984], 19)." Professionals also had to give credence to the mother's own perceptions about the state of her health and that of her baby. The transformation of pregnancy into a medical case by the medical system is the essence of the medicalization of pregnancy, according to Oakley (1986[1984]).

Barbara Katz Rothman, a sociologist by training, is quite postmodern with a good deal of self-reflexivity in her initial 1982 book, *In Labor: Women and Power in the Birthplace*. Rothman's voice and personal narrative are pivotal to her writing. She also draws heavily on history and philosophy in her analysis of childbirth in the United States. Rothman wrote at a time when sociology was still heavily quantitative. Few sociologists had yet to embrace qualitative methodology with its reliance on rich description, let alone the idea that the experience and role of the researcher should be central in research.

For Rothman, the fundamental characteristic of modern childbirth lies in the social phenomenon of hospital birth and the rapid, extreme transition in place of birth, from birthing in the home to the hospital. It is in the attempt to explain this phenomenon that she developed her analytic framework. Two "oppositional models" of care are in competition for control of childbirth—medicine and midwifery. Midwifery embraces a women's perspective, a perspective on birth "in which women are the subjects, the doers, the givers of birth. ... It is in the conflict between these two perspectives that the contradictions surrounding birth in America arise (Rothman 1982, 33-34)."

Rothman, in her initial 1982 writing, is the most overtly political in her analytic framework. There is a fundamental contradiction within the arena of childbirth. This medical model vs. midwifery model framework has both structural and ideological elements. First, central to the medical model is the ideology of technology, a mind-body dualism, where birth is conceived as a mechanical event. This is in opposition to the idea that pregnancy is a state of the woman, and that normal pregnancy should be the "working norm". Secondly, fundamental to the medical model is an ideology of patriarchy. "Not only is the male body taken as the norm by which the female body is understood, but the female reproductive processes are also understood in terms of men's needs. Thus, in the medical model, the woman is pregnant with the man's child (1982, 39)." Thirdly, a commodification of childbirth has taken place in medicine, particularly in the United States where health care is a business concern. Childbirth is a service that medicine provides rather than an activity that women engage in. Emboldened by commodification of the body, technology takes on a life of its own.

In Rothman's framework, there is a dialectical relationship between social structure and ideology. The medical model, the conception of the body as machine, arises out of technological society; the medical model then leads to more technology. "This approach to the body as machine, found in the medical model, both comes from the technical/industrial society and reflects that society, shaping it and its members (1982, 35)." The rise of the modern hospital system was key to this development for "the medical model of childbirth needed the hospital in order to develop to its logical conclusion (1982, 40)." A Cartesian analysis of the body as machine has been further developed by Emily Martin (2001[1987]}.

What I would add from my own observations, is that American childbirth does involve two very different ways of looking at care during pregnancy: an obstetric framework of labor that meets the requirements of an industrialized system and an opposing framework that recognizes birth as a human physiologic process. Rothman (1982) referred to this second framework as "the midwifery model of care". From my observations of nurse-midwives and interviews with both direct-entry midwives and nurse-midwives, I have perceived that American midwives of all types utilize a framework of birth as a physiologic process to varying degrees depending on their setting of practice. In the context of homebirth, midwives respect the physiologic process of birth to the extent possible given the realities of local power relations between midwifes, local obstetricians, and hospitals.

Davis-Floyd's (1992) analysis of modern childbirth in the United States has also been influential. Her central concern is to explain how and why American women have widely accepted and placed faith in the medical model of childbirth. After having interviewed over one hundred women on their birth experiences, Davis-Floyd concluded that it is the consistent acceptance of hospital birth, as well as the acceptance of medical procedures, that is characteristic of American birth. "It took me years to be able to hear that most of these women were not raising their voices in resistance and revisioning of the American way, but [were] in varying degrees of harmony and accord with that Way (1992, 5)."

Underlying this social phenomenon is our society's fundamental belief in the superiority of technology over nature. According to Davis-Floyd, the fear of the unpredictability and uncontrollability of nature exists to one extent or another in all societies but is particularly strong in American culture. Fundamental to the technocratic model, which our society embraces, is the belief that we can predict and control nature through technology, eliminating danger and risk. Yet birth is inherently unpredictable and can never be entirely controlled. "So the dilemma becomes," states Davis-Floyd, "how to create a sense of cultural control over birth, a natural process resistant to such control (1992, 60)?"

Davis-Floyd goes on to interpret birth stories and obstetrical procedures in terms of ritual. In her paradigm, it is through ritual that we as a society gain a sense of control over natural processes and accomplish a protection from perceived dangers. Obstetrical procedures, she says, "are in fact rational, ritual responses to our technocratic society's extreme fear of the natural processes on which it still depends for its continued existence (1992, 2)." Emily Martin's (2001[1987]) contribution in turn has been to deconstruct the metaphors within modern medicine that reveal the mechanization of the female body within our industrialized birth system.

All of these academics use the term *medicalization*. Initially used by Ivan Illich (1976), he observed that an ongoing process within modern society is the medicalization of life. The concept is fundamental to industrial/technological societies where the universe has come to be conceived in mechanistic terms. The body is then looked upon as a machine that can be altered, repaired, and controlled. The medicalization of childbirth is a process seen throughout the world although it has most strongly played out in the United States.

Following is a brief description of how each of these academics defines "medicalization".

Jordan: Birth is a physiologic event that is culturally shaped. Birth has become a "medical event" reinforced by authoritative knowledge.

Oakley: Medicalization represents the colonialization of the body by medicine (patriarchy) and the transformation of birth from a social event to a medical event.

Rothman: Medicalization has created two dialectical and oppositional models of childbirth: the medical model of care and the midwifery model. Patriarchy is the basis of the medical model care.

Davis-Floyd: Medicalization is a process consistent with our society's core cultural ideas and values. Medicalization is the means by which our society resolves our fear of childbirth.

Martin: Commonly accepted medical metaphors reveal the extent to which medicine has commodified women's bodies and turned women's bodies into a series of parts of a machine.

In her cross-cultural comparison of birth, Jordan views medicalization of birth as inherent to, and reflective of, Western society. Her concern is in the interface between western systems and the low technology, indigenous systems of less developed countries, as well as the tendency of high tech systems to overwhelm indigenous systems of care. For Davis-Floyd, medicalization is a development "consistent" with our society's conceptual frameworks. The medicalization of childbirth, "nurtures" our cultural need to believe that we have overcome the uncertainties inherent to nature (Davis Floyd 1992).

For Oakley (1980; 1986[1984]), medicalization represents "colonialization" of the body, "control" of men over reproduction, and the desire to control women. This colonialization is manifested in the doctor/patient relationship where the "conflict" between physician as expert and a woman's own knowledge is played out. Similarly, Rothman views the medical model and the midwifery model of care as actively opposing each other. "It is in the conflict between these two perspectives that the contradictions surrounding birth in America arise (1982, 33)."

Rothman views patriarchy as a fundamental element of the medicalization of birth. Similarly, Oakley also presents patriarchy as fundamental to modern childbirth in her 1980 academic work, *Women Confined: Towards a Sociology of Childbirth.* "Contemporary obstetric medicine has its roots in the 'scientific' and technological domination of male midwives over the empiricist and 'natural' methods of traditional female midwifery (1980, 26)." She continues, stating that, "Since it [obstetrics] was originally developed as a challenge to females modes of reproductive care, its ideology has historical roots in anti-feminism, in the creation of a mythology of women that represents them as a marginal group (Oakley 1980, 45)." At the time of Rothman and Oakley's initial writings, it was certainly true that modern obstetrics was overwhelmingly a male occupation. That is no longer true. The case for patriarchy as fundamental to modern society's turn towards technological birth is a reflection of the prevalent thinking of a specific era in the women's rights movement.

Where Rothman and Oakley see conflict and contradiction, Davis-Floyd and Jordan see consistency. The usefulness of Davis-Floyd's analysis is that it helps explain the strong appeal that high-tech birth holds for American women. Medicalization is something that women actively pursue as opposed to something that is forced upon them by our modern institutions. On the other hand, modern health care institutions offer women little choice.

While Rothman and Oakley tend to overemphasize the contradictions within our health care system, Davis-Floyd and Jordan tend to overemphasize the degree of stability. Their emphasis on the internal consistency of childbirth systems overlooks the subtlety of social conflict in the childbirth arena. Nor do these authors give credence to the agency of women to manipulate, resist, or utilize the medical system in ways that they find suitable.

The concept of culture flows throughout most analyses of modern childbirth and is used by theorists of childbirth to explain the overwhelming appeal of obstetrics. Within this analysis, women themselves are complicit in maintaining a system of care in which their bodies are relegated to the status of machines to be manipulated and managed. Everyday acts of resistance, as described by Scott (1985,1990) or the "measured judgments" of individuals as described by Morsy (1995) in actively engaging in decision-making, are theoretically dismissed as merely self-deceptions.

An overemphasis on cultural stability also misses the role of the individual in the social tensions that ultimately lead to social change. Labor rooms in American hospitals are anything but examples of the internal consistency of culture. In today's world, as I will describe in later chapters, mothers are still active players in our industrialized birth but in ways quite different from the era of these early theorists.

More recent works of critical anthropologists have included a critique of describing women as passive players in the growing use of technology during childbirth.

> Feminists have not always emphasized the ways in which women have simultaneously gained and lost with the lexicalization of their life problems. Nor have the scholars always noted the fact that women actively participated in the construction of the new medical definitions, nor discussed the reasons that led to their participation. Women were not simply passive victims of medical ascendancy. To cast them solely in a passive role is to perpetuate the very kinds of assumptions about women that feminists have been trying to challenge (Riessman 1998, 47).

Hegemony and Authoritative Knowledge

The concept of hegemony began with the Italian Marxist intellectual Antonio Gramsci. Along with many intellectuals in the early twentieth century, Gramsci was taken up with the question of why modern revolutions had not occurred in industrialized society as predicted by Marxists. Gramsci's analysis of hegemony developed out of a critique of orthodox Marxism, what he referred to as "mechanical historical materialism" or "economism". With economism, cultural change was interpreted as an inevitable result of structural changes (changes in the means of production). Gramsci's rejection of economic determinism led to an elevation of the significance of culture relative to social structure. Central to his analysis of power relations was that the dominant class in any society maintains its power through a cultural hegemony, a hegemonic apparatus from which values and ideas flow. Hegemony reflects and maintains the self-interest of the dominant class and is imposed upon society.

This hegemonic apparatus creates a "technically and morally unitary social organism (Forgacs 2000[1988], 34)." Society in general comes to see the worldview of the dominant class as normal, inevitable, and embraces this worldview as in their own self-interest: a form of self-deception or what some intellectuals have referred to as false consciousness. The oppressed, Gramsci proposed, "for reasons of submission and intellectual subordination [adopts] a conception which is not its own but is borrowed from another group; and it affirms this conception verbally and believes itself to be following it, because this is the conception which follows in 'normal times'—that is when its conduct is not independent and autonomous, but submissive and subordinate (Forgacs 2000[1988], 328)." In this way the oppressed cooperate in their own exploitation and "the ideological unity of the entire social bloc which that ideology serves to cement and to unify (p. 330)." Within this hegemonic apparatus, the intellectual class serves to legitimize the entire social system and is "an organizer of society in general, including all its complex organism of services (Gramsci 2005[1971], 5-6)."

A logical conclusion to this philosophical formulation is that, because culture does not inevitably flow from economic forces, there is always a potential for intentionality in political action where the cultural hegemony of the dominant class can be challenged. A reform of consciousness becomes possible "when one succeeds in introducing a new morality in conformity with a new conception of the world, one finishes by introducing the conception as well; in other words, one determines a reform of the whole of philosophy (Forgacs 2000[1988], 192)."

Gramsci, in his analysis of American culture and its impact on economic change, what he called "Fordism", was particularly prescient. If hegemony is used by the ruling class to create a "technically and morally unitary social system", then the United States (with its relatively unformed superstructure, a nascent cultural and social system, and open economic system) was prime for a more rapid, and complete, modern rationalization of society than was European society. The United States, with its wide-open, unregulated, unfettered industrialization, became the ultimate application of modern productivity and managerial techniques onto economic institutions, including American health care. It is the principle upon which the modern American economy developed into a dominant worldwide power.

> Hegemony here [in the United States] is born in the factory and requires for its exercise only a minute quantity of professional political and ideological intermediaries. The phenomenon of the "masses"… is nothing but the form taken by the "rationalized" society in which the "structure" dominates the superstructures more immediately and in which the latter are also "rationalized" (simplified and reduced in number) (Forgacs 2000[1988], 279).

In its infancy, the American medical profession was noted for its lack of regulation along with a local, pluralistic, entrepreneurial nature. Additionally, the American hospital system was primitive compared to industrialized European countries with their centuries old traditions of a regulated medical profession and advanced teaching hospitals (Starr 1982). The rapidity with which the American medical system has changed from an open system to a business monopoly has intrigued social scientists.

The increased rationalization and standardization of American hospitals as described by Perkins (2004) corresponds to Gramsci's concept of hegemony as born in the factory. (This is seen in the assembly-line nature of American childbirth and newborn care.) Hospitals are more and more bottom-line oriented and organized along modern business models. Emphasis is on the application of modern managerial techniques to enhance efficiency, productivity, and revenue generation. The implication for labor and delivery is the need for greater control (management) over childbirth in terms of time and cost. Supportive care is a cost while technological intervention and the use of technical implements, such as external fetal monitors, are revenue generators.

Each hour a woman spends in labor increases cost, cutting into profit, serving as a strong motivation to manage, and to standardize, labor with labor augmentation. Standardization and management of labor, in which as many interventions as possible are used, serve to increase profit. Each intervention represents a reimbursement (revenue).[12] Routine induction of labor, while associated with increased cesareans, helps maternity units cut labor costs (i.e. weekend overtime pay), relieves obstetricians from the inconvenience of weekend calls, while at the same time increasing revenue. Planned cesareans increase the ability of operating rooms to plan staffing levels in advance, optimizing the use of both staff and facilities. Healthy newborns are increasingly classified as at-risk and admitted to neonatal intensive care units for observation. These newborns are submitted to the risk of unnecessary testing. The overall effect is to increase the cost to society, while increasing revenue for the hospital. Of course, none of these health care decisions are discussed as economic—rather they are clinically justified, normalized in the form of protocols, and viewed as medical progress.

While economics is fundamental to the technicalization of American childbirth (Perkins 2004), a powerful cultural framework holds the entire system together, a framework that many American families have come to see as normal: the belief that childbirth is a pathological event that can and must be medically managed. Implicit is the promise and expectation of a guaranteed positive outcome, an expectation that has no basis in reality.

Used freely in academic discourse regarding childbirth, the meaning of the term "hegemony" has evolved over time. Comaroff and Comaroff (1991, 20) make the point that the concept has come to be "unspecified and inadequately situated in its conceptual context."

> We take hegemony to refer to that order of signs and practices, relations and distinctions, images and epistemologies—drawn from a historically situated cultural field—that come to be taken-for-granted as the natural and received shape of the world and everything that inhabit it. It consists, to paraphrase Bourdieu (1977:167), of things that go without saying because, being axiomatic, they come without saying; things that, being presumptively shared, are not normally the subject of explication or argument (Bourdieu 1977:9). This is why its power has so often been seen to lie in what it silences, what it prevents people from thinking and saying, what it puts beyond the limits of the rational and the credible. In a quite literal sense, hegemony is habit forming (Comaroff and Comaroff 1991, 23).

Van Hollen also uses this refined definition of hegemony in her discussion of childbirth in South Asia. "I use the term 'hegemony' to mean those systems of knowledge, symbols, and practices which are culturally constructed in the context of relations of power and which 'come to be taken for granted as the natural and received shape of the world and everything that inhabits it' (2003, 15). "

In the 1993 edition of her original work, Jordan adds a discussion on power and knowledge (what she calls "authoritative knowledge" rather than hegemony) to her analysis of the impact of biomedicine on indigenous systems of childbirth. Knowledge systems (authoritative knowledge), Jordan argues, hold power to the extent that they represent an "internal consistency", appear "natural, reasonable" and are "consensually constructed" (1993[1978], 153).

It is these characteristics, Jordan argues, that explain the power of biomedicine. It is through authoritative knowledge that hierarchical social structures are maintained and relations of power and authority are reproduced. She further argues that, to the extent that authoritative knowledge holds powerful sanctions, "People not only accept authoritative knowledge (which is thus validated and reinforced), but are actively and unselfconsciously engaged in its routine production and reproduction (1993[1978], 153)."

According to Jordan's analysis, the biomedical model of childbirth has become dominant to the extent that it is seen as normal, natural, and appropriate. It's dominance as a medical system lies first, in the high cultural value placed on technology within American society and secondly, in the cultural authority given to the obstetrical model as representing scientific truth.

Much of the thinking of social scientists with regard to childbirth has emphasized the power of biomedicine over the lives of individuals. The potential for resistance to biomedicine is deemphasized as is the progressive aspects of biomedicine, both in what it represents as well as the reality of what it offers to women. Jordan, with her theoretical paradigm of authoritative knowledge, does not offer adequate consideration to the possibility that American women perhaps embrace technology for the benefits that might accrue.

Leavitt (1983, 1986), a historian, documents how technology in childbirth was not merely forced upon women but actively sought out. Women were involved in seeking out the incorporation of technology into the American system of childbirth. In my observations, I find this to still be true. Social scientists are only beginning to develop a discerning analysis of the dynamic relationship between choice and constraint in relationship to childbirth and the ways in which women go about "negotiating the contradictory forces within which their lives are embedded (Ginsburg and Rapp 1991, 228)."

Biology and Culture

The relationship of biology and society has long been an area of debate within academia and so it is only to be expected that this would also be true in the social science of childbirth. Jordan (1993 [1978]) and Oakley (1980) both discuss biology and society but with differing approaches. Jordan is known for her biosocial paradigm, which describes biology and society as being interconnected.

> [Childbirth is a] phenomenon that is produced jointly and reflexively by (universal) biology and (particular) society. The distinction between what is biological and what is social is, in many ways, merely analytic. It has no ontological status. ... The physiology of birth and its interactional context (or the sociology of birth and its physiological context) constantly challenge all efforts to separate them.
>
> ... If we consider the sparse ethnographic record, we find that there is no known society where birth is treated, by the people involved in it's doing, as a merely physiological function. On the contrary, it is everywhere socially marked and shaped. To speak of birth as a biosocial event, then, suggests and recognizes at the same time the universal biological function and the culture-specific social matrix within which human biology is embedded (1993[1978], 3).

Oakley (1980, 6) puts forth a paradigm of women as reproducers where childbirth, or reproduction as she calls it, is first and foremost a social and cultural activity.

> Having a baby is a biological and cultural act. In bearing a child, a woman reproduces the species and performs an "animal function". Yet, human childbirth is accomplished in and shaped by culture, both in a general sense and in the particular sense of the varying definitions of reproduction offered by different cultures. How a society defines reproduction is closely linked with its articulation of women's position: the connections between female citizenship and the procreative role are social, not biological.

Oakley also places great emphasis on social arrangements. Childbirth is a "biological event ... the defining feature [of which] is [its] social character. ... Bodies function in a social world, and the parameters of this world supply an influence of their own (1980, 7)." In childbirth, the individual woman represents the "union of nature (biological reproducer) and culture (social person) directly (1980, 8)."

Oakley does give recognition to the "biological" element of childbirth but ultimately biology is about social relationships. "Particular childbirths create or break families, establish the ownership of property and entitlements to poverty or privilege; they may alter the statuses, rights and responsibilities of person, communities and nations (1980, 8)."

Jordan has the biology of childbirth embedded in the specific social matrix in which it is expressed. In contrast, even as Oakley speaks of biology, or reproduction, she is speaking not of physiology but of social roles and functions. In Oakley's paradigm, biology is subsumed within social relations and structure, particularly patriarchy.

> The management of reproduction has been throughout most of history and in most cultures, a female concern; what is characteristic about childbirth in the industrial world is, conversely, its control by men. The conversion of female-controlled community management to male–controlled medical management alone would suggest that the propagation of particular paradigms of women as maternity cases has been central to the whole development of medically dominated maternity care (Oakley 1980, 11).

Oakley, in her later work (1986[1984]), continues this theme that childbirth, while a biological event, is mainly defined by its social character. Rothman (1982) does not discuss biology nor physiology. In turn, for Davis-Floyd (1992) the significance of biology lies in her paradigm where the "technocratic" model of western society is seen as fundamentally the utilization of technology to overcome biology.

Emily Martin (2001[1987]), a critical anthropologist, has been influential with her cultural analysis of the "biomedical" model of childbirth, a metaphorical analysis of birth as "(re)production"— an analysis focusing on culture that also recognizes how economic and social forces shape our ideas, social expectations and institutions. Modern scientific thought, obstetrics being one example, is not "objective" but is a social and cultural construct where "facts" may in truth reflect cultural organization of experience as much as, or sometimes more than, actual physical reality.

Martin is a materialist in the sense that she traces how changes in the economic and social organization of society, particularly beginning with the Industrial Revolution and more recently the development of modern technology, have resulted in changes in the way we give meaning to and experience biological processes. Additionally, for Martin, words are the essence of how a society gives meaning to the world as we see it and are a reflection of worldview. Language and metaphor provide a basis upon which to understand the cultural assumptions fundamental to our social system and describes the meaning given to physical processes.

Martin describes the American childbirth system as a reflection of a cultural conception of the body functioning as a machine. This Cartesian model of the body as machine (separation of the body from the mind and spirit) has logically evolved into a conceptual model of the body as factory. Reflecting the larger social system, modern health care has evolved into a social system that relies heavily on technology and information, has lines of authority that are highly hierarchical, and is driven by profit. Under this system, the body is no longer merely a machine but the factory itself.

The doctor is no longer a "mechanic" but a "supervisor" or "owner". The mother is a laborer whose machine (body) produces an end product (baby). The entire focus of the process of childbirth (or reproduction in general) is now whether there has been successful or failed production (reproduction). Where the body is conceived as a series of parts, a profound body-self fragmentation occurs. "The organic unity [of the] fetus and mother can no longer be assumed and all these newly fragmented parts can now be subjected to market forces, ordered, produced, bought and sold (Martin 2001[1987], 20)."

Perkins' (2004) economic analysis of the rationalization of American health care in general, and maternal infant health care in particular, parallels that of Martin. However, her critique of Martin's analysis of the body as metaphor reveals a significant philosophical divide. According to Perkins, it is not the cultural metaphor of the body as machine that drives our childbirth system and obstetrical practices. Rather, it is the economic organization of our childbirth system that drives our cultural understanding. Furthermore, economic organization and cultural understandings are mutually reinforcing.

> With primary goals of accelerating throughout and enhancing productivity in the labor and delivery unit, active management and induction were inherently managerial techniques that enhanced the development of birth as a production process.
>
> I agree with Emily Martin's association of active management with production metaphors. But, as with other paradigm/intervention associations, it was not the metaphors [that] drove practices. Oxytocin use itself shaped the metaphors; active management prescribed oxytocin to strengthen uterine contraction and correspondingly diagnosed dystocia as a problem of inadequate contraction. This focus on uterine contraction ignored other factors contributing to prolonged labor, such as resistance of the cervix and birth canal. **Metaphors of production were just as much the result of structuring labor and delivery units like production units and using technology to enhance productivity, as they were its cause** [Emphasis mine]. Like the use of forceps, episiotomy, cesarean section, and intensive care before it, active management theory and practice coevolved with the economic organization of obstetrics. This means that reforming medical practice requires re-forming this organization (Perkins 2004, 155).

Perkins' criticism of Martin lies in the question of the relationship of social structure and culture, a question that has been debated among social scientists for decades. When we are discussing childbirth, there is also the question of the role of biology in relationship to culture, a question that has also been debated for years.

Trevathon (1987, 1997) has been the most influential anthropologist to bring biology as central to the discussion of childbirth. "Critical anthropology has pushed the body itself too far into the background," Trevathon (1997, 85) states. She makes the point that, while recognizing the universality of the social nature of human birth, most social scientists lack an appreciation of human birth as a fundamental biological human event and, furthermore, show a discomfort with the physicality of childbirth.

This discomfort with the reality of biology, a discomfort with the physicality of birth, is particularly apparent in the criticism of Odent by Emily Martin (2001[1987]). Both Martin and Odent share a criticism of the "biomedical" model of childbirth—a social and cultural model of childbirth that has brought alienation, a lack of control and autonomy by the mother, the separation of the mother and newborn as an "organic unity" (Martin 2001[1987}, 20). The biomedical model of childbirth also causes its own dangers (iatrogenesis) during childbirth, a fact emphasized by Illich (1976) in his critique of biomedicine.

Despite their agreement on this critical point, Martin criticizes Odent's emphasis on the physiology of birth as serving to essentialize women, to reduce women to our biological functions.

> In Odent's view, birthing women are perceived as moving back in time and down the evolutionary tree to a simpler, animal-like, unselfconscious state. This assessment must be viewed in light of the historical exclusion of women from 'culture'—that higher activity of men—and the exclusion of women's culture ... from the mainstream. It is ironic that Odent's efforts to give birthing back to women occur at the cost of reasserting a view of women as animal-like, part of nature, not of culture. Even though Odent has been made a hero by many birth activists in this country, we would do well to realize that his views share a lot with those of nineteenth-century writers who relegated women to the "natural" realm of the domestic (Martin 2001[1987], 164).

Martin's analysis of the connection between cultural metaphors and obstetrical practices has been instructive, adding to our understanding and critique of modern obstetrics. Her understanding of the cultural underpinnings of childbirth has been to analyze obstetrical metaphors and to show how the language used by obstetrics to describe the physiology of birth reflects cultural assumptions—an ideology of male superiority that views the female body as less than human, as a passive agent to our physiology, and an objectification of the woman as a reproducing machine.

However, when Martin extends this critique to Odent's contribution to our understanding of the physiology of birth, I believe that it reveals a discomfort with biology that is also seen in the work of many reproductive rights activists and academics alike. Biology is objectively seen as an inconvenience. The fact that childbirth is a physiological event can be easily lost when analyzed from the perspective of cultural variation and power relations. For many feminist academics, including Martin, nature (biology) is equated as subjugation. Martin's critique of Odent misses the essence of his writings. Physiologic birth does not have to take women backwards in the arena of human rights. Odent's critique of industrialized birth is instructive in how technology threatens the health of mothers and babies.

Odent emphasizes the instinctual nature of human birth to the extent that functional labor involves giving over of control, a shutting down of the neo-cortex (the thinking part of our brain), by the mother—a process necessary for the body to do its work This is the essential point made by Odent (1984, 1987, 2001, 2002, 2006), and before Odent, Niles Newton (1966a, 1966b, 1987). Undisrupted birth involves limiting stimulation of the neo-cortex so that the parasympathetic system can dominate, allowing for the uninhibited pulse-like secretion of oxytocin that is seen in successful labor (see Chapter Six). This point has been controversial among some feminists and academics. Martin (2001[19887]) in particular has articulated a discomfort with Odent's discussion of the physiology of birth.

Martin's viewpoint is not unique. It can be traced to some of the earlier feminist academics. Sherry Ortner's (1972) seminal article, *Is Female to Male as Nature is to Culture*, endures as an early stake of this intellectual position. Ortner's position, that women cross-culturally are viewed as part of lower order nature, while men are associated with the higher cultural activity, heavily influenced feminist social scientists. Based on this posit, it then seemed logical to state that as men see themselves as superior to nature, then women, seen as a part of nature, are considered to be subordinate to men based on our reproductive capacity. It can be argued that this ordering of culture as superior to nature has as much, if not more, to do with the human perspective that we (all humans) are of a higher order than other mammals.

Specifically with regards to Odent, Martin has criticized what she interprets as a regressive attitude that relegates women to an animal-like state. Odent's emphasis on the importance of, in effect, shutting down the neo-cortex to the extent possible is interpreted by Martin as reflecting an ideology of women as being of a lower order than men. Her fundamental criticism of Odent is that his analysis of the physiology of birth reduces the essence of women to our reproductive function. It is not helpful that scientists routinely refer to the sub-cortex as the "primitive" part of the brain. It is the part of the brain that controls the autonomic nervous system, is essential for life, and is a part of our biology that as humans we share with other mammals. While Odent emphasizes the significance of the parasympathetic system as well as the need to limit the activities of the neo-cortex during birth, it is a stretch to suggest that he views women as more primitive than men due to our reproductive capacities.

Odent's writings have captured the imagination and influenced childbirth activists throughout the Western world. An argument can be made that, within the alternative childbirth movement, his analysis has been used to romanticize childbirth. However, when women's reproductive biology is viewed as the basis of women's subjugation, as opposed to a part of our essential humanity and potential empowerment, it then follows that women are indeed inferior as a result of their own reproductive biology. Biology does, in fact, become destiny as a result. The only solution, then, for this conflict between culture and body is to fall back on Firestone's vision of technology completely taking over childbirth. This "nature-society dichotomy", as pointed out by Descolla and Pálsson (1996, 3), hinders "true ecological understanding".

It is easy from the lens of our technological society to forget the dangers faced by women during pregnancy and childbirth. Millions of women in underdeveloped countries still experience these dangers—as do women in our own society who do not have access to adequate health care and who live in poverty. It is all too easy, in the critique of the biomedical model, to downplay the dangers of childbirth. However, Odent's criticism of industrialized birth does not extend to a denial of the dangers faced by women who do not have access to life saving technology. Nor is it intellectually fair to state that Odent, with his emphasis on the physiology of birth, essentializes and reduces women to their role as reproducers.

The critiques of industrialized childbirth often fail to account for the reality that human birth is a fine-tuned physiologic process developed through years of evolution. Historically, anthropologists have long recognized the variation in the social organization of human birth. Trevathan (1997) provides a perspective that highlights a unique characteristic of humans: birth involves social organization, customs and interventions that are driven by an evolutionary imperative. "It was the evolutionary process itself," Trevathon says, "that first transformed birth from an individual to a social enterprise (1997, 81)."

Trevathan (1987) discusses how the evolution of human birth, so intricately tied to what it means to be human, relies on a series of physiologic events, each designed to facilitate the successful birth of the human baby. Human birth has evolved into a complicated biological event as compared to other mammals. Bipedalism and encephalization of the infant[13] together led to competing evolutionary tensions for successful human reproduction. Bipedalism changed the morphology of the human pelvis, narrowing the pelvis in relationship to the human fetus. At the same time, evolution favored the enlargement of the brain. The evolutionary compromise of these tensions was the birth of a relatively helpless infant, a characteristic specific to human infants.

An understanding of the uniqueness of the altriciality[14] of the human infant and how this characteristic forms the basis of what we know as human society—our cultures, social structures, our kinship systems—is missing from much of the literature on the social science of childbirth. Even Jordan (1993[1978]) with her biosocial paradigm, (birth is a universal physiologic event that is uniquely shaped by each individual culture), does not give adequate discussion to the particularities of the physiology of human birth and how this impacts the way that childbirth is shaped by society.

With her biological and evolutionary perspective, Trevathan (1997) provides a unique critique to this on-going discussion of authoritative knowledge and childbirth. She raises the question as to when, if ever, women have had unfettered power to make individual decisions with regards to pregnancy and childbirth. Trevathan makes the point that birth for most mammals is a solitary, private event led by an instinctive, physical drive for isolation. The trade-off between the physiologic drive for isolation in favor of social birth had to have been very strong and is associated with the development of "the consciousness of vulnerability" (1997, 83) that impelled women to seek and accept assistance during birth.[15]

Shostak (1983[1981]) and Konner and Shostak (1987) have documented that a cultural practice of solitary birth exists among the !Kung tribe of Africa. However, they point out that a laboring mother rarely gives birth alone during her first birth. Among the tribe, birthing alone, while not unusual, appears to be more a cultural "ideal" that represents physical courage. They do not conclude that it is the norm. At the time of Shostak and Konner's fieldwork, the !Kung and their reproductive strategies were viewed as possibly representative of human society during the Paleolithic period. This example of solitary birth does not by itself negate Trevathan's thesis.

The essential point made by Trevathan is that women share decision-making on some level during pregnancy and birth in all cultures. The laboring mother does not make decisions regarding her care, in any society, outside of cultural, social expectations, and norms. An evolutionary perspective on childbirth, "adds to our understanding of how birth today is constructed and experienced" and at the same time does not "inevitably lead to assuming that we are passive victims of our evolved bodies (Trevathan 1997, 80)."

Trevathon's thesis regarding social birth as a result of human evolution is supported by the work of Denis Walsh (2006a, 2006b), a British clinical researcher. Walsh has shown the significance of the presence of a trusted caregiver for normal progress of labor as well as to the development of matrescence, the embrace of mothering. Unique to the biomedical model, with its separation of the body from the mind, is the extreme disconnect between the mother-baby dyad. Also, the relationship that has existed in traditional societies between mother and birth attendant is lost in the midst of the modern industrial labor and delivery unit.

****

The intent of the above survey of academic literature is to provide a basis of understanding for the following description of American childbirth and nurse-midwifery. My approach has been eclectic, borrowing from all the academics discussed in this chapter. I have learned from them all and find each of them to be valid in their positions. I have chosen aspects of their models as I have deemed appropriate. It is apparent that there exists a need for more research to be carried out as to the variations and uniformity seen in human birth from a cultural, structural, as well as a biological standpoint.

---

[7] Direct-entry midwives, previously referred to historically as lay midwives, are empirically trained homebirth midwives in the United States that emerged from the homebirth social movement of the 1960s and 1970.

[8] The narratives referred to here are too numerous to cite in total. "Spiritual Midwifery" by Ina May Gaskin was one of the first. Others that have been well read, and the following include just a few: "Sisters On A Journey. Portraits of American Midwives" by Phyllis Chester; "Circle of Midwives" by Hilary Schlinger; and "Birth Without Doctors: Conversations with Traditional Midwives by Jacqueline Vincent-Priya. There has also been an avid interest in the stories of traditional South African-American midwives. These narratives include: Listen To Me Good. The Life Story of an Alabama Midwife by Margaret Charles Smith and Linda Janet Holmes; Motherwit. An Alabama Midwife's Story by Onnie Lee Logan; Beyond The Storm by Gladys Miton; and Why Not Me? The Story of Gladys Milton, midwife by Wendy Bovard and Gladys Milton.

[9] Founded in 1971, The Farm is an intentional community (also referred to as a commune) in Tennessee. As part of the counter culture movement of the 1960s and 1970s, it promoted and led the movement for out-of-hospital birth and direct-entry midwifery. The book *Spiritual Midwifery* was a collaborative effort by the midwives at The Farm, under the leadership of Ina May Gaskin.

10   In the past several years, the two American midwifery communities have begun to formally hold meetings seeking common ground. Significant differences continue to exist however: issues regarding credentialing and educational standards. Common ground has evolved over issues of promoting physiologic birth and support for home birth.

11   I recommend two academic works on the history of childbirth in the United States: *Brought to Bed. Childbearing in America, 1750-1950* by Judith Walzer Leavitt and Lying-In. A History of Childbirth in America by Richard and Dorothy Wertz.

12   An example of how epiduralized birth has revenue generation built into labor management: Anesthesia receives reimbursement for the insertion of the epidural catheter. Anesthesia then receives reimbursement for every fifteen minutes in which the epidural is running. The earlier an epidural is inserted, the greater the revenue generated.

13   Encephalization refers to an evolutionary trend in human newborns towards a larger and more complex brain relative to the overall body at birth. It also represents a shift in function in favor of the neocortex in the newborn.

14   It is postulated that human society was a response to the evolution of human newborns born in a state of altriciality. Altriciality refers to animals who are born relatively premature, helpless, and requiring intensive care for survival. The human newborn is unique among mammals with this characteristic of helplessness and continued brain development as an infant.

15   This is, of course, a theoretical concept put forth by Trevathan, one difficult to prove. However, I find her theory both logical and compelling.

Chapter Two

Childbirth at Community Hospital:
"Turning the Chapter Two Board Blue"

"It is a cultural contradiction that pregnant women in the United States will do so much to insure the health of their fetus and then, at the moment of birth, subject their baby to all the dangers of the drugs and devices of modern medicine (Devries et al. 2009, 51-52)."

I arrive at the labor and delivery unit shortly before 7:00 am, the morning shift change. Swiping my badge through the security monitor, the double door clicks open. I walk into the unit, which is clean and updated. I hear—silence: none of the expected sounds of birthing. Several nurses are sitting at the nurses' station. There is no activity in the halls of the L-shaped unit. I hear no noise coming from the patients' rooms. Noise did occasionally occur during a crisis, which happens on the rare occasion. Otherwise, one would not guess that this is a L&D (labor and delivery) unit. It felt more like a cardiac-care unit.

The silence of the labor and delivery unit is a significant characteristic of epiduralized birth. I was not alone in my unease at the quietness of the space. One midwife, with twenty-five years experience in a variety of birth settings, spoke of her own discomfort with this aspect of the maternity unit. She described her reaction to the quiet of L&D units, comparing Community Hospital to her experience at a hospital that had 14,000 births per year and an epidural rate of 75%.

> MAM: You used the term "baby factory". Could you tell me more what you mean by that?
>
> Midwife: When I walked into the unit [the unit she previously worked at], I was struck by how quiet it was. It was huge, with tons of labor and delivery rooms. Labor and Delivery was on two floors, it was so busy. I was struck by the quiet. It was because all the patients had epidurals. The bedside nursing ... there was no labor sitting. ...

MAM: So in the course of your career, you have really seen the changes. The epidural is one of the most obvious. The epidural has become so popular; patients come in demanding it immediately.

Midwife: Unfortunate.

MAM: How do you account for it?

Midwife: Number one: My thinking about it, having come through the whole process seeing the epidural rates go up and seeing C-section rates go up. It's discouraging, especially coming from the feminist movement. Owning and taking back your body. So I think a grass-roots movement is going to have to happen again.

I came to be discouraged at the births I observed, so many a prototype of others. There were days when I found myself tired of it all. I had been trained in the philosophy of physiologic birth. As one midwife had taught me, "Each woman births as she lives." I have seen the wide variation of normal birth as a midwife. The utter sameness of the births I witnessed at Community Hospital continued to unnerve me throughout my fieldwork.

The History of Community Hospital

Community Hospital is a small-scale, historic hospital that has existed for over one hundred years. For fifty of those years, an obstetric residency program was the foundation for the maternity service at the hospital. During those five decades, the maternity service operated along the lines typical of community hospitals at the time. Private physicians, at first general practitioners but increasingly obstetricians, held privileges at the hospital and admitted private patients to labor and delivery. These physicians increasingly entered into group practice rather than solo practice and provided cross-coverage for each other, arrangements that allowed for physicians to work fewer evenings and to plan vacations. It also created a lack of continuity; many women were delivered by a physician whom they had never met.

When an obstetrical residency program was established at Community Hospital, this lack of continuity was reinforced. A mother would often find herself delivered by a resident rather than her private physician. The obstetrical resident assessed patients, consulted with the patient's physician, managed the patient's labor, and often delivered the baby. The residents also carried out a variety of gynecologic procedures.

This organization of obstetrical care was common at the time. Private obstetricians preferred to have admitting privileges and refer clients to hospitals with residents for reasons of convenience and life style. Residents staffing an obstetrical service around the clock provided back-up service for private obstetricians, making night visits to the hospital less likely. This system guaranteed a strong feeder system of obstetrical patients, an important factor in the ability of a hospital and obstetrical service to remain competitive in the health care marketplace. The loss of an obstetrical residency program at Community Hospital threatened the very existence of maternity care at the hospital.

Throughout the last decades of the twentieth century, hospitals known as medical centers increasingly competed with smaller community hospitals. As these medical centers have attracted obstetricians (and the patients who come with them), maternity units at community hospitals have shut down. Community Hospital faced these same pressures. In 1998, the obstetrical residency program at Community Hospital shut down due to a lack of clinical activity. The hospital could no longer support the residency program due to a decrease in the number of deliveries and other obstetric/gynecologic procedures required for the education and training of residents.

The Midwifery Service at Community Hospital

Community Hospital's midwifery service was established to fill the void left by the closure of its residency program. The service was organized along the lines of what was called a "collaborative practice" between midwives and physicians. Midwives were hired to provide service—prenatal, intrapartum and well-woman care.[16] One nurse-midwife functioned as the Midwifery Service Director. It was the only full-scope, 24/7 (twenty-four hours, seven days a week), nurse-midwifery service in the community.

A group of obstetricians worked alongside the nurse-midwives. The midwifery service carried out most prenatal and intrapartum care but an obstetrician was on-site at all times, including nights. When only one physician was on-site, a nurse-midwife acted as first assist during surgery. In addition, the hospital contracted with a private anesthesiology service, which enabled the L&D service to provide emergency cesareans. The presence of 24/7 anesthesiology coverage also enabled the practice to provide epidural pain management. Anesthesiologists served the entire hospital, a disadvantage for the maternity service. Because the maternity unit did not have a dedicated anesthesiologist, it was not unusual for laboring mothers to wait for epidurals, particularly at night.

After initial assessment, and with subsequent assessments during prenatal care, patients were placed into one of three groups: (1) Appropriate for nurse-midwifery care, which generally meant no major risk factors; (2) Appropriate for nurse-midwifery care with physician collaboration. This designation sometimes meant that the mother would see both a physician and nurse-midwife during prenatal care. A nurse-midwife would more than likely deliver the mother with a physician in close proximity. (3) Appropriate for physician care only. Many of the mothers requiring a physician-attended delivery were transferred to a nearby tertiary-care maternity service. Nurse-midwives attended most vaginal deliveries with the physician called in for consultation or if a cesarean was necessary.

Prenatal and well-woman care were provided in an office suite at an office building next to the hospital. In the hospital itself, the labor and delivery unit held twenty beds (three of which were triage beds), a Level I newborn nursery, and an operation suite for cesareans and gynecologic procedures. Increasingly, the patients were referred by community health centers, or were self-referred, as opposed to earlier years when maternity patients came from private physicians. The maternity service increasingly relied on Medicaid payments and lacked diverse payment sources. The nearest maternity service was a high-volume tertiary-care center, which had a Level III neonatal unit. It had such a high volume of deliveries that it was not unusual for women to labor in a hallway bed. This service was known for its frequent and routine inductions. Rapid epidurals were available as a result of a dedicated obstetrical anesthesia service. What the midwifery service at Community Hospital offered in comparison was an intimate setting with highly individualized care.

The maternity service at Community Hospital was organized around the principle of what was called collaborative practice. The nurse-midwives at Community Hospital described collaborative practice as cooperation between midwives and obstetricians to serve their patients in an "inter-collegial and respectful" manner. Collaboration was further described as an "evolving understanding" of the standards and philosophy of the two professions. Monthly joint meetings were held to discuss a variety of issues—department policy, clinical cases with out-of-the-norm characteristics, as well as decisions regarding transfer of care to more specialized maternity care.

From the beginning there was, in principle, unity between the midwives and obstetricians with regards to physiological birth. Inductions were not routinely scheduled and would be carried out only when medically necessary, a major difference between Community Hospital and surrounding hospitals. VBAC (vaginal birth after cesarean) was encouraged, although a mother could freely choose to have a repeat cesarean. There was a commitment to avoid cesarean births except when medically necessary.

Policy and decisions regarding patient care were to be cooperative, with give and take on all sides. While a great deal of decision-making was carried out through discussion and consensus, ultimate decision-making rested with the staff obstetricians and with the Department Chair (an obstetrician). Staff obstetricians occasionally exercised their right to determine policy, albeit with consideration to the input of the midwifery group. When obstetricians and nurse-midwives disagreed, the opinions of the physicians trumped that of the midwives. The organizational model for the maternity service was, in fact, a subtle authoritarian, hierarchical model, even given the benevolence of the physicians.

The Midwifery Service Director served as liaison with the Department Chair, with frequent meetings between the two where concerns of the midwifery group were communicated. The ideal was to have "open communication". Despite the fact that most vaginal births were delivered by midwives, the maternity service was not a midwifery-led service in the sense described by Walsh (2006b, 2009) and Sandall et al. (2009, 2010). True midwifery-led care, according to these British researchers, is defined as maternity care where a midwife is the primary care provider for the mother, and where midwives have decision-making authority for midwifery patients. Their research suggests that midwifery-led units result in fewer interventions and improved relationships between mothers and midwives—maternal reports of empathetic care and increased satisfaction, At Community Hospital, most decision-making was carried in a respectful, co-operative manner. However, I witnessed exceptions that revealed collaborative practice to be less than a reality.

What the Epiduralized Birth Setting Looks Like

When I walk through the double doors of the L&D unit at Community Hospital, to the right is a hallway with rooms on both sides. At the beginning of this hallway are two rooms, one on the left and one on the right. Both are used for triage[17] of patients. Further down the hallway, on the left, are three labor rooms. The nurses' break room and an office are on the right. At the end of this hallway are double doors beyond which is the operating suite, kept ready for surgery at all times.

Facing straight ahead from the entrance to the unit is a hallway that forms the other leg of the L-shaped unit. Immediately to the left of the entrance is the "station", a common area in any L&D unit. This is the hub of the unit, where patient charts are kept. The area is surrounded with a continuous wall-desk at which people sit to chart and use computers. In one corner of the station, a whiteboard (referred to as "The Board") hangs on a wall, a central element of the unit. The Board is a crucial means of communication between the midwives, doctors and nurses in the unit.

On this board, information is added or erased throughout the shift. Room numbers run vertically down the Board. Essential pieces of information are listed horizontally: the patient's name; key pieces of obstetrical history (i.e. number of previous babies, weeks of gestation); if induced, when induction began and how; medications the patient is on (i.e. antibiotic for positive Beta Strep), rate of pitocin infusion; presence of epidural; last time that epidural medication was given and, if continuous, the flow rate; as well as other information of interest to the staff: how long the patient has been in labor and the condition of the cervix—dilation and effacement as well as position of the baby. (This is not an all-inclusive list of information provided on the Board.) At shift change, midwives (both outgoing and oncoming) and doctors gather around the Board to discuss each patient, exchange information, and discuss plan of management.

A laboring patient's information is written in green on the Board. Once a patient delivers, the information is erased and new information about the postpartum mother and baby is written in blue. Great significance was given to turning patients from green to blue on the board. I watched as midwifes marched up to the Board and with a dramatic swipe erased the green information, writing in blue the information about the newly delivered mother. While women did not have to advance along the lines of a rigidly implemented Friedman's curve as in the past, I observed that there was still a strong concern over how long labor was taking and a desire to move things along. This awareness of time in labor went beyond clinical issues and safety.

My awareness of how the Board was used to move things along according to the needs of the unit was an "aha" moment. I had finished an interview with one midwife and the tape was off. We were sitting in the midwife call room and chatting when she was called out. As she stood at the door, her hand on the door knob, I asked her, "I've noticed that there seems to be value placed on moving mothers along, getting the delivery done as quickly as possible. Is this true or is it my imagination? What is this thing about the board?" She turned and looked at me with surprise. "Oh. You've noticed that. You're talking about *turning the board blue*."[18] I thought to myself, "I should have known there's a term for it."

Turning the board blue is a representation of what occurs in the industrialized, assembly-line labor unit. At its best, it serves as a basis for communication among staff. It is also a process whereby staff can see how labor is "moving along". The concern about time in labor is real and valid. A good midwife is always concerned about keeping an eye on each mother's progress in labor. In quality midwifery care, the differentiation of normal vs. abnormal labor takes into account that each mother labors differently. At its worse, however, the Board is a visual tool for overall management of the unit: its goal being to clear beds for potential incoming patients, to make each patient's hospital stay as efficient as possible. Time spent in labor is a critical element of the cost per delivery, a crucial figure for meeting the departmental budget and a statistic paid attention to by hospital administrators.

Also hanging on the wall at the station were several large telemetry screens. These screens too were an important element of the birthing assembly-line of the unit. A monitoring machine at the mother's bedside sent all data to the nurses' station via telemetry, data that appeared on the screens on the wall of the station and the physician call room. From these screens, measurements of the mother and baby can be observed from a distance—the baby's heart pattern, the mother's contraction pattern, the mother's blood pressure and oxygen levels, the pitocin infusion level, the nurse's notes—the list goes on.

Walking past the station, to the left was the newborn nursery. Along both sides of this hallway were more labor rooms, all private except for one room that had two beds. This double room was rarely used. (It had been used for overflow during the early years of the service.) At the end of this hallway was a blank wall, "the wall to nowhere" as I called it: a wall that becomes important in this story when I discuss the closing of the service.

The labor and delivery rooms were spacious, clean, and stocked with supplies. Each room had a bed that could be broken down into a traditional delivery table, with stirrups. The midwives rarely broke down the bed. Each room also had a reclining armchair, a TV hanging from the ceiling, and a bathroom. Two rooms had large Jacuzzi tubs for water births. The midwives did occasionally deliver a water birth, although I was not lucky enough to see one while there. Most mothers wanted an epidural, which precluded a water birth.

Continuous external fetal monitoring was theoretically not a routine requirement. However, it was a requirement for epidural pain management and pitocin administration. As a result almost all women were continuously monitored as described below with their labor augmentation .

A central object in each labor room is what some call a Robo Nurse, a unit that has taken on nursing care responsibilities. It is a rectangular shaped cabinet next to the bed. This Robo Nurse serves as the central monitoring unit for the patient. On top of the box sits the fetal/maternal monitor. The mother is attached with two straps to this monitor, one of which holds a flat ultrasound sensor against her lower abdomen to monitor the fetal heart pattern. Another strap around the abdomen holds a toco disc to the upper fundus of the uterus and monitors the frequency and strength of the mother's contractions. A blood pressure cuff is attached to the mother's arm and a pulse oximeter to her finger (to measure oxygen saturation). Both are also hooked into the Robo Nurse. The staff nurse can set the machine to take blood pressure at established times.

All of the information provided by these instruments is seen on the monitor that sits on top of the Robo Nurse unit. Also on top of the box is a keyboard attached to the monitor. The staff nurse or midwife can type periodic notes into the monitor. This computer-like monitor replaces the outdated external fetal monitor from which strips of paper flowed. With the push of a button, the provider can move the electronic image on the monitor to compare the fetal heart rhythm and maternal contraction pattern over time. This computerized system, with the ability to type progress notes into the system, also replaces the long paper chart that was used in the past to chart labor progress.

Except in exceptional cases, mothers received at least one intravenous (IV) catheter. Also at the mother's side was at least one IV pump, often more. It is through IV pumps, lines, and catheters that the flow of IV fluids and medications (including pitocin, epidural infusion and antibiotics) are controlled. All this information is sent by telemetry to the monitors in the station.

A synergy is created by the use of technology in these epiduralized birth settings where the needs of all the players involved come together. The Department Chair estimated that over 80% of the women at Community Hospital chose to have an epidural. (The obstetrical department did not keep statistics on epidurals.) Most mothers entered prenatal care having already made the decision to have an epidural. From my observations, there was inadequate discussion of the pros and cons of epidural anesthesia.

Upon admission, the mother signed an informed consent form for epidural administration. However, the informed consent process tended to be pro forma. The midwives knew that the mothers were determined to have "my epidural" and were generally acquiescent to the woman's decision despite their professional belief in physiologic birth. It is after all a matter of the mother's "choice".

It is only recently that epidurals have become routine. In the past, many insurance companies did not pay for an epidural unless administered for a documented medical indication. Likewise, Medicaid in most states did not cover epidurals until recently. It was not uncommon for women, even those with private insurance, to pay out-of-pocket for an epidural. In the past, protocol for epidural anesthesia called for well-established labor: usually a minimum of five centimeters dilation and contractions that are regular, strong, and at least five minutes apart. When administered in this way, labor occasionally proceeded without pitocin augmentation.

Epidurals are often given as soon as possible when requested by the mother. I saw epidurals given with the initiation of induction, a time of minimal pain. Epidurals were often administered quite soon after admission even in the early phase of labor. Blood is drawn and sent to the lab. Once lab results are received, the anesthesiologist was notified. Anesthesia was available 24/7 for the administration of epidurals, although often not as quickly as the mother would wish. The anesthesiologists arrived at their convenience. How long a mother waited for her epidural depended partially on whether the anesthesiologist was held up in surgery.

Large maternity units now usually have dedicated anesthesiology for the maternity unit. From the standpoint of anesthesiologists, obstetrical epidurals are a mixed blessing. They are considered a nuisance by some anesthesiologists, particularly if they are woken up at night. At the same time, obstetrical epidurals have become the bread and butter of many anesthesia departments. Epidurals keep anesthesiology busy making it economically feasible for a hospital to have in-house anesthesia 24/7.

The routinization of childbirth made possible with the epidural makes for a smooth-running unit that involves urinary catheterization, augmentation of labor with pitocin and continuous fetal monitoring. Once an epidural is given, the mother is immobilized, even with the so-called walking epidurals.[19] An IV becomes necessary to avoid decreased blood pressure, a possible side effect of epidural anesthesia. IV fluids also guarantee that the mother is kept hydrated, a care process that was once a function of bedside nursing care. A urinary catheter becomes necessary, as the epidural medication results in a flaccid bladder tone. Also, the mother cannot walk to the toilet. Sitting on a urinal is problematic, and requires nursing care, as the mother has difficulty moving.

Prior to routine epidurals, continuous external fetal monitoring and monitoring of contractions, was a bothersome clinical activity. As the mother would move around, particularly during contractions, it was necessary for nurses to continually readjust the straps in order to maintain an adequate strip (a tracing). In epiduralized birth, the immobility of the mother makes for a more accurate, undisturbed image of the fetal heart rhythm and contraction pattern. (It is no longer a paper strip. With telemetry it is more accurately called an image or tracing.)

As previously described, technology has advanced so that information from the bedside monitor is transmitted via telemetry to the central monitoring unit in the station. The image one sees upon entering the labor room is that of the pregnant mother, (perhaps on her side, sometimes on her back), immobile, her pregnant womb apparent, with numerous lines attached to her. The Robo Nurse unit becomes a central focus. The anesthetic from the epidural usually slows down contractions, particularly when given in early labor, and so almost everyone with an epidural now receives pitocin. With the blocking of pain by the epidural, pitocin can now be titrated to higher levels. Contractions and progress of labor become more predictable through the careful titration of pitocin. Through titration of pitocin, the midwife can often predict when the mother will be fully dilated. As the mother usually feels little to no pain, bedside care in the form of labor support is barely needed.

The delivery of the baby itself is usually equally routine. As the mother has difficulty moving, she typically delivers on her back, in a semi-recumbent position, with several people holding up her legs. The mother usually has little or no sensation of contractions and does not feel the physiologic fetal ejection reflex (the involuntary need to push) and so is often told to begin pushing based on determination of full dilation by cervix check. The pace of pushing is determined by the contractions seen on the monitor. This directed pushing can take longer because of the lack of sensation.[20] The absence of the physiologic fetal ejection reflex can be significant as there is evidence that this critical phase of labor involves a hormonal surge, both maternal and fetal, a surge that is central to maternal-infant bonding (see Chapter Six).

In physiologic labor, the involuntary urge to push can occur later than full dilation. The period of time between full dilation and the fetal ejection reflex is an important interval when the fetus settles into a final position within the birth canal, one that is optimal for both the baby and the mother's pelvic architecture. As a result, epidurals are associated with prolonged second stage (pushing) and the use of forceps or vacuum extraction during delivery.

The Centrality of the Epidural

Figure One
The Centrality of the Epidural

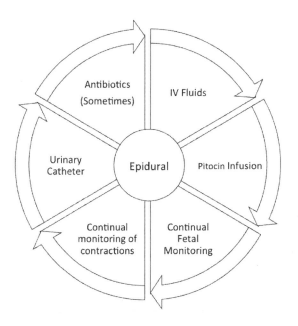

The cascade of interventions is no more. There now exists a complex, unitary, interconnected set of interventions. Figure One, *The Centrality of the Epidural,* is a representation of this interconnection of interventions. This unitary set of interventions is held together by the routine use of the epidural. If a mother has an epidural, she *will* automatically have an IV catheter. She *will* have IV fluids. She *will* have augmentation of labor with pitocin. She *will* have a urinary catheter.

Without the epidural, this complete totality of management of labor would be quite difficult. The epidural is the hub of this wheel of interventions. In a non-interventive birth, where an epidural is not administered, these subsequent interventions are not inevitable. The epidural is central to the uniformity of what is now the norm for birth in America's system of birth.

Under these conditions, the labor and delivery unit runs like a well-oiled machine. Another analogy would be that of a well-run industrial assembly-line monitored by computer technology. The entire system is a Gleichschaltung of birth. As mentioned in the Introduction, I do not use the term in the political sense. I use the term in its original mechanical meaning—a process that is so well-coordinated, with each element in accordance, that the pieces are inseparable and work in perfect harmony as a whole.

From the standpoint of efficiency, turning the board blue is an essential organizational principle of the labor and delivery unit. Industrial efficiency is involved in the large number of routine inductions as well as augmented labors in many maternity units. Pitocin is titrated to manage the timing of deliveries to fit the need of the unit, adjusted to slow down or speed up labor. Each hour that a patient spends in a bed during labor, and during the postpartum period, represents a cost to the hospital and ultimately the labor and delivery unit. Turning over beds in a timely fashion is critical for the overall cost efficiency of the unit. Turning over beds is also an attempt to prevent the situation where a laboring patient arrives to find no available bed. Routine inductions and repeat cesareans provide a greater degree of certainty in the staffing of a maternity unit, which in turn helps the bottom line in a maternity service's budget.

I had a discussion with one midwife about the pressure to move patients along—to "turn the board blue". I wanted to see how prevalent this practice was in the midwifery service. As our discussion proceeded she became more forthcoming, stating that there was, in fact, some degree of pressure to manage labor in order to move things along—a pressure having nothing to do with safe practice and everything to do with convenience. A standard for the midwifery service, although one not openly articulated, was the ideal to have the board as empty as possible at shift change.

> MAM: Do you feel pressure to move someone along so that she delivers before the next midwife comes on?
>
> Midwife: Sometimes. Because some people will comment on that. Like, "Well, clean it up before I get there."
>
> MAM: Meaning get someone delivered?

Midwife: ... There is sometimes the implication that I would like you to "clean it all up for me" before I get there. That's the implied ideal. But you can't really.

MAM: And by saying "cleaning it up"?

Midwife: It means get them delivered. But these are just comments. I don't know how you really *do* that. ... But I've done things that I wouldn't necessarily have otherwise done because I knew [the midwife at shift change] would want me to move on it. And I don't like that feeling. And I've had to tell myself to just hold back.

MAM: What are the things you would do in order to "move on it"?

Midwife: Like start pitocin. Break somebody's water. And I've regretted it. I think it happened once that I broke somebody's water because I knew [another midwife] was coming on. And the patient was seven. [She means seven centimeters.] I don't like to break someone's water because I just don't think it makes a difference.

This pressure to manage labor and move things along is a function of the needs of the industrialized unit with its shift work, staffing needs, the desire to be prepared for the inevitable new patient coming in, and ultimately the cost efficiency of the unit. The way to manage production in the labor and delivery unit is to incorporate the complex of interventions, the epiduralized birth: the Gleichschaltung of birth.

Walsh (2006b, 2009), a British medical ethnographer, describes the same phenomenon, referring to it as assembly-line childbirth. Hospital birth has come to be process-oriented and out-of-sync with the "temporality of labor and birth". Without interventions, physiologic birth is individual, highly variable, and unpredictable. The industrial model of childbirth, with its focus on standardization and management of the progress of labor, is designed to move women through the system, a particular concern in large hospitals. Walsh (2009, 166) describes the commonalities of industrialized birth with Fordism.

> Both arrange activity around disassembled stages and with clear demarcation for employees' roles. As a car is 'birthed' following linear and discrete processes on an assembly line, so laboring women are processed through 'stages' using a mechanistic model. Both has a timescale for completion of the product, and both have a highly sophisticated regulatory framework. ...

> Procrastination and delay cannot be accommodated, because of a cascade effect for other stages. In their study of a large delivery suite, Hunt and Symonds (1995) observed that the labor procrastinators ("nigglers", or women in early labor) did not constitute real work in the eyes of the midwives in their study and that this activity needs sifting out if the system is to work efficiently. Delays after a process is started are dealt with by acceleratory interventions such as artificial rupture of membranes.

The Agency of Mothers in Epiduralized Birth: "Induce Me Now!"

> "I came in one night and they told me I was only one centimeter and that the pain I felt was cramping but not real contractions, so they sent me home. But I was so uncomfortable at home. I came back in and I was going to make sure they kept me this time."

The above words, spoken to me spontaneously by a mother, represent the back and forth between midwives and mothers witnessed throughout my fieldwork. Women are active players in the industrialized system of birth. This can be seen in the demand for epidurals and induction, as well as the desire to have as many ultrasounds as possible.

Three ultrasounds during pregnancy were the norm. Typically, the first ultrasound obtains the best dating possible for the pregnancy, establishing an estimated due date. (This is often done in the first trimester, prior to twelve weeks.) The next ultrasound, performed during the second trimester, determines if the baby has any anomalies and the location of the placenta. The third, closer to the estimated due date, verifies the position of the baby, as well as the condition of the placenta and the health of the fetus. If a mother goes beyond her due date, or if there is any medical condition to be ruled out, it is not unusual for the mother to have a fourth or even fifth ultrasound in the form of a biophysical profile. [21]

The meaning of the term "due date" is in flux. The very concept of a due date is one that has fundamentally changed as a result of industrialized birth. What was once an *estimated* date with five weeks of potential variation has come to be viewed as a *date certain* by both doctors and mothers alike. (In later chapters, I discuss how this five-week period has now been categorized into three distinct periods—early full term, full term, and late full term—justifying greater use of prenatal testing in normal pregnancy.)

The midwifery service at Community Hospital had a policy against routine induction. Protocol mandated that induction require a medical indication. Indications would include postdates, concern that a baby was growing too large, low amniotic fluid, maternal hypertension, etc. This policy against routine induction was based on the desire of the service to keep down its cesarean section rate. Some mothers demanded to be induced, only to be sent home. Many would come back two or three times before they were finally admitted. Some would present to a nearby hospital where they knew that they would be admitted.

The relationship between inductions and the rising cesarean rate is debated, but most studies do show a correlation. In a review of medical literature, the American Congress of Obstetrics and Gynecology (ACOG 2014)) has recognized the correlation. Cesareans lead to significant morbidity and even mortality including maternal infection, maternal hemorrhage, neonatal respiratory difficulty, and neonatal infection (Liu et al. 2007; Belizán et al. 2007). During my fieldwork, I observed an increase in inductions for medical indications, particularly for decreased amniotic fluid index (AFI). (Discussions between midwives and physicians regarding decreased AFI are explored in later chapters.)

Some mothers had difficulty accepting the induction policy and attempted to find ways around it. During my time with the midwifery service, I began to see the service accept an erosion in its policy regarding elective induction. One reason admitted to me by midwives: they were losing patients because of the service's induction policy. The pressure to accept routine induction was great and it was coming from the patients as well as some physicians.

I began to witness discussions at the Board at morning shift change regarding what was called "social induction". Patients would appeal to physicians to be induced. A physician would state that a patient was being brought in that day to be induced for social reasons. The midwife might demure that it was against policy, but the decision by the physician was really not up for question, even though it was the midwife who had to carry out the induction.

The first time I witnessed this, the reason given for the social induction was that the husband needed to be out of town in several days. As I witnessed an increase in the number of social inductions, the reasons varied. For example, the day of induction might be the only day that the patient could find someone to care for her children or it was the only day she could be assured of transportation. Routine inductions, now the norm in most hospitals, bring an element of control to what has in the past been an experience that involves anxious waiting. Routine induction, having a set date for delivery, allows the modern mother the ability to organize all the various social demands on her time.

The stated reason for induction, at times, would be the desire to not loose a patient to a competing hospital. According to the state Medicaid rules, a mother could go to any hospital for delivery. Medicaid reimbursement was differentiated between prenatal and intrapartum care. As a result, a mother could receive prenatal care at Community Hospital and then present to another hospital for delivery. That hospital then received the portion of Medicaid payment for delivery. Competing hospitals were quite willing to induce a mother who walked into their unit. Mothers knew the right things to say: "I haven't slept in three days." "My back pain is severe." The rationalizations were numerous.

Community Hospital would become aware that they had lost a patient when they received a fax from a competing hospital requesting a copy of a mother's prenatal records and stating the mother had been admitted for induction. The Midwifery Director of the service admitted to me towards the end of 2012 that in one month alone they had expected seventy deliveries, while the actual number of deliveries was sixty. Ten out of seventy patients had presented to another hospital asking to be induced and their request was carried out.

One evening a patient came into the labor and delivery unit stating she was in labor, insisting she be admitted. The midwife on duty assessed her condition. The mother was having an occasional contraction. The midwife was in a quandary and decided to induce labor. "This mother," she told me, "came in two days ago. She was four centimeters then and she's still four centimeters. She isn't having regular contractions but she's in a lot of discomfort. If I send her home, she says she is going to another hospital where she knows she'll be admitted. Her cervix is favorable. I know once I start pitocin she'll go fast. So I've decided to augment her labor."

I looked at the midwife and said, "You realize that you are not augmenting her labor. You are inducing her labor. She's not in true labor. She has had no cervical changes since her last visit and she's not having regular contractions." The midwife looked at me sheepishly, sighed, and shrugged her shoulders. She was correct; once pitocin was administered, the mother began to have regular contractions and quickly delivered. However, the midwife documented this induction of labor as an augmented labor. It was not the first time I have seen an induction of labor called augmentation of labor—one reason why it is difficult for researchers to determine how often induction occurs.

There is no reliable estimate for induction rates due to this confusion over how to categorize the start of pitocin administration. Is it an induction or augmentation of labor? One academic article estimated induction rates in the U.S. to be from 9.5% to 33.7% of all pregnancies (Tenmore 2003). This estimate is indeed a wide-span and reflects the difficulty in knowing precisely what is going on in our labor and delivery units. What has been recognized is that the increased practice of routine labor induction has resulted in a progressive trend towards birth at lower gestational ages. This trend toward decreased gestational age at birth appears to have slowed with the recent ACOG recommendation limiting routine induction to 39 weeks (Osterman and Martin 2014). It must be recognized, however, that even under the best circumstances (i.e. a ripe cervix) induction of labor involves risks.

The midwife quoted above later discussed her conundrum in an interview.

> Midwife: We have sent people home because we pride ourselves on our low C-section rates and not intervening. However, there have been patients not in active labor sent home. They might be multips at four or five centimeters but if after several hours it's judged that there hasn't been any changes, or their labor hasn't picked up, they were sent home. And subsequently we find out that they go to another hospital and are admitted.
>
> So is it that important to send people home or keep them and give them a whiff of pitocin when they are four to five centimeters and we're not busy? Where do we draw the line? ... A client will say, "Wait a minute. I thought we get admitted. I thought you admit people at six centimeters." And I say, "Well, it's nice to be in labor too."... Because I've known people to walk around for a week or two at six centimeters.

Twenty years ago, mothers would have been told to go home and return when contractions are regular and at least five minutes apart. A patient might have been given medication to help her sleep in order to cope with the common discomfort of late pregnancy. But she would not be induced merely for her convenience or the convenience of the L&D unit.

I was discussing this pressure to induce labor with several of the midwives and what they said was illuminating. One midwife spoke about what was lost when a mother is given a routine induction—the significance of the anticipatory period before the start of labor.

> I think it's surrendering. To have a natural childbirth, you have to have a confidence. What I saw in my last practice, this core of high achieving, workaholic, goal-oriented women ... shooting off emails on their way to the hospital. ... That's different from here that's for sure.

... but they did self-select to nurse-midwifery because they wanted support. ... I think they were trying to do so many things; they weren't totally putting as much [into it] or getting into that place of quietness. For some of them, I would have to work with them to put on the brakes. I would say, "I think it's good to take a week off before your due date just to tie yourself together and get yourself into the place where you need to be to take on labor and stuff." ... It's an approach to life.

Of course, "taking a week off" to get into a quiet space was a privilege available to few mothers at Community Hospital. Another midwife compared the inductions at Community Hospital to other settings where she had worked, stating that the induction rate was much higher in other settings.

Midwife: I don't know if they've looked at the national induction rate, but it's way higher than here. [In some hospitals] people fight over spots for inductions.

MAM: What do you mean, "fight over inductions"?

Midwife: Physician practices. Because induction schedules get filled. That's why ACOG made that rule, and a lot of insurance companies. That you can't induce before 39 weeks. Because it had become such a problem.

MAM: So you're saying, women are routinely being scheduled for inductions at other places?

Midwife: Maybe it isn't called that. People are kept who are not truly in labor because they want to be.

MAM: And then it's called augmentation of labor when it's really induction?

Midwife: Right. I don't think we're doing that. I mean. Sure sometimes it happens. You know it happens. But it doesn't happen routinely. And because you are in the hospital and you have access to pitocin, it's easy to just say, "Look. You are still at six and it has been four hours." ... So maybe the numbers here are not ideal. But if you compare it to the standard, it is a lot better. A *lot* better. People aren't going to give you induction numbers. Because as I was saying, there isn't a schedule. And physicians will say to the patients sometimes, "If you want an induction, go in, complain of x, y, z and you'll get admitted." It's like a sneak induction.

MAM: What kinds of things would a woman say for a sneak induction?

Midwife: The baby's not moving. If you're 40 weeks and the baby isn't moving as much, chances are you're going to have an induction. They'll just sneak it in somehow. It's an easy way for the doctor to say, "Let's just induce her." And then he has his induction in. ... The larger hospitals will have daytime induction and nighttime induction. They have five spots for the day and five spots for the night. And they are scheduled weeks in advance.

MAM: And they have places on the schedule for induction just like they schedule operating rooms for repeat sections far in advance?

Midwife: Yeah. Yeah. And you better get them on the book weeks early because if you don't get it on the book early, you're not going to get in.

MAM: Here what tends to happen is that somebody will be seen in clinic and they'll be sent over.

Midwife: They'll be sent over. And some of it are the physicians because Dr. X sends over a lot of people. And maybe that's something we have to tease out. Because we're delivering the physician's patients also.

... I've worked at a small community hospital in (City X) but it was busier than here. It was kind of similar. There were both nurse-midwives and physicians. So some of the way things were done, you could see the way that physicians did things. And then I worked in a large tertiary care center in (City Y) that did 7,000 deliveries a year.

... The community hospital wasn't bad. You could see that nurse-midwives did things one way and the physicians did things another way. Although some nurse-midwives did things the physician way. But we had inductions every single day. Like multiple. And at the big hospital, forget it. And they were all nonsense.

MAM: So in your experience, you worked at the busy large hospital where there were a lot of routine, scheduled inductions. Did you see the correlation between inductions and cesareans?

Midwife: Oh absolutely. Absolutely. First of all, with a primip you are already putting her at risk. Because it just takes longer for a primip. And once you're at the hospital, the clock starts ticking. And people aren't patient. They're checking people every two hours, which is unfair. They are not necessarily thinking in terms of ripening a cervix. Because ripening of a cervix can take multiple days. It can take two days. They are ripening a cervix for twelve hours over night and starting pitocin regardless of whether her cervix is ready. And they also don't want to be there at night. So if it hasn't happened by a certain time… It's horrible. It's ridiculous. I couldn't stand it. I had to get out of there. [To be clear, she is talking about her experience at a different hospital.]

When this midwife said that Community Hospital would go days without an induction, from my observations her statement is not correct. To be fair, the midwives at Community Hospital were quite aware of the risks of induction—usually taking measures to ripen the cervix (when necessary), having patience, and trying to avoid the tradition of being driven by the clock. My observation, however, was that it was not uncommon to see a nurse-midwife begin an induction with one dose only of prostaglandin gel to ripen a cervix, and to then begin pitocin regardless of the Bishop's Score of the cervix. (A cervical Bishop's Score is an assessment of how favorable a cervix is for induction.) [22]

I observed only one young obstetrician who insisted on using the Bishop's Score in determining when to begin induction. A nurse had come to him, requesting to begin pitocin on an induction. He asked, "What is her Bishop's Score?" I did not hear the nurse's response, but I did hear him respond to her with an agitated voice. "Don't ask me to start pitocin until you can give me a Bishop's Score of at least seven. Give her another dose of gel. I won't start pitocin without a favorable cervix. I don't care how long it takes." He was the only obstetrician that I observed insisting on this standard of care.

The most important point to take from the above midwife's comment is that in many hospitals, routine scheduling of induction has become the norm. At Community Hospital, it was rare to see a mother admitted and allowed more than a day for cervical ripening, a process that might require multiple applications of a prostaglandin cervical gel in order to be successful. The obstetrical system just does not allow for the expense of patience as an approach to cervical ripening.

As the midwife above noted, at many hospitals where routine inductions are normative, there are a fixed number of openings for induction. Competition among physician practices over induction schedules lead to the scheduling of induction at the twenty-week prenatal visit. Hospitals schedule inductions in the way they schedule elective surgeries. In the past, if there was no opening for a 39-week induction, obstetricians then worked backwards scheduling the induction for 38 or even 37 weeks.

A due date is nothing more than an estimate. With early induction, it is not unusual for a baby to be delivered who is assessed after birth to be premature, less than 37 weeks gestation. It was because of this growing trend that ACOG came out with a position declaring induction for non-medical indications to be unsafe prior to 39 weeks (ACOG 2013a). Routine scheduling of inductions was not protocol at Community Hospital. Yet I began to observe an increase in inductions during my year of fieldwork, where I frequently saw inductions on the Board.

I encouraged one midwife to talk about the phenomenon of the social inductions that I witnessed—inductions carried out for social reasons rather than medical indications.

> MAM: I overheard a discussion between several midwives and several physicians during report, during shift change, about induction. And I got the sense that some of the physicians were more supportive of induction. They used an interesting term that I hadn't heard before: social induction.

> Midwife: Yes. It's used when an induction is considered but there is not a medical indication. Maybe the patient is tired. They're ... People come up with all kinds of things. "My husband works. He can only be there on this day." "I'm afraid it's going to snow." Now that it's winter, that will be a big one. "What if I can't get here?" "I have childcare issues."

... It's like people are begging to have the baby. ... The due date is an end point. ... For me, part of the magic of it [birth] is that it is something in which you have no control. You don't know when it's going to start. [But] it's anxiety provoking for some people. ... Women here have so many hard issues to deal with. Transportation here is such a large issue. And that is a big issue. "I'm not sure how I'm going to get there but I'll figure it out when it happens." I find that does happen here.

... People complain. "I want to have my baby now," and they are 37 weeks. And they will go to another hospital. But to me ... I find myself having to explain, and explain, and explain. Because it is good practice. It is not good practice to induce at 38 weeks. It's crazy. And you don't give into that.

MAM: And even if it is your due date. It's still not good.

Midwife: Right. Absolutely not. It's so much better to go into labor on your own. And if someone comes in and they are two centimeters but they are not contracting, they are not in labor. They are *not* in labor. And I have done my job. Some of the midwives worry that we are losing patients. I don't have that responsibility so it doesn't bother me. Because I feel that in the end we are better off doing the right thing.

The pressure on the midwives to give in to unnecessary induction came, not only from patients but also came from some of the physicians, who held the philosophy that inductions were an overall positive for the service. This was borne out in a debate that occurred at a staff meeting between a midwife and a physician. The debate was over the midwife's decision to send a mother home, refusing to carry out the mother's request for an induction that was not medically justified. The Department Chair berated her decision and made clear that the decision should ultimately come down to the issue of efficient utilization of labor beds. "There is no reason to turn away a mother who wants an induction. We are underutilized," the Department Chair scolded.

One midwife argued that there was a problem in the department with physicians giving orders for inductions without consultation with the midwife on-duty. Yet it is the midwife who is responsible for carrying out the induction and is held responsible for any outcomes that may result.

> Midwife: [The midwife has the right] to know if someone is coming in for an induction. And they have the right to know what the reason is. And if there is no medical reason ... In my way of thinking, there will be times when it makes sense but it should not just be willy-nilly. Well, we've learned our lessons there. So we're less likely to do the willy-nilly. But we still do inductions from time to time. And some of it is the docs sending their patient in for induction. Partly because of the numbers, we're not going to turn it down.

> MAM: That was what Dr. X said to me. "The service can't afford to turn away patients."

> Midwife: Midwives wind up doing some of the management of the induction and get feisty about it because it's never for the reason that is put in the book. LGA [Large for Gestational Age]. Postdates. And then they [the mothers] are neither when they come in. It's for the doc's convenience. But we try to hold the line at 39 weeks at least.

> MAM: It was interesting, this interchange in the meeting. The midwife said she had sent somebody home saying, "No. I'm not going to do an induction." I think the patient was 39 weeks.

> Midwife: Was it busy?

> MAM: She said it had been very busy. But Dr. X said, "That should never be an excuse. We're underutilized."

> Midwife: ...We have sent people home because we pride ourselves on our low C-section rates and not intervening. There have been patients not in active labor sent home. They might be multips at four or five centimeters but if after several hours it's judged that there hasn't been any changes, or their labor hasn't picked up, they were sent home. And subsequently, we find out that they go to another hospital and are admitted.

The escalation in the number of inductions could be one explanation for the increased cesarean rate at Community

Hospital, which occurred even as the census rate decreased. (This increase in the cesarean rate over time is discussed in a later chapter.) Another explanation for this rise in cesareans within the practice was discussed in a staff meeting, where the Department Chair presented data on the trend of rising obesity, failure to descend, and increased newborn birth weight among their clientele. When I asked if the failure to descend might be related to epidural administration, the Department Chair stated that a correlation was possible but unclear.

The nurse-midwifery service at Community Hospital provided care to an increasingly high-risk population due to a greater number of extremely obese mothers with accompanying co-morbidity. The fact that the maternity service at Community Hospital continued to show positive neonatal outcomes (also discussed in a later chapter) is a reflection of the quality care provided, despite the high-risk of many patients due to the incidence of obesity, and other chronic health problems, among the clientele.

"Give Me My Epidural Now!"

As previously noted, 80% to 90% of women chose to have an epidural, and it was an intervention about which many mothers were most adamant. It was *"my"* epidural. While the vast majority of women received an epidural, there was often a delay in when a mother might receive her pain relief. Community Hospital contracted with a private anesthesia practice to provide hospital-wide anesthesia. When the anesthesia department received a call from the L&D unit for an epidural to be administered, the timing of when the anesthesiologist arrived depended on the overall demands of the hospital, particularly what was going on in the operative suite. At night there was only one anesthesiologist on site. If the anesthesiologist was tied up in an emergency operation there could be a time lag in arrival to the unit. Additionally, blood work had to be drawn and the results received before the anesthesiologist administered an epidural.

One incident I witnessed illustrates the extent to which the mothers at Community Hospitals worked at getting "my epidural". A woman had come to the unit during the evening, diagnosed as being in early labor, and admitted to the unit. It was not her first baby. As she was wheeled towards her room, she was screaming and writhing in pain. "I want my epidural *now*! You call that little Indian doctor and tell him to get up here *now* and give me my epidural." The nurses were respectful but at the same time teasing the mother. "Now Miss X," one nurse teasingly said. "How do you know that Dr. X is on duty tonight? And you know we have to draw blood and wait for the lab results before we call Dr. X to come give you an epidural. He's going to want to see your results."

As the mother was helped into the bed, she continued to scream in pain, rocking back and forth, screaming that she was in terrible pain and needed her epidural. A family member took hold of the rolling bedside table, positioned it, and placed upon it a camcorder that he proceeded to turn on. One of the nurses informed him that he could not tape the birth, that it was against hospital policy. He turned off the camcorder, but within several minutes the red light was back on. Another nurse told him once again to turn it off. At this, the mother quickly sat straight up in bed. She was no longer screaming and rocking in pain. She furiously said to the nurse, "Girl. You can't tell him what to do. He is going to tape my entire birth." Gone was the screaming pain. Her entire behavior seemed to have been an attempt to speed up the process of obtaining epidural anesthesia. What I observed were mothers actively influencing the system to receive the care that *they* desired. These mothers were far from powerless victims of the system.

I found that mothers knew and utilized medical terminology in a way that patients did not know twenty years ago. Like the young mother discussed above, patients would use words such as "rupture of membranes". "Dehydration". I am "high-risk". "Maternal exhaustion". "Vacuum extraction". "Induce". "Dilation". "Effacement". I heard mothers use these words and phrases quite freely and with ease. They spoke in terms of weeks of gestation rather than months, which was common in the past.

The use of medical terminology by patients was a means of negotiating their way through the birth system. One midwife said to me, "People know the buzz words to get themselves into the hospital, to get themselves onto the monitor."

I observed numerous instances of the agency of mothers who were determined to give birth in *their* way. Some midwives were conflicted when faced with the contradiction between their own beliefs and that of the mother demanding interventions. I observed one young, first-time, seventeen-year-old mother take over control of the birthing room. In this instance, she had the typical epiduralized birth and having reached full dilation of the cervix was encouraged to start pushing. The young mother decided she was not going to push. She lay back on the labor bed, sipping her water, and just refused to push. "I have maternal exhaustion," she said. "Call the doctor. Tell her that I have maternal exhaustion. Tell her to bring the vacuum. She is going to have to vacuum the baby out." (She was referring here to vacuum extraction, a procedure used during second stage of labor when a mother has not been successful in delivering the baby. The use of instruments to deliver the baby, either forceps or vacuum extraction, is one of the potential risks with an epidural.)

It was close to shift change and the midwife on duty, a midwife of many years experience, was quietly and patiently trying to encourage this young mother to try to push, but to no avail. Finally, she threw up her hands and left the room. The new midwife on duty came into the room, appraised the situation, looked at the mother, placed her hands on her hips and firmly said, "You *are* going to push and you are going to push *now.*" And push she did with the baby delivered thirty minutes later.

In epiduralized birth, the pushing stage can be difficult because a nurse or midwife has to actively talk the mother through the mechanical motions of pushing. For the mother it can be frustrating because it is often difficult to make progress, pushing the baby through the birth canal when she does not have sensation. This is in opposition to the way that a woman's body normally works without an epidural, where spontaneous and ultimately uncontrollable urges to push occur. With the epidural, so much of the pushing becomes a matter of position and mechanics.

I observed mothers at Community Hospital, though a definite minority, request birth with little or no intervention. These choices were honored whenever possible. VBACs were not uncommon and I witnessed one twin vaginal birth by a nurse-midwife, with the obstetrician close by in the hallway. The epiduralized births that were the norm at Community Hospital seemed to be as much about the social environment in which we find ourselves, not merely a result of an authoritative hand of the medical professionals at the midwifery service. Mothers were demanding the care that *they* wanted, even when the nurse-midwifes disagreed with their decisions. Yes, there are social forces at work that many mothers do not recognize or understand. For the mothers at Community Hospital, however, it seemed that what was important to them was that *they* were making the decisions.

It's All About The Relationship

I observed mothers who strived to establish a relationship with a single midwife, impairing the team approach used by the midwifery service at Community Hospital. One midwife was a particular favorite. Other midwives and doctors shared with me that her prenatal schedule was quickly filled up and she had a very low no-show rate compared to other midwives. When she was on duty at night, the doctors complained. One doctor openly stated, "She tells her patients when she is going to be on. I know she does. We are going to be so busy during the night. No sleep tonight."

It was not difficult to see why she was a favorite. On labor and delivery she did not rest, moving from room to room, spending as much time with each laboring woman as possible. Numerous researchers have discussed the significance of a one-on-one relationship where the mother develops trust in her provider. British researchers, in particular, have looked at this characteristic of care and point to the relationship between mother and midwife as a significant element for a successful, safe delivery and for promotion of maternal satisfaction and maternal-infant bonding (Sandall 1997; Sandall et al. 2009, 2010, 2012; Walsh 2006a, 2006b, 2009).

One of the limitations of the team approach to maternity care is that it is difficult to establish an intimate relationship between midwife and client. Yet, it is within an intimate relationship that a mother is most likely to feel cared for and to have the feeling of safety that is so important for physiologic labor. Hunter et al. (2008) use a metaphor, the "hidden threads in the tapestry of maternity care", to describe the significance of the midwife-mother relationship. "The quality of relationships is fundamental to the quality of maternity care. Although this might appear to be stating the obvious, it is notable how rarely relationships are overtly identified as causal factors, particularly in macro-level discussions of maternity care (Hunter et al. 2008, 132)."

In addition to the continuity of care between midwife and mother, Huber and Sandall (2009) have identified the element of "calm", the "freedom from agitation or excitement", as another important aspect of physiologic birth. They point out that these characteristics of care are intrinsically related to the midwife/mother relationship. When a pregnant woman has established a relationship of trust with her provider, information is more likely to be accepted and heard. This helps to create relief from the anxiety that is so often the cause of abnormal labor. It is one thing to say to a mother, "This is your show. You do it your way." This is only one side of the equation of a trusting relationship. There needs to be trust; the job of a midwife is to provide accurate information during informed consent and to manage the birth environment so that the mother has the calm and privacy so necessary for the progress of birth.

The fragmentation of care seen in a team approach to maternity care, which was the model of care at Community Hospital, makes it difficult to establish these intimate relationships between provider and patient. A mother may come to the hospital in labor and be cared for by a midwife she has never seen. The midwifery service did try to have all midwifes meet each patient at some point during prenatal care. However, this goal was difficult to fully implement due to scheduling and the use of part-time midwives. One strategy used at Community Hospital was for midwives to share information about clients informally and at staff meetings. Additionally, the careful documentation that I observed during prenatal care helped in communication between midwives about patients. When a mother arrived at the labor and delivery unit, the midwife-on-call usually knew about her even if they had never met. This does not, however, take the place of the continuity of care and the trust that develops when each patient is assigned a primary midwife. However, caseload organization of care, where a patient has a primary midwife, can be costly.

It was during prenatal care that the midwives at Community Hospital truly shined and the values of nurse-midwifery were most evident. During prenatal visits, I observed how midwives listened; they shared of themselves, provided important information and education. Patients were treated with respect and dignity.

Caseload midwifery care, the organizational term for when a mother has a primary midwife, is shown by McLachlan et al. (2000) to result in decreased augmentation and epidural rates when randomly compared to a study group of mothers who receive a traditional team, or shared-care approach, to maternity care. Another positive aspect of caseload midwifery is what Walsh (2006a) calls matrescence, the process of becoming a mother. This process of matrescence is "relationally mediated". In traditional childbirth, this process of becoming a mother involves cultural and social practices where a pregnant woman is surrounded and cared for by other women. The traditional period of "lying in" as described by Leavitt (1986) and Wertz and Wertz (1989[1977]) served a dual purpose. First, it created a period of time for the mother-to-be to prepare mentally for the birth, to limit stimulation, thereby beginning the process of shutting down the cerebral cortex (Odent 2002). It also provided a time for nurturing and care, a mothering of the mother.

The favored midwife described to me her philosophy, her approach to care. It led to an intimacy with mothers, where she could say things that other midwives found difficult.

MAM: One thing I've noticed in observing you, *you* can say things to people that other midwives don't or won't. Why is that? What do you think it is?

Midwife: Well, you have to be nice. You have to be straightforward. But if you want people to listen to you, you can't talk down to them. Because I'm a defiant person by nature. If you tell me I *can't* do something, I'll do it just to prove to you that I *can*. It's a "you're not the boss of me" type thing. But yeah. If you want people to take you seriously, and listen to what you have to say, you have to say it in a way that doesn't piss them off.

MAM: You can be blunt and yet have the caring come across at the same time. It's a skill that I think you have.

Midwife: Part of it is that I *do* care. I do care. I do care that these women aren't getting what they need and it makes me mad. Maybe it's something having to do with championing the underdog. But I do care. I do want them to have a good experience. They deserve to have the best experience, just like any woman at some highfalutin hospital. But they have to meet me half-way. Just don't be an idiot. Don't be stupid. Again, don't be stupid. If you do crack, guess what? Your baby is going to be investigated.

The above is an example of what Walsh (2006a) is talking about when he discusses matrescence as a distinct feature of optimal maternity care. Mothers-to-be, particularly younger women as well as women who have been inadequately nurtured themselves, need to feel cared for. Along with this care comes the trust that enables the mother to accept the advice of her provider and that prepares the mother to, in kind, mother her child.

Odent (2002) talks about the importance of creating an environment of quiet and safety as a means of facilitating physiologic birth. Some midwives at Community Hospital had difficulty managing the environment of the birthing room. The perceived right of the autonomy of the mother, her choice of whom to have in the room, as well as the extent to which social media was brought into the birthing room, these all at times came into conflict with the midwifery value of physiologic birth. There were some exceptions: One midwife, coming into a room with numerous people sitting around creating commotion, simply told people to get out. "This is not a sport event," she said. "Only two people can stay." Still yet another midwife came into a room where a mother was pushing. "Turn that TV off," she said in an authoritative voice. "No baby deserves to be born hearing Jerry Springer in the background." She would also reprimand family members who would be creating disorder, for example talking loudly on their cell phones and busily snapping pictures. "It is the mother who is important here. Put that away." "You can take pictures after the baby is born. No crotch shots."

Another midwife described walking into a room where a mother was having difficulty with a prolonged second stage. "There were numerous family members in the room, just sitting there doing nothing. One family member was sitting in front of the TV, his legs propped up, eating Cheetos, and watching the movie Scarface. I had most of the family leave and had the TV turned off." Still yet another midwife commented, "It's almost as if they [the family] are modeling [the birth] on what they see on TV, acting like they are on a reality show." Another midwife agreed. "I forget the really nice birth that I last had, because there aren't that many these days. ... There was one. It was just constant. People were on their phones, and talking, facebooking, and notifying the entire city. And I was like, 'Uh. There *is* a mother and baby here.' "

Choice and Consent

As mentioned previously, the Chief of Obstetrics at Community Hospital estimated that 80% of the patients received an epidural, verifying my observations that epiduralized birth was the norm at Community Hospital. From my interviews, it is apparent that interventions such as epidurals, planned induction, augmentation of labor, and elective cesareans are widespread in American hospitals. It is difficult to find precise statistics on the scale of these interventions due to the lack of data. Cahill et al. (2010) estimate a 90% epidural rate in many maternity units nationwide. Osterman and Martin (2011) estimate a 60% epidural rate nationwide. What is known is that there are wide variations in the use of epidurals: variations by race, class, and age, as well as region (Osterman and Martin 2011). Women are told that an epidural is safe. The appeal of a painless childbirth is obvious.

The work of Gertrude Fraser is significant in any discussion of birth, race and decision-making. Fraser (1995, 1998) makes the point that when discussing the pros and cons of the medical model of childbirth, it is important to recognize that maternity care can look very different, and provide a different balance of benefits and limitations, to the white, middle-class woman as compared to an African-American woman. A social and historical prism factors into how each mother approaches childbirth. For example, homebirth and/or a midwife delivery may be a form of resistance to the hegemony of modern obstetrics among some white, middle-class women. For the equally self-aware, middle-class, African-American woman, homebirth and midwifery may symbolize the humiliating and dangerous health care disparities during the era of segregation. Most relevant to this discussion, relief of pain during childbirth with an epidural is seen by many women of color as a right, not a hegemonic intervention. Poor and minority women can view the absence of such pain relief as discriminatory. They can remember a time, not so long ago, when the epidural was available only to a few, elite women with a generous medical insurance policy.

Nurse-midwives tend to justify their engagement in epiduralized birth on the basis of the concepts of control and choice. The justification is that they (nurse-midwives), by accepting the status quo of epiduralized birth, are honoring the choice of mothers and the need of mothers to have control over their birth experience. However, these terms are used without agreement as to their meaning.

The concepts of choice and control need to be problematized, as both are nebulous even as they are widely used without adequate definition. The term *control* is used quite a bit in childbirth literature. While the concept is identified as important to childbearing women, it is "rarely defined" and there is ambiguity in the ways that the term is utilized. The concept of control is also ambiguous, holding numerous meanings for women in the context of childbearing. The term *control* variously refers to options, self-determination, respect, personal security, attachment, and knowledge. Each of these words, in turn, holds a variety of meanings for different women (Namey and Lyerly 2010).

Choice is an illusion in the absence of knowledge. For example, the nurse-midwives I observed often failed to emphasize significant information regarding the potential adverse effects of both the epidural and pitocin administration. The choice made by women for epiduralized birth is often not a genuine choice. In many situations in our complex world, we are frequently not presented with the complete information and knowledge needed to make a true informed choice. In the face of complexity and uncertainty, individuals often accept the information given to them by authority figures as being truthful, particularly in vulnerable situations. In the context of a set of givens within a certain environment, available choices are often confusing and unclear.

In the context of the modern hospital, mothers are not making a truly informed choice to have an epiduralized birth. Informed consent for an epidural, as I observed, involved in some cases the holding back of information. Equally offensive, although on its face seemingly innocuous, informed consent often involved the trivializing of information. In the face of the normalization of medicalized birth by society as a whole, and in the face of experts deemphasizing the risks, it is easy to see the rationality in a mother choosing the ease of an epiduralized birth. Some nurse-midwives then use the mother's choice as their justification for acquiescence to our system of epiduralized birth.

In choosing epiduralized birth, women are not misled in the sense of the Marxist concept of false consciousness. Rather, American women have become extremely welded to the epidural and to routine induction. Certainly, larger forces are at work. Perhaps what we are looking at is the neo-liberal concept of the patient as an individual consumer. Women enter into prenatal care already "deeply acculturated" (Heelan 2013, 156) to technological interventions.

This phenomenon has been researched. In one British study, fifty-eight midwives were observed as they provided informed consent to mothers as to options for fetal monitoring during labor. What the researchers found was a profound disconnect between the ideal of informed consent and the reality. The midwives "favoured the application of informed consent and shared a unanimous consensus on the definition. However, the idealistic perception of informed choice, which included contemporary notions of empowerment and autonomy for women expressing an informed choice, was not reportedly translated into practice (Hindley and Thomson 2005, 306)." "In reality, informed choice for women is a slogan that often does not apply to practice (p. 313)." Hindley and Thomson further attributed this disconnect between the ideal and reality to "deeply ingrained cultural expectations" (p. 313), as well as to a "deeply ingrained pre-occupation with technological methods," which has "placed limits on the facilitation of informed choice and autonomous decision making for women (p. 306)."

Ultimately, the failure of midwives to provide robust informed consent is a reality of working within the confines of a Western obstetrical system of care.

> [Informed choice was carried out] within a competing set of health service agendas, i.e. medically driven protocols and a political climate of actively managed childbearing. This resulted in the manipulation of information during the midwives' interactions with women. This ultimately meant that the women often got the choice the midwives wanted them to have (Hindley and Thomson 2005, 306).

Choice has become an empty word in the context within which it is used in the modern world, merely "rhetoric" as stated by Hindley and Thomson (2005). In modern society, choice is often a "bare choice" and of little value because it is so often used outside of the context of what we are choosing between. No society allows unfettered individual choice. One can argue for the primacy of a woman's right to choose, but in reality a woman's choice is rarely divorced from her relationships and her environment. It becomes a meaningless concept when thought of outside the context of social life.

> It is clear that to have any kind of livable society some
> choices have to be restricted, some authorities have to be
> respected and some individual responsibility has to be
> assumed. The issue should always be which choices,
> authorities and responsibilities, and at what cost. In
> other words, falling back on slogans ... hides from us the
> dilemma we have to navigate between in our choices
> (Taylor 2007, 479).

Is there any such thing as an absolute right to individual
choice? Choice has come to be used as the ultimate justification
for almost anything. For example, is it in the interests of society
that women have the right to choose an elective primary cesarean,
a position supported by ACOG (2013b)? The question needs to be
asked: to what degree are women truly choosing their
epiduralized births? Given the fact that epidural and pitocin
administration can pose significant risks, should women have the
right to choose an epiduralized birth as a routine intervention,
with no medical indication? Should they at least be thoroughly
advised as to what the medical literature shows regarding the
safety of epidurals and pitocin administration?

The issue of informed consent goes to the heart of the right to
the autonomy of women to birth as they choose, a core value of
nurse-midwifery. These values—choice, control, autonomy, and
right to informed consent—are deeply enmeshed within the
nurse-midwifery profession and culture. However, there appears
to be a disconnect between theory and practice in the case of
informed consent. Without true informed consent, where *all*
pertinent information is provided, there can be no true autonomy.

> Informed consent is a legal process central to the
> protection of patient autonomy. The idea of shared
> decision-making is an ethical correlate to the legal term
> of informed consent, both of which exist to enhance
> patient participation and control in his/her medical care
> (Cahill et al. 2010, 125).

The concept of shared decision-making can be a cop-out—a way
of avoiding difficult conversations while maintaining a facade of
autonomy. When a medical decision involves an intervention

with potential side effects, it is imperative that a patient receives all relevant information. Without full disclosure of risks and benefits, and the *weight* of each risk in relation to benefit, the decision to have an epidural becomes normative, accommodating the needs of the maternity care system while abdicating the rights and autonomy that the patient believes is present (Whitney et al. 2003).

---

16   Well-woman care refers to primary care provided to women who are not pregnant—typically the care that healthy women expect from a yearly visit to a provider. This care would include a pap smear, breast exam, and contraception if needed. Diagnosis and treatment of sexually transmitted infections and urinary tract infections are included in the scope of practice of CNM as well.

17   Triage of patients occurred for a variety of reasons. If a patient had any complaint at all, she could walk into the unit and ask to be assessed. One example might be that the mother was concerned the baby was not moving as often as was normal. Another common reason for triage was that the mother would come to the unit without calling stating that she was in labor and asking to be admitted. She would be assessed in a triage room, including having external fetal monitoring which would show the fetal heart pattern and the maternal contraction pattern. As I describe later, these interactions between mother and midwife were difficult. Often the mother came in hoping to be induced. The midwife service had a policy against induction of labor without a medical indication. The medical studies showing direct correlation between induction and cesarean rates are numerous. One midwife informed me of what she called "sneak inductions" where women would walk in and know what to say in order to be admitted and induced.

18   Anthropologists place great significance on language. So much about human society can be discerned by the identification of a culture's use of words to describe the environment.

19   Even with the so-called "walking epidural", I never saw a mother taken out of bed when having an epidural. One midwife did talk about getting women up into a chair at times when they had a walking epidural. To do such a thing required the help of three staff and so it occurred quite infrequently.

20   Several midwives did share with me that they tried to avoid this practice of directed pushing, encouraging a process they called "laboring down". This involved having the mother continue to labor after full dilation, allowing for a period when the baby would begin to make its way into the birth canal. This practice was discouraged by some of the physicians and nurses.

21   A biophysical profile is a diagnostic procedure simultaneously using ultrasound and electronic fetal monitoring. It provides an analysis of the wellbeing of the fetus. A score is provided based on five measurements – fetal heart rate in relation to fetal movement, frequency of fetal movement, fetal muscle tone, fetal respirations and the amount of amniotic fluid (also called the amniotic fluid index or AFI).

22   Bishop's Score is a scoring assessment of the cervix using five criteria—cervical dilation, effacement, consistency, position, as well as fetal position. It has been shown to be predictive for how likely a mother's cervix will respond positively to induction, leading to a successful vaginal delivery following induction.

Chapter Three
Negotiating Birth

"I think we did women a disservice, à la Lamaze, by suggesting that there can be birth without any pain (A midwife)."

"I [am] no longer in charge of my own independent midwifery service, ... at least I [am] still catching babies (Vincent 2003, 321)."

The desire for independence and autonomy among nurse-midwives is often in conflict with the realities of daily clinical practice. In most clinical settings, nurse-midwives work side-by-side with obstetricians, many of whom still believe in a staff hierarchy where they function in a supervisory position. When nurse-midwives and obstetricians do not agree on how to carry out care, difficult situations arise, requiring negotiation. In many cases, obstetricians essentially trump the decision-making of nurse-midwives; despite the desire by midwives for equal collaboration. Physician hegemony is still the reality for many nurse-midwives. There remains for nurse-midwives a "conflicting claim to occupational jurisdiction." Within the hospital setting in particular, nurse-midwives are too often essentially "subordinate" (Teasley 1983, 1).

At Community Hospital, not all obstetricians interfered with the decision-making of nurse-midwives in the care of low-risk patients. Most of the physicians were respectful and genial. Each nurse-midwife had her own strategy for dealing with interference and control by some of these same physicians. The point is that the concept of collaboration only works to the extent that each individual obstetrician does, in fact, see the nurse-midwife as an equal professional player. That is not always the case. At the same time, for many nurse-midwives, collaboration is an escape clause from taking responsibility.

One CNM, a homebirth midwife with an independent practice, spoke to me about the conflict between CNMs and obstetricians around the issue of independence. Criticizing the concepts of a back-up physician and written practice agreements, she described the requirement of a written practice agreement as "a permission slip from your father". On the other hand, she was critical of the approach of some independent midwives who see the practice agreement as a form of protection, a way to "pass the buck" if something goes wrong.

> We want to be independent but, at the same time, we want the physician to take the ultimate responsibility. It's what they are accusing us of, that we want them to be our deep pocket. If that's the midwife's attitude, then we are never going to be an autonomous, independent practitioner. ... And until midwifery schools start teaching midwifery as an autonomous profession, we're going to continue to have that hierarchical relationship.

This same homebirth CNM criticized nurse-midwifery education for not exposing students to homebirth, where she believes midwives learn independence and come to recognize what physiologic birth looks like.

> Homebirth is the gold standard. It is only in the home that you truly see physiologic birth. How many midwifery students actually see a physiologic birth in the hospital? And it is only in the home where you learn to be truly independent. ... When I go to a mother's home I have everything I need with me. ... In the hospital they have their securities, the safety net, the sense that there's a doctor down the hall five minutes away. The machines ... And that's what they rely on. ... That's what makes them feel safe.

A midwife at Community Hospital made a similar point: that there is a fundamental tension between independence and subordination and that some midwives feel they need permission to make decisions that are actually within their professional purview.

> Midwife: It is unfortunate that we avoid the issues rather than having a conversation. I feel like saying, "You know. We have good outcomes here. And we get these good outcomes by acting this way. So just leave us alone."

> It's just several physicians who act that way. The other ones let you do what [you want] with inducing somebody. [In one case] a midwife had started with one agent [for promoting cervical ripening]. And the patient wasn't making any progress. So I wanted to switch to something else. And I asked her, "What do you think?" And she said, "Yeah, if Dr. X is okay with it." And I wondered, "Why would I need to ask?" I personally felt that I didn't need to ask. I didn't. I just felt, "What the hell." And nobody had a problem with it in the morning.

Another midwife described her frustration with her position, having a great deal of responsibility but little institutional support.

> Sometimes I feel that I'm spinning my wheels. ... Looking at the admin [administration] angle that I've been pressed into. OMG. Where's the support? Where's the communication? Why am I learning all the time about one more committee meeting, or one more pass through, to get someone credentialed? And why does it take four to six months to get people on board? And why don't we have better staffing? Why is the clinic so disrupted? Why do they keep changing leadership? Why don't we have adequate supplies? Who does the ordering for supplies? Because half the time it's somebody who is out sick and the stuff isn't there.

The midwife above listed a series of problems that reflected a lack of commitment to the nurse-midwifery service on the part of hospital administration. Problems she mentioned included: a lack of support for meeting the needs of the service; being left out of meetings; a lack of communication; a floating nursing staff as opposed to a consistent, specifically trained support staff resulting in a disorganized clinic setting; and the difficulty in being resupplied in a timely fashion.

The hospital undermined the midwifery service in various ways. The prenatal clinic was disorganized and poorly staffed, a significant problem. The staffing of nurse-assistants was sporadic with no permanent assistants assigned to the prenatal office (the hospital utilized a staffing system of floating nurse-assistants). Without permanent staff, the prenatal clinic often relied on staff that did not know the complex specifics of prenatal care. It was not unusual for me to come into the office and find the midwifery service director in the chart room preparing the charts for that day's clients—a job that should have been carried out by a clerk. However, the clerk, similar to the nurse-assistants, was from a floating pool and often did not fully understand the needs of the clinic. The service director sadly commented, "I'm not sure why but I'm losing my passion for it all."

The nurse-midwives and obstetricians wanted the office to look and feel like a private office, as opposed to a clinic. This was in line with their hope that eventually they would begin to attract women with forms of insurance other than Medicaid. Theoretically, the clinic was organized like a private office. It had a comfortable waiting room and clean exam rooms. Perhaps most importantly, patients were given specific appointment times. Yet the patients, 95% of whom were on Medicaid, continued to behave as if the office was a clinic, ignoring their appointment times, and showing up at their convenience, expecting to be seen. In contrast, at many private obstetrical offices, if a patient is fifteen minutes late they are required to reschedule their visit.

Negotiating birth is a daily reality for nurse-midwives as they work to establish their profession within a division of labor, a jurisdiction (the modern obstetrical unit), which is ultimately controlled by physicians. Time and again, nurse-midwives described how they employed the skills of patience, negotiation, and subtle manipulation of the technocratic obstetrical model to bring the midwifery model of care to the many women who birth in the hospital. One nurse-midwife described to me her relationship with an obstetrician and how she is able to "handle my guy". Their relationship was difficult for her at first because he "micromanaged my care. But over time he came to trust my judgment, and I now can do pretty much what I want without his interference. When I want to do something that I think he might not go along with, I know how to handle my guy. I can call him and talk him into going along with just about whatever I think is best."

This strategy—establishing a relationship with an obstetrician, "my guy", the benevolent physician, who then backs off enough to allow the midwife room to practice her model of care—is repeatedly expressed by nurse-midwives as key to survival in the hospital setting. The danger they note is that the instinct of flexibility and compromise, so intrinsic to nurse-midwifery, can turn into its opposite: hesitance and a fear of rocking the boat. The relationship between survival and change remains a central theme in the discourse of nurse-midwives.

Veteran nurse-midwives defend their culture in terms of surviving in order to bring about change. In order to bring about change, one has to still "be there", that being *here* involves "shifting and survival". Future midwives need to be prepared for the "reality" that they must be "better than". Facing that reality involves having a clear view of "what you truly can and can't do". These are words I have heard spoken over and over. At the same time, other nurse-midwives express frustration with what they see as an ultimately self-destructive acquiescence to medicine.

Resistance to subordination does not come easily to some nurse-midwives but there are exceptional moments. At one private meeting of staff midwives, there were complaints about a change in benefits. As part of a cost-cutting plan, hospital administration informed nurse-midwives that they would no longer be subsidized to go to professional meetings. The obstetricians, in the meantime, had retained this benefit. The midwives were complaining to each other about this blatant inequality. One midwife spoke up. "Why don't we do something? We don't have to just accept it." Several days later, the service director reported that in a meeting with the OB chief she spoke strongly against the inequality in benefits. The benefit was given back.

This conflict between the desire to practice with independence and a long history of acquiescence continues to play itself out within the profession. Lawrence et al. (2012) call for interdisciplinary "teamwork" in order to provide safer maternity care. The ACNM (2011a) advocates "the principle of collaboration", collaboration involving consultation and joint management of care (ACNM 2012b). The reality of maternity care, however, is that the ability to practice as an independent profession, while working in a respectful, collaborative relationship with obstetricians, depends on the proclivity of the individual obstetricians. This was true at Community Hospital where some obstetricians recognized the midwives as experts in normal birth, seeing their own role as that of specialists in high-risk obstetrics. Yet other physicians saw themselves as serving the function of supervisor of an obstetric team that included the nurse-midwife.

ACNM's viewpoint in its position statement, *Reproductive Health Choices,* is that "every woman has the right to make reproductive health choices that meet her individual needs" in addition to the right to factual information. That right includes the right of the mother to choose elective induction of labor when provided with informed consent (ACNM 2010). These positions, taken as a whole, create an inevitable conflict in the real life world of clinical practice for nurse-midwives who increasingly find themselves caught between the various demands of all players within the American system of childbirth. Kennedy (2010, 199) asserts that for many nurse-midwives, "normal as it pertains to childbirth, is problematic." Interventions, she states, have been normalized. Women "bristle" when it is suggested that a cesarean or epidural is not normal. "Why have we made the normal abnormal and the abnormal normal in this perverse way?" Kennedy asks (2010, 199).

Certainly, other professionals face similar conflicts between the ideals of a profession and the reality of day-to-day practice but it is quite pronounced for nurse-midwives. Kennedy (2006), in a study of nurse-midwifery students, has shown a "theory-practice" gap. In her study, 50% of student respondents identified the divergence, or an incongruity, between what they are taught and the reality of the clinical practice they had seen. Nurse-midwives *believe* in physiologic birth but in many clinical settings are unable to put into *practice* the values and beliefs they hold dear.

It was difficult for the midwives at Community Hospital to respond to questions about the theory-practice gap so apparent in their own service. Their commitment to physiologic birth was clear in their care: their focus on avoiding induction when possible, facilitating VBACs, and working to keep down the hospital's cesarean rate. However, their ability to do so ultimately came down to the commitment and cooperation of the individual obstetricians.

The influence of tradition-bound practice (as opposed to evidence-based practice) as a value in the obstetrical profession is also a barrier between obstetricians and nurse-midwives. The debate at Community Hospital surrounding VBAC unveiled the fact that some obstetricians are quite reluctant to give up protocols to which they are wedded, despite scientific evidence and even despite the recommendations of their own profession. And that reluctance impacted the ability of nurse-midwives to practice independently.

At a monthly staff meeting, ACOG's (2010) latest position on VBAC was under discussion. ACOG's position on VBAC states that in the case of a healthy pregnancy, women with a history of two low-transverse cesareans, as opposed to one, might safely attempt a VBAC. (As will be discussed later, increasing the incidence of VBAC is an important element in decreasing cesarean rates.) The obstetricians and nurse-midwives were discussing if this new ACOG recommendation should become policy at Community Hospital. The nurse-midwives all spoke in favor of changing the VBAC policy as did several obstetricians. Two obstetricians were adamantly opposed to changing the policy to allow for VBAC after two cesareans, in any case. Their clinical judgment was based on the fact that they did not "feel comfortable" with the change. As a result, the policy of VBAC after only one low transverse cesarean remained departmental policy.

The fact that only the obstetricians were allowed to vote on the matter corresponded to the reality that the relationship between midwives and obstetricians was not an equal one. Amazingly enough, "comfort level" was the basis for clinical policy rather than scientific evidence. It would appear that some obstetricians profess evidence-based practice only when it supports practices that are within their "comfort level", a concept that was never quite explained and therefore left unjustified.

The 2010 ACOG position on VBAC had been a result of several years of intensive study and debate by a committee of obstetrical leaders. If a profession does not act as one, based on an understanding of the best available evidence, what we have is a clinical anarchy—a term used by critics within obstetrics itself. What I was observing during this debate over VBAC is a fundamental weakness in medicine as a whole, even if more pronounced within obstetrics. Some clinicians give lip service to evidence-based practice. In reality, some physicians make clinical decisions based on personal opinion, comfort level, convenience, and tradition (continuing to do what one has always done), as much as on science. This ideological basis for clinical decision-making is described well by the social scientist, Raymond DeVries.

> Ideological differences about the most appropriate way to give birth ... give rise to irresolvable disagreements about what constitutes evidence and how that evidence is to be interpreted. "Evidence" cannot settle scientific disputes in any simple way. Rather, it becomes a rhetorical justification for whatever particular groups were going to do anyway. Scientific evidence rests on clinical practice, which in turn is rooted in structural arrangements and cultural ideas (Devries 2004a, 595).

Another debate among the providers at a staff meeting had to do with induction of labor following rupture of membranes (ROM). The nurse-midwives argued for watchful observation of these mothers, as evidence shows that most will spontaneously go into labor within twelve hours and induction of labor increases the possibility of cesarean. On the other hand, prolonged rupture of membranes increases the possibility of maternal infection. One obstetrician argued for immediate induction stating that waiting twelve hours left only twelve more hours for the mother to deliver. The traditional clinical practice has been to perform a cesarean if a mother has not delivered within twenty-four hours following rupture of membranes. However, this practice is highly controversial within the obstetrical community and is not supported by evidence when there is a lack of signs of infection .

At Community Hospital, the decision when to induce labor following ROM depended entirely on the judgment of each individual obstetrician and was highly arbitrary. Decisions were based on convenience and arbitrary beliefs as opposed to scientific evidence as put forth in professional position statements. In discussing the back and forth between the obstetricians and midwives regarding clinical management of ROM, one midwife used the term "mediation". The use of the term "mediation" as a part of midwifery in relation to obstetrics implies a reality that nurse-midwifery practice is not always independent in clinical areas that are within the professional purview of midwifery care.

The following discussion took place in the middle of a night shift in the midwives' call room.

> Midwife: There is a definite feeling I get at the meetings that the doctors would like to be able to tell the midwives what to do. For example, they came up with their pap smear policy. Dr. X came up with a new policy following new recommendations on pap smears. He asked the physicians, "Are you comfortable with this?" But we weren't asked, although we have to enact it.

> [Regarding premature rupture of membranes (PROM).] The midwives wanted to give people twelve hours. People who wanted to wait, like for twenty-four hours, the midwives were comfortable with that. But the doctors were like, "No." There was some discussion. Dr. X can be quite collaborative but sometimes in the meetings can be authoritative. Even though working with him he can often be quite good.

> It's a problem. About 25% of women will rupture membranes spontaneously before labor begins. One midwife said in the meeting that 90% of these women go into labor within twenty-four hours. But then Dr. X said, "Yes. But they will not have delivered within that twenty-four hours." His concern was infection.

> MAM: And then we're back to the old rule that you must deliver within twenty-four hours.

> Midwife: I'd be fine with sending somebody home. But the hospital would have a problem with that. But we do have a lot of sporadic … no transportation. Some people don't even have a thermometer. We can't even go there. But I think all the midwives would be fine with, "Let's just hang out here and wait." And not examine until … I think the patient is thinking, "Why are we doing this when I could get induced?" That is where we would have to do some education about what we are doing.

> There is a mediation that goes on. Because Dr. X, he was the one who offered twelve hours, which believe me was like paradise in the OB world. [She is saying that Dr. X was suggesting that the practice have a protocol to wait for twelve hours after premature rupture of membranes before intervention.] Oh my God. We weren't even talking about patients who were GBS positive. But Dr. Y

> is more conservative about that. I work a lot with him. ... [But] I could be sitting on someone [who is] ruptured right now for the next twelve hours and he [the physician] would be unconcerned.

Let us mull over this statement: "I could be sitting on someone [who is] ruptured right now for the next twelve hours and he [the physician] would be unconcerned." It is the middle of the night. This midwife is stating that because it is nighttime and the physician is asleep, she can make decisions that the obstetrician might find objectionable during the day shift. She can hold off on induction of a mother with ruptured membranes, if at night. Instead, she can maintain a careful observation for infection while avoiding cervix checks. The midwife knows, because of both scientific evidence and experience, that the mother will most likely begin labor on her own. Without induction, the mother is more likely to have a vaginal delivery.

The midwife has the luxury of doing this because it is night and the physician would rather sleep than awaken for consultation. This obstetrician argued against delay of induction with premature rupture of membranes. However, in practice, he changes his opinion about intervention in the case of rupture of membranes depending on whether it is day or night shift. He may talk about the need to deliver within twenty-four hours, arguing that his opinion is based on science. In reality, his decisions had nothing to do with safe practice or scientific evidence. His decision-making had everything to do with time of day, convenience, and being able to sleep through the night.

Another midwife, with many years experience, described her frustration with the fact that there were still some physicians who believed they needed to "supervise" her work, literally being in the room as she delivered a baby. Ultimately, it was all about money—being able to charge Medicaid for the delivery.

> Midwife: [The Doctors from Community Clinic X] claim that they're owed the money for all the deliveries they do on their shift, even though they don't know the patient, they don't manage the patient, they don't deliver the patient. They claim that by stepping into the room at delivery time, they can claim the delivery fee. It's made us very upset.

But it's usually on weekends, and especially Sundays. ... They tend to be hungry for deliveries. They want to come into the rooms and claim that they are supervising and it's driving me crazy. It's making me feel secondary. I brought this to [an administrator] and he's on my side. And he said, "How much do they have to do to claim this. This must be fraud." I'm doing all the work and they want to claim this [the reimbursement].

So I go to the [OB] Chief and he says, "No. You're still doing what you're doing. It's just about money. We're making money on the admission, not the delivery.[23] And we can't afford to kick them out the door." And I'm saying, "Why do you need a midwife there at all when they're the attending?" I'm going to say, "Hey. If this is the way it's going to go, I'll be in the call room. You can call me for first assist. [She is referring to first assisting in a cesarean.] ... *You* can take the calls." I haven't done it yet. But I'm thinking this will be my scenario. But am I endangering the other midwives then?

An increasing number of inductions occurred during my year of fieldwork. This shift towards more inductions may explain the increasing cesarean rate noted in a later chapter. One midwife complained about the fact that physicians make the decision to induce labor while it is the midwife who has to carry out the induction. Another midwife complained about what she called "sneak inductions" where the physicians coach a patient on what to say in order to be induced. Ultimately, it became the work of the nurse-midwife to carry out what is essentially a decision made by a physician.

Physicians routinely ordered an ultrasound at forty weeks for estimated fetal weight, although the predictive value of determining fetal weight through ultrasound at term is poor (Caughey 2012). Often, these ultrasounds resulted in a finding of decreased amniotic fluid index (AFI) and the obstetrician subsequently would order an induction. AFI is known to be highly inaccurate for the diagnosis of oligohydramnios (decreased amniotic fluid) as opposed to the measurement of the single deepest vertical pocket (SDVP). The continued use of AFI as a measurement of amniotic fluid results in "an increase in obstetric interventions without any documented improvement in perinatal outcome (Magann et al. 2007, 554)." A possible reason for obstetricians using clinical tests proven to provide faulty information and to result in unnecessary intervention is that they, in fact, need or want a reason to order an induction. Or is is perhaps a matter of doing what one has always done ignoring the up-to-date evidence. The contention surrounding inductions, and the fact that it was a physician order that had to be carried out by the nurse-midwife, added to the clinical conflict between nurse-midwives and obstetricians.

The conflict between nurse-midwives and obstetricians is likely to become even more problematic with ACOG's (2013b) new definition of term pregnancy. Traditionally, a term pregnancy was defined as 37 to 42 weeks, three weeks before and two weeks after the estimated due date. The growing trend for routine induction as early as 37 weeks led to an evolution of thinking, certainly among mothers, that the estimated due date (EDC) is not what it implies, merely an estimate. The EDC has come to be seen as "an end point", as one midwife put it. This has added to confusion, with mothers thinking that they are late if they go one day beyond their estimated due date.

This evolution of the EDC as an end point, rather than an estimate, has created confusion among physicians and mothers alike. There was a growing awareness that labor induction has been scheduled on the edge of term labor. Given the fact that a due date is merely an estimate, even with the best dating process an induction to often results in the birth of a premature baby. ACOG (2013a; 2013b) responded to this troubling development by adding to the confusion: ACOG merely changed the definition of term pregnancy providing further justification for interventions. We now have "early term" representing 37 0/7 weeks (37 weeks plus zero days) to 38 6/7 weeks gestation (38 weeks plus six days). 39 0/7 to 40 6/7 is now "full term" and 41 0/7 to 41 6/7 weeks gestation is considered *late term*—an implication that a gestation past 41 weeks is somehow not entirely normal. The recognition that term pregnancy has a variation of 37 weeks to 42 weeks gestation is gone. As one nurse-midwife said to me, "What ever happened to 42 weeks?" ACOG justifies this change in definition on evidence that babies born between 39 0/7 and 40 6/7 weeks gestation have fewer adverse neonatal outcomes. It is possible that this change in terminology will justify greater interventions, rather than observation, during the latter period of normal variation of term gestation. These interventions will inevitably challenge nurse-midwifery's commitment to physiologic birth.

Each individual midwife had a different way of dealing with the inevitable conflicts with obstetricians with whom they work. One young midwife simply stated to an obstetrician who attempted to supervise her clinical activities, "Who is managing this patient, you or me? If you want to manage this patient's care then you take over the care. If not, then let me do my job." Another midwife described a more subtle way of dealing with this conflict and resisting interference by the obstetrician.

> MAM: I would like to talk about collaborative practice. I know that this midwifery practice defines its practice as a collaborative practice. What does that mean to you?
>
> Midwife: Sometimes I don't want collaborative practice. ... I feel I would like to be able to do what we do and be able to call in the physician when we need to. There are some patients that are high-risk, such as a patient with high blood pressure that should be seen by a physician. But I don't want them dictating our practice.
>
> MAM: Do you think that collaborative practice involves the physician dictating your practice?
>
> Midwife: I can see how that can happen but it doesn't have to be. Although I've heard people say, "My resident." "My nurse." "My midwife." It's the person that I have who I tell what to do. I would want collaborative practice to be where they have their job, which is to take care of the higher risk or surgical situations. And the midwives are the experts in vaginal delivery. And that is our realm and we know how to handle that. That's how I would see the ideal. We can consult with each other. I like the fact that the midwives do the vaginal deliveries. That's an appropriate way of ... but collaborative ... I don't want collaborative to be that the midwives do the delivery the way the obstetricians want them to.

MAM: And do you think that is the way it's done here?

Midwife: I think that there are things that the midwives have been able to do. But there are situations where the doctors ask, "Have you broken her water yet?" And you just ignore the questions and do what you're going to do. ... Or you lie and say, "It's high." [She is referring here to the station of the fetus. Rupture of membranes is not generally advisable if the baby is still high in the pelvis due to the risk of umbilical cord prolapse.]

But it's unfortunate that you just can't say ... Because there have been times where I will say, "You know. I don't believe in doing that." And I'll get a response, "What do you mean?" ... It is unfortunate that we avoid the issues rather than having a conversation. I feel like saying, "You know. We have good outcomes here. And we get these good outcomes by acting this way. So just leave us alone. ..."

MAM: I think there is a fine line between collaboration and supervision and sometimes it's hard to know the difference.

Midwife: Now I would agree with that. And medicine has a culture of ... what is it I'm wanting to say ..."Dammit. I worked hard to get where I am. And somebody yelled at me. And now I get to go out and order."

These midwifes articulated several strategies employed by nurse-midwives that are very much a part of the nurse-midwifery professional culture. One midwife described directly facing and engaging the obstetrician. The second described quiet resistance, avoiding conflict, ignoring the doctor and quietly following her clinical judgment. She also describes outright lying to a doctor in order to carry out best practice.

Another strategy for dealing with the conflict between autonomy and subordination is that of acquiescence. The following story is difficult to tell. It is not representative of the care provided by nurse-midwives at Community Hospital, care that was overwhelmingly safe and respectful. There were times, however, when nurse-midwives were faced with negotiating decision-making, when the obstetrician had made a decision based on convenience as opposed to safety. These moments revealed the mettle of the nurse-midwife. Would she stand up for safety? How do you make a decision when the needs of a mother and the desires of the obstetrician conflict?

It was evening shift, about 9:00 p.m. A mother in active labor, (I will call her Patient A), was moving along nicely. Her labor had been nonmedicated and she was making progress, as would be expected in a multip.[24] (It was her fifth baby.) Suddenly a nurse walked quickly into the station, clearly agitated. Another mother (patient B) had just been admitted in labor and had informed the nurse that she had changed her mind about having a VBAC. She did not want to deliver vaginally but wanted to have a repeat cesarean, as was her right. The problem: Her cesarean needed to done fairly soon because she was already in labor. If there was too long of a delay she might deliver vaginally against her wishes.

The doctor on call, Dr. X was notified and came out of the physician call room. Anesthesiology was called, but the only anesthesiologist in-house was currently involved in an operation. He sent a message that when he came to labor and delivery, he wanted the operation to occur immediately. He stated he wanted to be in bed by midnight.

Most of the players were whispering about all of this and so it took a while for me to understand this kerfuffle. Patient A was progressing rapidly, while Patient B was demanding to know what was holding up her cesarean. She did not appreciate having her contractions become stronger when her plan was to have no labor pain. Dr. X kept asking the nurse to get an ETA on the anesthesiologist. In the meantime, the nurse-midwife and Dr. X sat in front of the Board, staring at it as they watched the nurses change the numbers on the progress of the two mothers. They stared at the Board as if willing a solution, as if watching two planes collide and not knowing how to stop the collision. I heard Dr. X keep mumbling something about "twelve o'clock". I asked the nurse-midwife, "What's with this thing about twelve o'clock?" The nurse-midwife looked at me and said, "She wants to be in bed by midnight." The priority for both physicians, obstetrician and anesthesiologist, seemed to be getting into bed by midnight.

The anesthesiologist finally arrived and there was frantic movement to get Patient B into the operating room. In the meantime, a delivery table with equipment needed to deliver patient A had already been placed beside the door to her room—she was expected to deliver at any moment. As the nurse-midwife entered the OR to first assist with the elective repeat cesarean, she said to a nurse, "Make sure that Patient A receives pitocin IM after the delivery. This is her fifth baby. Once I'm scrubbed in, I can't break sterile." She then walked through the double doors into the operating room.

Within minutes of the obstetrician and the nurse-midwife disappearing into the OR, a nurse who had never before delivered a baby delivered Patient A. After closing Patient B's cesarean incision, the obstetrician and midwife came into Patient A's room. The mother was lying in bed holding her baby. A pediatrician rushed in to assess the baby. This birth had now become a high-risk incident because there was no obstetrical provider present at the birth.

"Why were you not at the delivery?" Patient A asked the obstetrician and the nurse-midwife. The obstetrician apologized profusely, but told her, "We had an emergency cesarean." It was an outright lie. The nurse-midwife stood there, not saying a word. Later she said to me, "You know. The two babies were born at the exact same time." It did not have to be that way. An elective repeat cesarean for a woman in early labor trumped the needs of a multip mother about to deliver vaginally.

This was a good midwife, one that I admire greatly. I know from experience that we all make compromises but there should be limits to our willingness to compromise. The two doctors (obstetrician and anesthesiologist) had made a decision to leave a patient, one who was to give birth momentarily, in the hands of a nurse who had never before delivered a baby. The repeat cesarean could have been put off until Patient A had delivered. Patient A's delivery was imminent, while patient B had time before she was ready to deliver. I thought to myself, "What if there had been a hemorrhage? What if there had been a shoulder dystocia?" All of this because the doctors involved want to be in bed by midnight? And convincing Patient B to wait for perhaps thirty more minutes would have been awkward. Convenience of the physician trumped safety and the nurse-midwife acquiesced, going along with something she knew was wrong.

How did they decide that the best solution to this problem was to have a mother delivered by an inexperienced nurse? If the team had waited for patient A to deliver, the worst case scenario would be that patient B might labor longer than she wanted before having her repeat cesarean. Or Patient B, although unlikely, might have had a VBAC that she did not want. Which situation presented the greater danger? The answer was obvious. Everyone should have patiently waited for patient A to deliver, which occurred within ten minutes after the physicians and nurse-midwife disappeared into the OR. Both patients delivered at the same moment but at the expense of the mother who delivered vaginally with an inexperienced nurse.

When later discussing this event, the nurse-midwife stated, "I could have been more assertive." The purpose of this narrative is not to disparage the care provided by this group of excellent midwives. The narrative reflects how difficult it is for a nurse-midwife with twenty-five years experience to stand up to two determined and aggressive physicians.

The Normality Paradox for Nurse-Midwifery

Nurse-midwives face an existential paradox: a strong belief in the normality of physiologic birth while holding as a core value the right of a woman to self-determination and autonomy. The majority of nurse-midwives work in birth settings where epiduralized birth is now the norm. They are often unable to provide the type of care that is required to create the undisturbed birth that is essential for a physiologic birth.

Holly Kennedy, past President of the ACNM, has written about the "problematic" nature of natural birth, or what she encourages midwives to call physiologic birth.

> I suggest that our culture has situated childbirth fully in risk and normalized childbirth interventions. It is a paradox in which tremendous resources are poured into preventing rare events rather than supporting most

women to avail themselves of resources to sustain and improve their health. Fear of birth has become the foundation of childbearing in US culture. We do not usually fear things that are normal, and therefore childbirth has become culturally pathologic: it is something to be "fixed." We live in a society where women are likely to have heard only birth stories that include epidurals and cesareans. It is a culture that deifies technology and control, with no room for uncertainty of any kind or for less than perfect outcomes (Kennedy 2010, 299).

How is the average nurse-midwife to stand up against the pressures of our system of epiduralized birth? Kennedy (2010) suggests that the solution must include "midwifery-led" maternity units. These types of maternity clinics have become a cause for birth activists and midwives in England. In the United States, freestanding birth centers, a U.S. version of midwifery-led maternity units, have been slowly gaining ground despite enormous political and economic obstacles.

Some nurse-midwives at Community Hospital privately expressed their concerns about the epiduralized births that were so routine at Community Hospital. One midwife who has practiced for many years and was previously a childbirth educator stated,

> I think we helped bring it on in a sense. We did a disservice to women. The birthing community was convinced that there should be, as Dr. Lamaze originally said, childbirth without pain. But breathing and relaxation really didn't do it. With the Lamaze movement, we put it in women's minds that there could be such a thing as birth without pain. But that was not true. There was still some pain. And so women looked elsewhere for pain relief.

When asked how and when epidurals became so ubiquitous, she became thoughtful and said, "It happened so slowly I don't know how it happened because often I wasn't involved in the decision. It was the doctor who had the discussion with the patient. I just knew that this patient was going to have an epidural and that patient was not going to have one. I was never sure why."

"Did it have to do with reimbursement?" I asked. "It probably was," she said. "But I was unaware of those issues back then." She went on to say, "It's true that the epidural was first used in surgery on adults. And in the nineties the epidural was only given once the mother was quite far along in labor and so the exposure to the anesthetic was much less. Now we are giving it when the mother is two or three centimeters and that's unproven technology for sure. The mother is receiving the epidural for ten, twelve hours. We really don't know what it does to the baby."

Another nurse-midwife described her perception of how the epidural has come to be central to the industrialized childbirth unit.

> I'm not convinced it's safe. It's easier for the nurses. Even if a mother doesn't have an epidural, if I get her out of bed to walk with her a bit the nurses get upset. "She's off the monitor!" Because they want all the patients to be continuously on the monitor, otherwise they get nervous. ... But it's interesting. People are expecting to be hooked up to all these things. So maybe I'm not being assertive enough. Maybe some of the fight has gone out of me too.

Several other midwives had quite practical responses as to why they did not do more to discourage the use of epidurals.

> It's tough. It's hard. There are so many other issues these women have also. If no one has educated them about their choices ... Sometimes just getting the baby out healthy becomes a top priority.

When it was pointed out that most of the mothers came in expecting an epidural, another midwife said:

> Well I can't hardly blame them. Their lives are so crappy. They have such crappy lives. They work hard. It sucks. It's a way of escaping. Why add one more thing. Although some do surprise me. Especially our Jehovah's Witness women. They don't want epidurals. But it's true. We know that the epidural causes that cascade of events.

Yet another midwife talked about how difficult it was to focus on education about epidurals when so much else is going on in the mothers' lives.

> Midwife: I think a lot of the mothers are not ready to consider not having an epidural. They just can't go there. There is so much going on in their lives. They're stuck. I don't fight. If I can figure out a way to empower a person in another way, then that's a good thing. To try to get them to feel proud of their bodies. Or to get their partner involved. Or to think about what they're eating in order to avoid later diabetes. Anything like that I consider to be a more important focus than worrying about the epidural. Even if I prep them, they come in with their minds made up. ...
>
> MAM: And that's discouraging.
>
> Midwife: It is. And unfortunately, you've already lost time and you are playing catch up. To somehow make an impact on their lives. If you can get them to breastfeed, great. ... It's hard to talk about epidural. We tell them that they're perfectly capable of having the baby without pain medicine. If you can get them in the right time frame, sometimes you're successful. Often, they just don't want to hear it.
>
> There were places in the country ... there was a time when a poor woman couldn't get an epidural. So they want it. It's, "I'm going to get it" type of thing. They feel that it is their right to have all the bells and whistles.
>
> At least we try to protect the rest of the process. You still have good birth outcomes. We still have the lowest C-section rate in our area. So something is going right. But the epidural ... We're not pushing for an induction. We are trying to facilitate as long as possible not giving the epidural.

These comments reflect a true caring and commitment on the part of the nurse-midwives at Community Hospital for mothers. However, the relationship of physiologic birth to maternal/infant bonding, along with the ability of the baby to breastfeed, are somehow lost in the discussion. Or perhaps these midwives believe that these are things they are unable to control in the current birth environment. They sound resigned to the way things are and present an appearance of acquiescence. They are very busy, working hard to provide humane, safe, and supportive care. They want every woman to feel "empowered". So often I came away from these discussions with the feeling that nurse-midwives are so busy empowering their patients, they forget to empower themselves.

Why is there not a more robust system of informed consent regarding the unknowns of epidurals? Perhaps the entire system of epiduralized birth, the interests of physicians (both obstetricians and anesthesiologists), nurses and, too often, the mothers, is too powerful. Perhaps, in too many cases, nurse-midwives know that they have to go along with the assembly-line or they will have to leave. Late at night, one midwife was reflecting on a newly trained midwife who did not last long at the service. "She just couldn't get use to the way things are. She would try to convince mothers to not have an epidural. She would walk her patients up and down the hall. She was a good midwife. She just didn't fit in."

Peggy Vincent (2003), in her narrative *Baby Catcher,* describes her difficulty in adjusting to hospital maternity care. Vincent is a veteran nurse-midwife who provided homebirth service to the Berkeley community for several decades, catching over two thousand babies. She was named in a malpractice lawsuit along with other providers. After settling the lawsuit, her insurance carrier dropped her liability coverage. Unable to obtain affordable insurance, she shut down her homebirth practice and began shift work as a nurse-midwife at a Kaiser Permanente hospital.

Vincent describes, through many stories, the intimacy and attachment that occurs between the mother and midwife in homebirth during the course of prenatal care. She describes how that translates into trust and working together for, in most cases, a successful vaginal delivery and maternal/infant bonding. She also describes her dismay at the differences she encountered between homebirth and hospital birth after she began the new phase in her career as a hospital-based nurse-midwife.

> I love homebirths. I love their unexpected diversity.
> Women react with perfect freedom in the comfort of
> their own homes and I learned long ago not to try

> predicting who would be quiet or noisy, stoical or
> dramatic. ... At Kaiser, nearly all uncomplicated women
> were assigned to a midwife upon admission. I never
> met them till they came through the doors of Labor and
> Delivery. Most of them had no real interest in
> experiencing the raw passion of childbirth with a
> midwife to guide them. ... "This is an obstetrical
> factory," I said to my husband. "I check these women,
> order an epidural so they won't feel pain, deliver them,
> and move on to the next room. I'll never see them
> again." (Vincent 2003, 315-316)

Vincent goes on the express the nurse-midwife's paradox, the attempt to practice based on her belief system vs. the barriers placed upon her by a system of epiduralized birth.

> But some things hadn't changed. I still got my kicks
> from hanging out with women having babies. In the
> name of compassion and common sense, I still bent rules
> right and left, and I hadn't lost my appetite for drama.
> The rush of the unexpected, the thrill of living on the
> edge, the heart-stoppingly tender moments, the surprise
> of laughter in the midst of pain—these all charged my
> batteries with the energy to endure yet another sleepless
> night. I was no longer in charge of my own independent
> midwifery service, but at least I was still catching babies
> (Vincent 2003, 321).

"In the name of compassion and common sense, I still bent rules right and left, and I hadn't lost my appetite for drama." In one sentence, Peggy Vincent captures the essence of nurse-midwifery culture—the ever constant commitment to the care of mothers and babies, everyday acts of resistance to unreasonable rules, and a passion for the miracle of birth.

The stress on midwives who work in birth environments controlled by obstetricians is well-documented. Keating and Fleming (2007) interviewed midwives in three large Irish hospitals, focusing on the feelings and strategies of midwives working within a medical model of obstetric care. By statute in Ireland, the obstetrician is the lead professional in all maternity hospital units. Most Irish midwives work in large maternity units with a very hierarchical organization. Obstetricians wield a great deal of power and prestige. Keating and Fleming describe "a logic of domination" revealed in their interviews. They also identify strategies used by midwives to subvert the obstetrical approach.

> Some of the midwives avoided obstetric interventions during labour but did so quietly, avoiding direct confrontation with obstetricians about the rationale for the increased interventions used during normal birth. ... Midwives may have difficulty promoting evidence-based practices where medical evidence and technology are highly valued (Keating and Fleming 2007, 519).

There it is again: the everyday acts of resistance to obstetric hegemony. Quietly avoiding obstetric interventions. "Quietly avoiding direct confrontation with obstetricians," yet still ultimately having difficulty "promoting evidence-based practices" in the face of highly valued technology (Keating and Fleming 2007, 519).

Keating and Fleming, in their interviews of Irish midwives, heard in the voices of their subjects the frustration and difficulties in attempting to promote normal birth in a maternity unit dominated by obstetricians. "Midwives inability to utilize their midwifery skills in a hospital ... [was] a source of frustration and stress," Keating and Fleming (2007, 520) found. One midwife stated that it takes "strength" to stand against the medical model. "Sometimes you need strength. ... It does take a bit of guts really to be able to say, 'I am happy enough to let her carry on (2007, 523)." In other words, there are times when quiet resistance does not work. At times, straight-forward resistance is needed but this takes strength of character.

Another identified resistance strategy used was to work nights, a time when the midwife would not be supervised closely. One midwife is quoted as saying; "You can make decisions on night duty. It is easier, less hierarchical (Keating and Fleming 2007, 524)." Another midwife utilized the same strategy.

> But it is much easier to facilitate that [non-interventive birth] on night duty because you don't have people coming in and saying, "Why is this woman screaming?" and obviously you are not a good midwife if this women is, what they think is out of control.

A third midwife expressed a similar strategy.

> I do try to facilitate normal physiological birth as much as I can. I find it easier in night duty, probably 'cause there is not so many doctors and people around so you can get into your room and be with your woman and try to do as much as you can normally.

"Some midwives did contest obstetric rationale *discretely* [emphasis mine]," state Keating and Fleming (2007, 525), "with the goal of maintaining a non-medical approach to birth, but this was difficult within the constraints of hospital practice. ... The midwife's ability to facilitate normal birth was impeded by the culture of the birth environment and a hierarchy of health personnel who subscribed to the medical philosophy of birth."

Nurse-midwives at Community Hospital were subsumed into a culture of medicalization, in conditions very similar to that described by Keating and Fleming. However, Keating and Fleming present mothers as passive players in industrialized birth, which was certainly not the case at Community Hospital. The similarities are the inability of the midwives at Community Hospital to practice according to their belief system and what they knew to be true about the risks involved in epiduralized birth.

****

Central to the professional culture of nurse-midwifery is an internal conflict—holding physiologic birth as an ideal while having to survive within a childbirth system that has organized itself around epiduralized birth. This cultural tension played out in the everyday clinical practice of nurse-midwives at Community Hospital as they attempted to practice with as much autonomy as possible within the confines of a collaborative relationship with the staff physicians. Interprofessionalism, collaboration, partnership—these are all words that minimize the reality of the continued marginalization of nurse-midwives at the clinical level. Autonomy and an independent midwifery remain an ideal rather than a reality.

The midwives I observed were passionate in their care of the mothers at Community Hospital and that care is reflected in nurse-midwifery's tradition: their mission of being with, and standing with, women. As I have described, these midwives used various types of strategies to subvert obstetrical ways of birth in order to implement their own value system. In this they are no different than midwives in many countries, for example what we have seen described in Ireland. In the end, they still face the paradox of having to implement medicalized care that is contrary to their own belief system.

To a great extent, women have been led to believe in the safety of epidurals and pitocin. The convenience of both is highly attractive to mothers. However, the acquiescence of nurse-midwives to epiduralized birth, acquiescence that is difficult to work around, shows that the ideal of a collaborative relationship between obstetricians and midwives remains less than an actuality. Community Hospital was ultimately an obstetrician-led maternity unit and midwives relied on the benevolence of certain physicians to influence departmental policies. The nurse-midwives, in truth, had little independent impact on policy.

---

23 Reimbursement for hospital births involves two components. There is a separate reimbursement for the facility fee. There is then a second reimbursement to the provider of the delivery, one for vaginal delivery and a larger fee for cesarean.

24 Multip: Meaning multiparous. A woman who has given birth to more than one baby.

Chapter Four

The Closure of Maternity Care at Community Hospital:
The Business of Birth

"I knew things had been bad. I just didn't know how bad (A midwife)."

This story does not end on a positive note. The midwifery service discussed in this book has been shut down, a victim of the transformation of maternity care that has occurred throughout the United States. (Each midwife has subsequently found employment elsewhere.) Through the lens of the closure of the maternity service at Community Hospital, we can see the impact upon maternity care by the centralization of maternity care and consolidation of hospitals (resulting in fewer but larger maternity care units). We also can see the impact of regionalization on maternity care (referral of high-risk pregnancies to maternal-fetal centers). The physical space previously used by Community Hospital's maternity service will now be used as spillover by the medical center within which the hospital has merged. It will be used as space for patients that need to be discharged from the medical center but are not yet well enough to go home: a skilled nursing care center for patients who need a step-down unit or who have little support for recuperation at home. [25]

The closure of Community Hospital's maternity center is part of a recent fundamental transformation of the American hospital system: a transformation that involves a shift away from small community hospitals, both urban and rural, to larger tertiary-care medical centers. The small hospitals that survive have often done so by merging into a larger, nearby medical hospital system. This merger usually involves the reorganization of services provided by the community hospital to meet the overall needs of the medical center system.

A prime example of this trend towards centralization, through the merger of hospitals, is the recent merger of two medical networks in New York City into one entity (Mt. Sinai Medical Center and Continuuam Health Partners, itself a network of smaller hospitals). The merger resulted in New York City served by only two large, non-profit health care networks of providers and hospitals (Hartcollis 2013). The exception to these two giant networks is the New York City Health and Hospital System (HHC).

Proponents of centralization and consolidation have predicted that these large networks of interconnected hospitals and health care providers will result in greater efficiency, providing an integrated system that results in a single point-of-care for individuals. Skeptics state that communities where intensive hospital consolidation has occurred have experienced increased medical costs due to lack of competition. In many sectors of the economy, consolidation results in efficiency of scale, placing downward pressure on consumer costs. However, some economists have shown that the American health care system does not operate under the same rules as other sectors of the economy. Consolidation, they say, promises efficiency but in actuality results in escalation of health care costs. The debate remains unresolved. What is clear, however, is that the impact of consolidation on maternity care has been the nationwide closure of small labor and delivery units at Community Hospitals. The result is that, in many communities, mothers must travel long distances to access the nearest maternity care service.

This major reorganization of American hospitals, one that has seen the closure of small community hospitals (or their merger into larger hospitals), began in the last three decades of the twentieth century. It is closely tied to the growth of medical centers with highly specialized services. In New York City, for example, thirty-nine hospitals (one third of New York hospitals) closed between the years 1970 and 1981. This reorganization is fundamentally as much about health care financing as it is about technological changes and demographic changes (McLafferty 1982, 1986).

Financial pressures and other stressors faced by community hospitals have included: decreased reimbursement, limited reimbursement streams, the shifting of care into community hospital emergency rooms for uninsured/underinsured patients, and the growth of larger hospitals with specialties that receive enhanced reimbursement. The lack of specialty clinical services (and the resident physicians that come with such services) is a characteristic of community hospitals and is associated with weak reimbursement (Shonick 1979).

Other factors are involved in hospital closure as well. Additional factors involved in hospital closures include: occupancy rates, the socio-economic status of the neighborhood served by the hospital, infant mortality rates of the neighborhood, and hospital size. The size of a hospital is significant: the larger the size of a hospital, the less likely that it will face closure. McLafferty (1982, 1986) proposes that the number of uninsured/underinsured patients (a proxy for poverty) included in a hospital's catchment area is a significant underlying cause of hospital closures, hence the association with infant mortality. "What we are seeing, in analyzing closures, is the result of a highly competitive process in which those facilities best able to adapt to the rapidly changing health environment are most likely to survive (McLafferty 1982, 1668)."

Hospitals that are at a competitive disadvantage have used a variety of survival strategies, one of which is merger into a larger medical center that provides the sharing of staff and facilities. The advantages of such a merger for a small hospital includes: economies of scale in the purchase of supplies and equipment, access and utilization of specialty services at the medical center, and the use of residents from the larger facility (McLafferty 1986). All of these factors came into play in the decision for Community Hospital to merge with a nearby major medical hospital, a hospital referred to in this book as Medical Center 2 (MC2), a hospital associated with a medical school.

The Closure of the Midwifery Service at Community Hospital

The impetus behind the nurse-midwifery service at Community Hospital had been the loss of an obstetrical residency program. As Community Hospital's maternity service transitioned to a nurse-midwifery service, it incorporated the latest technological advances while remaining small and intimate.

At its zenith in 2006, the midwifery service had almost 1,300 annual deliveries. From that time onwards the service saw a steady decline in births.

The problem of decreased patient numbers was openly discussed within the maternity service. The Department Chair consistently talked about the problem of "underutilization" during department meetings. The Midwifery Service Director confided that she was under pressure from hospital administration to "do something about the numbers" but was offered no administrative support through marketing, and little in other areas of administration. Her time was increasingly taken up with tasks that could (and should) have been taken up by lower-level employees.

Only after gathering statistics from the state, did I become aware of the degree to which Community Hospital had steadily lost its clientele year after year. Not long after the closure of the service, I shared with one midwife the chart comparing delivery numbers between four hospitals, including Community Hospital (see Figure Two). She was shocked by the numbers. "I had no idea," she stated to me. "I knew we were losing patients, but not to this extent."

Figure Two (next page) compares the number of deliveries at four hospitals for the years 2005 to 2012—Community Hospital (CH) and three other hospitals. All hospitals were within several miles of each other. Medical Center 1 (MC1) is a large hospital with a Level II neonatal unit and a maternity service quite similar to Community Hospital in that it serves a low-risk maternity clientele. It was staffed by an obstetrical resident service as opposed to a nurse-midwifery service. MC2 and MC3 are both Level III hospitals with high-risk neonatal care units and both are associated with medical schools.

Figure Two shows a steady decrease in deliveries at Community Hospital (CH) beginning in 2007. At the same time, there were increased numbers of deliveries for MC1, MC2 and MC3. By 2012, all hospitals, with the notable exception of Community Hospital (CH) had deliveries at or above 1500 per year. The number of deliveries at MC2 and MC3 (the two hospitals associated with medical schools and having maternal-fetal centers for high-risk mothers) remained relatively stable, although slightly increased.

Figure Two
# of Deliveries at Four Hospitals:
2005 — 2012

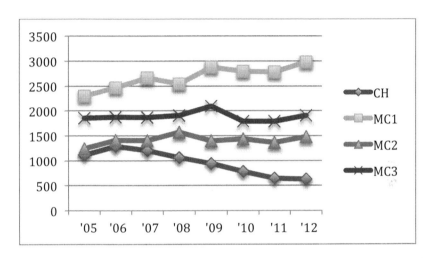

MC1 had the greatest increase in market share throughout the years 2005–2012. In 2006, Community Hospital (CH) had its largest number of deliveries (1,289 deliveries), followed by a steady decline to only 622 deliveries in 2012. Community Hospital was budgeted for a minimum of 800 annual deliveries; so within five to six years Community Hospital was under-budget. By comparison, Maternity Center 1 (MC1) had a steady increase from 2,300 deliveries in 2005 to 2,981 in 2012.

These numbers support the suspicion, expressed to me by midwives at Community Hospital, that they were losing market share to MC1, a low-risk, high-volume maternity service. It appears that MC1 became the main competitor for Community Hospital during the years of the maternity service at Community Hospital. It is the maternity service most resembling Community Hospital, except that MC1 maintained an OB/GYN residency program. MC1 provided routine and elective inductions. It also carried out VBACs during this time, although not to the extent found at Community Hospital.

MC1 had a more robust feeder system, probably due to its residency program, which made its service more attractive to obstetricians in private practice and at community health centers. From 2005 to 212, Community Hospital lost its referral arrangement with several community health centers. In addition, MC1 had a larger anesthesiology group; its delivery numbers were such that it was able to provide dedicated anesthesiology to the labor and delivery unit. This made the epidural service for MC1's labor and delivery unit more timely and efficient—an attractive feature for many pregnant women in the community.

The decline in client base had significant impact on the long-term sustainability of the midwifery service at Community Hospital. Hospital administration spoke in terms of underutilization, code for increased cost per delivery due to lack of efficiency. The decrease in deliveries also placed the service under scrutiny with regards to safety. There were no statistics to suggest the service was unsafe but it has become accepted dogma within obstetrics that small maternity centers by their very nature are unsafe. (A later chapter discusses CH's excellent outcomes.)

Regionalization, Centralization and NICU Categorization

Two trends in health care have impacted small maternity units, those similar to Community Hospital. The first, regionalization, has involved the integration and coordination of prenatal care throughout a defined region. Ideally, all pregnant women identified as high-risk are referred out of small community hospitals: receiving prenatal care and delivering at larger medical centers with specialists (including neonatologists and perinatologists) and a neonatal intensive care newborn unit (NICU). Regionalization, which has been rapidly embraced by most developed countries, is credited with a decrease in newborn mortality rates.[26]

Regionalization has also involved the reorganization of maternity units into three rankings based on the level of care available to the newborn—Level I, Level II, and Level III. Attempts at creating a uniform system for categorization of maternal and newborn care remain ongoing. Regionalization has brought with it centralization of maternity care, with ever larger maternity units. Hospitals compete to be designated as a Level III hospital. With centralization of maternity care, there has also been "an increase in the number of neonatal intensive care units (NICUs) and neonatologists, without a consistent relationship to the percentage of high-risk infants," as well as "a proliferation of small NICUs in the same regions as large NICUs (Committee on Fetus and Newborn 2012, 588)."[27]

This expansion of NICUs has made a consistent categorization of maternity services difficult. Proponents of regionalization of care for at-risk neonates view this proliferation of NICUs at lower-volume hospitals as compromising the overall effort to direct at-risk neonates into the most advanced neonatal services. Comparative qualifications of hospitals claiming to have NICUs have become increasingly difficult to determine, resulting in a subcategorization of Level III hospitals (Committee on Fetus and Newborn 2012).

Level I hospitals (hospitals with basic neonatal care: the ability to resuscitate, stabilize and transfer neonates for life-threatening problems) are now few and far between in the United States. Community Hospital was objectively a Level I hospital, although staff stated it was a Level II facility. Level II maternity units are those with a neonatal care unit and in-house pediatric service. Level III maternity services are those having subspecialty care including the capability to carry out neonatal surgery. Level II and Level III hospitals have further subcategories, including the ability to carry out surgery on the fetus during pregnancy. The significant point here is that the care of the newborn has become so specialized, neonatologists have difficulty arriving at a consistent system for classification of neonatal intensive care units (Committee on Fetus and Newborn 2012).

The advantage of regionalization has been the transfer of mothers prior to delivery, those who have been identified through prenatal screening as high-risk, so that at-risk newborns and mothers receive specialty care before, during, and immediately after birth. The trend of screening and referral to Level III maternity services during the prenatal period has been a result of the development of the medical specialties of neonatology and perinatology. These are sub-specialties within pediatrics and obstetrics, focusing on care of high-risk pregnancies and the newborn with predetermined life-threatening problems (Papiernik and Keith 1995).

Regionalization of maternity care has taken place in two distinct stages. The first stage involved increased numbers of newborn transfers to Level III hospitals for treatment and/or evaluation. In the United States, this regionalization stage occurred throughout the 1970s and 1980s. The second stage gained ground during the 1990s, with pregnant women increasingly screened and transferred to Level III high-risk maternal-fetal services prior to delivery. Studies have shown that neonatal mortality and morbidity rates have decreased in direct relation to shifts toward the use of intensive neonatal care service: through both increased neonatal transfers as well as increased maternal transfer in the prenatal period (Papiernik and Keith 1995). The consequence, however, has also been the closing of maternity units at smaller Community Hospitals.

In some countries, not all health care policy experts are convinced that the vigorous transfer of mothers out of smaller maternity units results in decreased perinatal deaths. France, for instance, has yet to embrace a universal policy of regionalization of maternity care and has a perinatal death rate similar to that of other European countries (Papiernik and Keith 1995).

The Role of Cost-Inefficiency at Community Hospital

Prenatal care at Community Hospital involved rigorous screening appropriate for a Level I maternity service—history, physical examination, lab testing, and ultrasound at specified weeks of gestation, along with other testing. Prenatal care is a comparative process. Appropriate screening, at specific points in time during pregnancy, has become one benchmark for quality prenatal care. My observation of prenatal care by the midwives verified that the service carefully followed safe and consistent screening of patients.

Many mothers came to the midwifery service already high-risk for both medical and socio-economic reasons. Academics debate the concept of "risk". The reality is that poverty does, in fact, create risks in pregnancy that place uncertainties for the long-term health and life of the baby and mother. Responsible, quality prenatal care requires screening even as the individual experience is taken into account.

Quite a few patients were referred to the nearby high-risk, maternal-fetal care center (MC2) for a variety of reasons—screening with advanced 3-D ultrasound for fetal abnormalities, genetic counseling, and assessment for conditions that can adversely impact on the mother or fetus such as diabetes or hypertension. Some of these patients were assessed by the high-risk center as appropriate for low-risk care and referred back to Community Hospital. Some were not. The midwifery service did not have statistics as to how many patients were lost to their care as a result of this aggressive referral system. (The reader will see later that the newborn outcomes for the midwifery service were excellent suggesting that this assertive referral system worked.)

Size of a maternity unit is important to the quality of maternity care—the ability of all staff to know each patient intimately, to know what is going on, the ease of communication. However even at small maternity units, the out-of-control use of technology is a major problem. It is the routinization and standardization of care (made possible with ever larger numbers of patients) that makes intensive technology efficient: care that resembles the hospital equivalent of the assembly-line. What we are seeing, particularly with large hospitals and maternity units brought about by regionalization and centralization, is the assembly-line of Fordism as initially described by Antonio Gramsci (Walsh 2006b, 2009). It is also the industrialization and mechanization of birth as described by Odent (2002).

Level I maternity units have tended to be smaller and more intimate. Community Hospital was the only Level I maternity unit still in existence in its community. Its closure was characteristic of the nationwide trend toward larger maternity units. Regionalization and centralization of hospitals has resulted in a decrease in the number of hospital maternity services. The relationship of the regionalization of maternity care to the decrease in Level I hospitals is apparent. Sixty percent of maternity unit closures occur at hospitals within thirty miles of another hospital offering a similar or higher level maternity service (Zhao 2007). Smaller units have found it difficult to maintain the staffing requirements provided at Level II and III services (i.e. 24/7 onsite specialists such as pediatricians, obstetricians, anesthesiologists, neonatologists, and perinatologists).

Reasons for this trend in closure of Level I maternity units are multifactorial. Obstetrics has become a highly litigious area of medicine and smaller number of deliveries present challenges in maintaining skills for all staff. Infrequent use of skills such as neonatal resuscitation can result in a perception of increased liability. Hospitals with smaller numbers of deliveries have difficulty maintaining economies of scale and financial efficiency when trying to keep up with changes in technology. Capital costs and staffing requirements enter into the issue of efficiency. Hospitals that primarily serve mothers receiving Medicaid are particularly vulnerable to closure as a result of insufficient reimbursement. This was true at Community Hospital, which relied heavily upon Medicaid reimbursement. (Medicaid reimbursement in most states averages 50% of the actual cost of care.)

Other systemic factors are at work in the closure of maternity units nationwide and the subsequent centralization of maternity care. Inherent changes in the medical profession itself are significant, underlying reasons for such closures. Hospital administrators at community hospitals, those with small maternity units, consistently suggest that the decision to close their maternity service had much to do with the inability to attract family physicians and obstetricians. As an explanation of such closures, one hospital administrator is quoted as stating, "It is more likely that other factors such as the 24/7 duty intrinsic to OB services and the desire of Ob/Gyns and family practitioners to maintain a more family-friendly balance between work and family/leisure are at work (Zhao 2007, v)."

The decision to close Community Hospital's maternity service, and to transform its physical space into a skilled care unit, appeared to be based on finances, or underutilization as it was continually referred to.

Figure Three
Delivery Costs:
Fiscal Year 2011 — 2012

	L&D Beds	# of Births	Birth per Bed	# Vaginal Births	Cost per Vaginal Delivery	# Cesareans	Cost per Cesarean
CH	20	605	30.3	435	$7,729	170	$11,763
MC1	26	2,813	108.2	1,954	$6,108	859	$ 8,988
MC2	30	1,438	47.9	1,011	$10,866	426	$15,524
MC3	35	1,845	52.7	1,293	$10,206	552	$15,130

The lower cost per vaginal delivery at MC1 shows a possible cost-efficiency associated with its higher number of deliveries per bed. Community Hospital had 30.3 births per maternity bed in fiscal year 2011-2012 compared to 108.2 births per maternity bed for its competitor, MC1—an astonishing difference in cost-efficiency (see Figure Three). In fact, the maternity service at Community Hospital often had empty beds. By comparison, MC1 was described to me as a "baby factory", with mothers laboring in the hallway.

The cost differential for cesarean births showed a similar difference in cost-efficiency. The cost-per-cesarean at Community Hospital was $11,763 compared to its main competitor MC1, which had a much less cost-per-cesarean at $8,988. (These are actual costs, not reimbursement.) These cost statistics reveal the financial stress faced by the midwifery service at Community Hospital, a stress caused by the service's underutilization.

One factor in increased costs, and the poor competitive position of Community Hospital vis-à-vis MC1, can be explained by Community Hospital's VBAC policy. Figure Four reflects the difference in VBAC rates and provides a comparison of the VBAC rate for Community Hospital and MC1. [28]

Figure Four
VBAC Rates for Community Hospital & MC1:
2005 — 2012

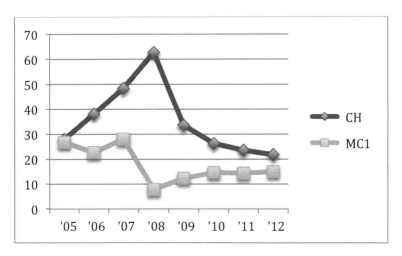

The commitment to vaginal birth after cesarean is reflected in the VBAC rate in the early years of Community Hospital's midwifery service. While MC1 did carry out VBACs during the years 2005-2012, the VBAC rate at Community Hospital was consistently greater, a direct result of an ongoing commitment and a strong pro-VBAC policy. Community Hospital's VBAC rate climbed to 62.7 per 100 women (VBAC candidates) in the year 2008.

The cesarean rate for these two hospitals began to converge (as seen in Figure Five on the following page). In 2008, Community Hospital had its lowest C-section rate—20.1%, while MC1 reached its highest cesarean rate of 40% in the same year. By 2012, only four years later, the cesarean rate for the two hospitals had converged at 27.7 vs. 30.2, respectively.

Figure Five
Cesarean Rates for Community Hospital & MC1:
2005 — 2012

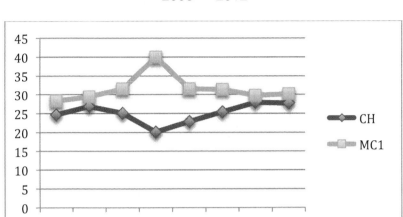

These trends become more apparent when the number of deliveries at both Community Hospital and its competitor, MC1, are teased out.

Figure Six
# of deliveries at Community Hospital & MC1:
2005 — 2012

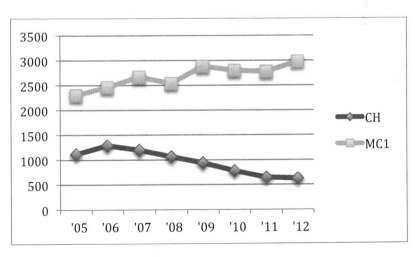

135

The trend of losing market share to MC1 is seen in Figure Two but is even more apparent when the statistics from only the two hospitals are shown in Figure Six. The increase in deliveries for MC1 mirrors the decline for Community Hospital.

When three statistics for 2005 and 2012 are considered together—the VBAC rate, cesarean rates, and number of deliveries—an interesting trend is noted. As Community Hospital's patient population decreased, it's cesarean rate increased. At the same time, its VBAC rate decreased. In contrast, as MC1 had an increase in deliveries, its cesarean rate and VBAC rate remained relatively stable.

The midwifery service did significantly decrease its cesarean rate at the beginning, with 20.07% in 2008—well below the national average. By comparison, MC1 had a cesarean rate of 40% that same year. However, by 2012 the cesarean rates for the two hospitals began to converge, with Community Hospital showing a 27.63% cesarean rate compared to 30.19% at MC1 (see Figure Five on the pervious page).

The trend at Community Hospital, where the cesarean rate increased as deliveries decreased, is counterintuitive. It runs contrary to what the Midwifery Service Director thought was going on. "Our cesarean rate is decreasing," she stated to me in 2011. "As our numbers go down, we can give more individualized attention to each patient." As it turned out, she was unaware of the statistics for her service.

One explanation for the convergence of the cesarean rates at the two hospitals may be found by analyzing the primary cesarean rates (see Figure Seven on following page). The primary cesarean rate is an important measure because it is a key factor in lowering overall cesarean rates. Community Hospital accomplished a significant decrease in its primary cesarean rate beginning in 2006, reaching its all-time low of less than 15% in 2009. However, the rate then began to climb. MC1 showed a similar decrease in primary cesareans during these years, and by 2012 had achieved approximately the same primary cesarean rate as Community Hospital. At the same time, the midwifery service at Community Hospital showed a significant decrease in its VBAC rate. It would seem that the increased primary cesarean rate, as well as the decreased VBAC rate, was quite significant in the overall upturn of cesarean rates at Community Hospital.

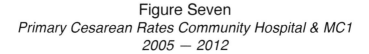

Figure Seven
Primary Cesarean Rates Community Hospital & MC1
2005 — 2012

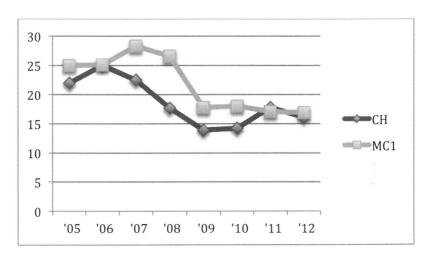

One midwife confided that she saw a change over time in physician attitude regarding VBACs and cesareans in general. There was a growing reliance on per-diem obstetricians during these years, obstetricians who may not have shared a commitment to preventing cesareans. The staff obstetricians also began to undermine the service's commitment to avoid unnecessary inductions. Additionally, midwives and obstetricians alike observed a growing number of extremely obese mothers, another possible factor in the increased cesarean rates due to prolonged and obstructed labor. All of these influences most likely had an impact on the ability of the service to keep down its cesarean rate. By 2012, there was little difference between Community Hospital and MC1 with regard to measures related to cesarean.

The increased cesarean rate also shows a subtle change in the culture at the midwifery service. It reflects the reality of ultimate decision-making in collaborative relationships between midwife and obstetrician. It also reflects the change in attitude regarding induction. Unnecessary induction of labor is consistently shown to be associated with subsequent cesareans.

Is Larger Safer?

The trend toward regionalization (the channeling of high-risk mothers to regional hospitals with Level III neonatal services), along with the trend toward centralization (fewer maternity units with larger number of annual deliveries), has worked synergistically in the closure of small maternity services at community hospitals. The two trends have advanced the shift toward fewer and larger maternity services (increased volume/number of deliveries per service). With increased centralization of maternity services, the comparative safety of larger vs. small maternity service has been debated. Proponents of centralization of maternity services maintain that labor and delivery units with fewer than 1,000 deliveries per year have poor safety records, justifying their closure. Others claim that centralization has been a solution looking for a problem.

The earliest studies during the regionalization phase of maternity service reorganization documented a direct correlation between fewer neonatal death rates among low-birth-weight infants at large maternity units, which tend to have neonatal intensive care units (NICUs) staffed by perinatologists (Moster et al. 2001; Holmstrom and Phibbs 2009). (Neonatal mortality is defined as death prior to day 28 following birth.) There is consensus that regionalization, with organized referral of high-risk pregnancies to perinatal centers, has resulted in a significant decrease in perinatal mortality in developed countries. There is less agreement on the issue of centralization of maternity services.

Is there a correlation between neonatal death rates in full-term, normal weight, healthy babies and size of maternity unit? One of the first quantitative studies to look at this issue was that of Heller et al. (2002) analyzing birth data in Hesse, Germany from 1990-1999. (The study has come to be referred to as the *Hesse Study.*) Data from 582,655 births was collected retrospectively from the perinatal birth registry for the German state of Hesse. The Hesse Study had the advantage over earlier research by having the ability to look at a specific geographic area with a highly regionalized maternity care system, thereby correcting for urban/rural bias.

A system of regionalization was in place in Hess, Germany. Pregnant women categorized as high-risk were aggressively transferred to perinatal centers, as were newborns born with life-threatening problems. Maternity centers were categorized by number of births per year: very small units with 500 or fewer births; small with 501-1000; intermediate with 1001-1500; and large with more than 1500 births per year. Under this system, the midwifery service at Community Hospital would be categorized as intermediate between the years 2005 to 2008, and small in subsequent years.

The Hesse Study found that the size of a maternity unit was associated with early-neonatal mortality. A system of referral to large units resulted in decreased early-neonatal mortality rates (newborn deaths within the first seven days of life). "Very small units showed the highest death rate...whereas in large delivery units the lowest early-neonatal deaths ... [were] seen (Heller et al. 2002, 1063)." The study then looked at the question whether volume of births impacted the neonatal death rate of normal newborns, those born of normal size at term (weight > 2500 gms/> 5 lbs 8 oz). When analyzing newborn mortality rates of low-risk, normal-weight, term babies, there was shown to be an inverse relationship between the volume of a maternity site and newborn mortality rates. The larger the volume of births, the lower the early-neonatal mortality rate for normal size, full-term, low-risk newborns. A relationship between maternity unit size and early-neonatal mortality was found at all volume levels.

Researchers were surprised by the Hesse Study, as the deliveries at smaller maternity units tended to be low-risk. One weakness of the study is that it excluded maternity services that were exclusively staffed by midwives. The Hesse Study, however, began a vehement policy debate as to whether there is a volume/outcome relationship in maternity care systems. Should regionalization and centralization of maternity care be aggressively extended to all pregnancies?

A study of perinatal mortality rates in Norway, a study that also used birth registry data (Moster et al. 1999), came to the same conclusion as the Hesse Study. A further study evaluating neonatal mortality in Norway (Moster et al. 2001) also arrived at the same conclusion: a small but significant decrease in neonatal death is associated with larger maternity units. However, the differences in the volume/outcome relationship were not as significant in the Norway study as were found in the Hesse Study.

Moster suggests that attention to issues of expertise, equipment, and experience can ease the impact of volume on neonatal outcomes in small maternity centers. The improved outcomes seen in larger maternity sites may be explained by "better care and access to rapid intervention during delivery, resuscitation of the newborn, and identification and management of newborn infants with unexpected malformations and various illnesses (Moster et al. 2001, 908)." Holmstrom and Phipps (2009) suggest that, although the Hesse Study and the Moster research utilized a large database, the perinatal mortality rate among full-term, normal-weight, low-risk newborns was so low as to lack statistical power.

Phibbs (2002) recommends that studies be replicated using larger study groups. Even if the Hesse Study is found to be valid, Phibbs (2002) questions the ability of some countries and regions to safely concentrate all maternity patients into large regional units. What are the costs—social, personal and financial—of such a shift in maternity care? Are these costs worth the small number of lives potentially saved? How large must a maternity unit be in order to gain the advantages that may account for a decreased neonatal mortality rate? Critics of the Hesse Study state that it does not give careful thought to the potential unintended consequences when its findings are used as a basis for maternity care policy.

At this time, the Hesse Study has not been consistently replicated. In Australia, an analysis of the relationship between neonatal mortality and size of maternity units did not show adverse outcomes for normal newborns born in small units (Tracy et al. 2006). The Australian study did show a relationship between the increased interventions during birth with larger maternity units. In New Zealand, a small country with a tightly organized and regionalized maternity system, Rosenblatt et al.

(1985) also found results contradictory to that of the Hesse Study. "In New Zealand, women who deliver in small, mostly rural Level 1 hospitals have the highest likelihood of bearing children who will survive the first week of life (Rosenblatt 1985, 430)." Rosenblatt also states that, "It is also possible that there is an advantage, particularly for normal birth-weight children, in being born in smaller obstetric units. There is no evidence that a satisfactory outcome depends on a minimum number of deliveries (1985, 429)."

Studies that analyze the relationship of obstetric volume to perinatal mortality ignore the increase in the unnecessary use of technological interventions associated with large volume maternity units . Another comparison study of maternity units by size (Coulm et al. 2012), shows that the larger the maternity unit, the greater the use of interventions—for example, increased induction, cesarean delivery, episiotomy, and forceps.

The unintended consequences inherent in regionalization and centralization of maternity care have been identified in Quebec. A long-standing policy for evacuating all rural Inuit mothers to urban hospitals with high-risk maternal-fetal services resulted in poor neonatal outcomes and severe stress on communities and families. A radical change of health care policy has been implemented, with most mothers cared for at community-based birth centers staffed with trained, indigenous midwives. These birth centers are truly midwifery-led. This public health policy is contrary to the implementation of ever-larger maternity services. The result has been improved neonatal and maternal outcomes in Inuit communities. Mothers are screened for risk and a small minority, mainly those with severe health issues or preterm labor, are still flown out of the community to perinatal centers. However, the policy for this community reflects the philosophy that risk involves more than biomedical markers.

> Risk screening is a fundamental principle of safe care in this remote setting. The whole concept of risk in birth, however, is conceptualized in a much broader context than protocols or risk scoring systems. *Risk screening is seen as a social, cultural and community process rather than simply a biomedical one* [italics mine] (Van Wagner et al, 2007, 387).

The Canadian experience, one of decentralization of birth within the Inuit community, brings into question the idea of an inevitable correlation between regionalization/centralization of maternity care and improved outcomes. The Inuit community experiment resulted in an improved perinatal mortality rate of nine deaths per 1,000 births. This compares favorably to the overall Canadian neonatal death rate of 8-10 deaths per 1,000 births (Van Wagner et al. 2007).

A study of regionalization in California (Snowden et al. 2012) did find a relationship between unit volume and newborn asphyxia. This was true for all births, including normal-weight newborns. However, no correlation was found between unit volume and neonatal mortality rates among low-risk, normal newborns. The authors of this study point to the difficulty inherent in large cohort studies that draw exclusively on discharge data. Such data invariably miss significant, but subtle, and potentially confounding, variables, such as staff expertise, staffing levels and patient characteristics. Snowden et al. (2012) call for observational studies in order to gain a more nuanced understanding of the issue of safety in small maternity units.

Can There Be Safety in Small Numbers?

Studies claiming a correlation between small maternity units and poor outcomes have been methodologically weak, and have failed to account for important, nuanced variables including: 1) staff experience and longevity; 2) protocols for neonatal resuscitation drills; 3) universal regional protocols; 4) conformity of practice guidelines; 5) lack of distinction between physician vs. midwifery-led units; and 6) uniformity in referrals of high-risk pregnancy.

Given the fact that Community Hospital was a small maternity unit, it is interesting to look at data regarding neonatal outcomes. Because of Community Hospital's careful referral system, a fair comparison can only be made with outcomes for normal, full-term newborns. The available data that best reflected neonatal outcomes born at a low-risk small maternity unit, compared to other hospitals, is the measure represented by the category "normal full-term infants born with life-threatening problems". This measure is broader than newborn mortality as life-threatening problems included a range of potentially life-threatening newborn problems, i.e. difficulty breathing and hypoxia.

The below data was maintained by the state and it is possible to compare Community Hospital's outcomes in this category with that of the three nearby hospitals. Each hospital coded newborns within specific categories. The number of deliveries for each hospital, per year, was too small to establish outcome statistics of any significance. As a result, Figure Eight shows aggregate data for the seven years of 2005–2012.

Figure Eight

Percentage of Normal, Full Term Newborns Born With Life-Threatening Problems: 2005– 2012

	# of Normal, Full Term Newborns	# of Normal, Full Term Newborns with Life-Threatening Problems	% Normal, Full Term Newborns with Life-Threatening Problems
CH	5160	223	4.32
MC1	9011	1658	18.40
MC2	2598	1487	57.24
MC3	4045	2172	57.70

The above data on newborn outcomes suggests that large and efficient does not necessarily translate into safer care. MC1 is the largest maternity service, as well as the service most comparable to Community Hospital with regards to the acuity level of its maternity patients. Despite a larger number of deliveries, and clear cost efficiency, the maternity service at MC1 did not provide better outcomes for full-term babies when compared to Community Hospital. Normal, full-term newborns born at MC1 were more than four times likely to suffer life-threatening problems than similar newborns born at Community Hospital's midwifery service. (Community Hospital 4.32 per 100; MC1 18.4 per 100)

We can only speculate as to the reasons for this discrepancy in safety. The assertive protocols for referral at Community Hospital perhaps contributed to its excellent neonatal outcomes. Perhaps the presence of residents at MC1 led to a false sense of security, leading to a mischaracterization of newborns as "normal, full-term", and a failure to adequately identify and refer out the truly high-risk mothers to one of the two Level III maternal-fetal centers.

Centralization of maternity services continues throughout the developed world. Due to the closure of most hospital maternity services with volumes less than 1,000 deliveries per year, it is difficult to assess the issue of safety in relation to volume size for hospital births in the United States with any degree of validity. However, in the case of the midwifery service at Community Hospital, when compared to a large, low-risk hospital (MC1), centralization and increased size of a maternity unit did not lead to improved outcomes when comparing normal, full-term newborns.

Freestanding Birth Centers and Outcomes

The reported outcomes for freestanding birth centers in the United States, maternity services that best mirror that of small maternity units in community hospitals, show an alternative to large maternity centers. Data obtained through a registry maintained by the American Association of Birth Centers (AABC) has been used to evaluate newborn outcomes from 2007–2010 at seventy-nine American birth centers (Stapleton et al. 2013). Data included 22,403 client records with a final data set of 15,574 mothers. The final study sample of birth center births represented mothers who were eligible for delivery at a birth center at onset of labor. (Subjects removed from the data set included first trimester loss, nonmedical transfers, or transfers to physician care for medical reasons.)

In the Stapleton et al. (2013) study, the outcomes at credentialed freestanding birth centers compare favorably to other studies of low-risk vaginal deliveries. The neonatal mortality rate for freestanding birth centers in the study's 2007–2010 cohort (0.40/1,000 births), is lower than the overall U.S. neonatal mortality rate for full-term, normal-weight newborns (0.75/1,000 in 2007).[29] The authors point out that overall neonatal outcomes occur in a maternity environment that involves increased use of interventions and technology, including increased inductions and cesareans. Their findings are consistent with previous studies of American freestanding birth centers. "This consistency speaks to the durability of the birth center model over time, despite increases in the rates of intervention and cesarean birth nationwide during the same period (Stapleton et al. 2013, 8)." Of equal importance, the authors highlight that "The cesarean birth rate in this cohort was 6% versus the estimated rate of 25% for similarly low-risk women in a hospital setting (2013, 9)."

Beyond the important issue of neonatal outcomes, there is the issue of cost. The cost of childbirth is not insignificant. Five out of the ten most common procedures performed in hospitals are associated with childbirth. In 2008, childbirth accounted for 23% of hospital discharges. With regard to cost, "In 2008, hospitalization for pregnancy, birth, and care of the newborn resulted in total hospital charges of $97.4 billion, making it the single largest contributor as a health condition to the national hospital bill (Stapleton et al. 2013, 8)." The authors claim that when their study is considered in conjunction with previous outcome studies of birth centers, 85% of pregnant women in the United States could be cared for and delivered safely at freestanding birth centers with less intervention and greater patient satisfaction resulting in significant savings in health care expenditures.

The high cost of hospital birth in the United States occurs in the context of a system that utilizes highly technological birth. "The potential savings from the cost of care and lower intervention rates highlight birth centers as an important option for providing high-value maternity care (Stapleton et al. 2013, 9)." Arguing for the viability of freestanding birth centers as a safe, cost-effective alternative, the authors state that a review of the Cochrane Database shows that "British studies of place of birth, and US studies comparing midwifery and obstetric care... suggest that midwifery-led birth center care is a safe and effective option for medically low-risk women (2013, 8)." They also conclude that given the documented outcomes, "Birth centers and their midwifery-led, collaborative model of maternity care continue to offer an important solution to any of the issues affecting the quality and cost of maternity care in the United States (2013, 9)."

The Closure

The midwifery service at Community Hospital began to systematically loose its client base, despite its positive outcomes. There are a variety of reasons for this. The intense competition that existed between hospitals for maternity patients has been discussed. Some women in Community Hospital's catchment area were at personal odds with the midwifery service's philosophy to not carry out routine, elective induction. This was significant. The desire for a social induction is quite real and rational. Many patients were without private transportation. For many women the uncertainties and discomforts that come with the end of pregnancy are not mere inconveniences. The reality of life for many patients requires planning—arranging care of children while in the hospital, arranging transportation.

Mothers covered by Medicaid had the right to choose which hospital to go to for delivery. The patients who chose to come to the nurse-midwifery service at Community Hospital did so knowing that they would have humane and respectful care along with the technological procedures they desired. There were other patients who held the view that the hospital was behind the times and desired the more technocratic model offered by nearby hospitals. They wanted their induction. They wanted their epidural as quickly as possible. In their minds, they would receive inferior care at Community Hospital with regards to these considerations.

Nurse-midwives at Community Hospital were focused on providing optimal care to their patients, all the while aware that larger forces placed their service at risk. In the end, the demise of their service had nothing to do with the quality of care. The service provided an intimate maternity service with excellent patient satisfaction and outcomes. The closure of the maternity service had to do with demographic changes as well as inefficiency and underutilization. Their ground, literally their physical space, was needed for a medical service more in line with the hospital's need to make budget. A small, intimate maternity center with good outcomes was not a priority for the hospital administration.

The first time I became aware that the hospital administration had plans to shut down the maternity service, I was walking around the unit with the Midwifery Service Director. I commented on the fact that there were so many family members crammed into a patient's room during a delivery. It seemed in many cases that the mother did not necessarily desire so many people to be present. It also interfered with care by the midwife and nursing staff. "Isn't there a place for some family members to wait?" I asked. The Director sighed and said, "Do you know what is on the other side of this wall?" She pointed to the wall we were standing in front of, the wall at the end of the hallway that I previously referred to as "the wall to nowhere".

"There is nothing on the other side of this wall," she said. "Half of this floor is empty. When the hospital renovated this unit we begged for a waiting room but we didn't get it. If and when they finally shut us down, this wall will come down and the entire floor of this hospital will become a skilled nursing care unit."

This was at a time when the hospital administration kept telling the midwifery service that they needed to "do something" to increase their number of deliveries. The hospital administration did nothing to help increase the census, complained of underutilization, and then used underutilization to justify shutting down the maternity service.

The description of this one hospital, and its position vis-à-vis the local medical system, is by no means representative of maternity care throughout the country. In many areas, pregnant women must drive many miles to the nearest labor and delivery service. This picture of women being able to pick and choose between hospitals, and hospitals competing to deliver their babies, will be out of the ordinary for women in many communities. For many women, there is no such ability to pick and choose a hospital. Induction is often a choice made by a family because the nearest maternity service is miles away and induction prevents having to rush for miles to the hospital at the onset of labor.

What this story does reflect is the business nature of childbirth in the United States and the financial incentives involved. Cesarean section has become the most frequently performed surgical procedure carried out in hospitals. Planned and unplanned cesareans, planned inductions (with the routine epidural and the interventions that accompany it) not only account for rising hospital costs of childbirth. They also account for the growing importance of labor and delivery as a cash cow for hospitals. Dr. Jeff Thompson, a Fellow within ACOG and a strong proponent of childbirth reform, has been quoted on the financial significance of American childbirth practices to our system of childbirth. "Birth," he says, "keeps the lights on in hospitals (Weeks 2012)."

Community Hospital slowly hemorrhaged patients as mothers chose to go to nearby medical centers to deliver their babies rather than deliver at a small, intimate, clean, maternity center led by empathetic, highly-trained nurse-midwives. Community Hospital was literally a short walk away from large maternity centers. The maternity floor at MC1 was so busy that mothers would often be placed in a bed in the hallway waiting for a labor room bed to come open. MC1's maternity unit was so busy, it was not uncommon for a baby to born in the hallway. Babies would be delivered by a resident who would mark the delivery in his book, counting the delivery as one more towards his required number of deliveries. An episiotomy? All the better. Another check. Low forceps or vacuum extraction? Check again. Another cesarean? Check again.

The women turning their backs on Community Hospital; taking these steps away from a small, intimate maternity setting; choosing to give birth in a large, inhospitable, cold setting; were for the most part African-American women on public insurance. It was entirely their choice and that choice was made quite self-consciously. It is a complicated phenomenon, that American women, including poor women of color, are embracing epiduralized birth to such a large extent.

At the same time, birth activists in the community—overwhelmingly white middle-class women—blogged about their struggles, their difficulty in finding a doctor willing to provide VBAC as an option.[30] These activists complained that their obstetrician demanded, and scheduled, a routine induction at their twenty week visit. When it was pointed out to birth activists that Community Hospital held a commitment to VBAC, what ensued were criticisms of Community Hospital that did not attempt to hide the racism lurking behind their comments. Community Hospital, historically seen as a black hospital, was "unclean" birth activists routinely claimed. This was not true. The maternity floor far exceeded standards of cleanliness. The labor and delivery rooms were as spacious and clean as I had ever seen. It was claimed that someone, who knew someone, who was told by someone else, that security guards at the emergency room entrance at Community Hospital smoked marijuana on the job: again untrue. There was then the pièce de resistance: "I would not drive through *that* part of town to go to a hospital."

Among the local birth activists, these racist statements went unchallenged and were accepted as reasonable excuses for not availing themselves of the very service that could provide the care they professed to want so badly. Essentially, the reasoning was: "I'll take my chance at such-and-such a hospital knowing they will insist on inducing me, knowing that my chances of having a cesarean are increased, knowing that I will not be able to have the VBAC I so badly want—all because I do not want to drive through *that* part of town."

The closure of the service, and the growth of larger hospitals nearby, begs the question: Are there reasonable limits to regionalization and centralization of maternity care? By 2002, women in 44% of non-metropolitan counties had absolutely no maternity care as compared with 24% in 1985 (Zhao 2007). The continued concentration of maternity services, along with the burgeoning of NICUs, is not uniquely American. Other Western countries have seen similar trends, although to a lesser extent. Our reliance on technology and NICUs as a disproportionate part of our prenatal and perinatal care, has translated into greater health care costs but without improved neonatal and infant outcomes (Thompson et al. 2002).

The concentration of births into larger maternity units is justified by its proponents not only by arguments regarding safety. It is justified as economical based on the ability to capture economies of scale. However, with the technological imperative that comes with centralization of care, childbirth has become more expensive.

> The hospitalization of birth encourages the use of technologies that can only feasibly be applied in a hospital. As the twentieth century progressed, hospitals became centers where new technologies could be easily tested and then applied to large numbers of women. The concentration of women in one place made the training and staffing needed to maintain the technologies clinically safer and economical feasible: the presence of the latest scientific technologies (e.g. fetal monitors and epidural anesthesia) in hospitals served to enhance their prestige as centers of science.

> Hospitalization of birth also has a variety of economic and social consequences. It makes feasible a larger client base for providers, a particularly important issue in those countries whose funding system rewards physicians for the size of their practice. It also eases the demands on providers and allows health planners to make care more "efficient." Bringing large numbers of patients to a central location is much more economical for providers and planners – than providing care in homes or in a series of small "cottage hospitals". *If one considers birthing mothers to be economic units, the larger the site, the greater the potential for economies of scale. The irony of this approach is that it often leads to large birthing hospitals also becoming centers of elaborate, and very expensive, technology, the use of which makes birth more costly* [Emphasis mine] (Declercq et al. 2001, 8)

Does the continued concentration of maternity care into large medical centers serve well our mothers and children? The case of Community Hospital's midwifery service suggests that it does not. Hospital administrators, when presented by the midwives with strategies to improve the community's impression of the maternity service, were intransigent. The closing of a community outreach clinic precipitated the initial decline in deliveries. The underutilization of the service was to some extent the result of long-term decisions made by health care bureaucrats who cared not a wit about what the midwives at Community Hospital were attempting—keeping hold a safe place for normal birth within their community. Nor was the welfare of mothers and babies in the community a consideration.

At an annual meeting of the American College of Nurse-Midwives, I encountered one the midwives who had worked at Community Hospital. I had spent hours observing her provide dedicated care to mothers and had also interviewed her for hours. We ran into each other in front of the elevators and I hugged her. "I hear you have moved to Hospital X and you are making more money. You know the closing of the service at Community Hospital was inevitable," I said. She looked at me with a sad face and said, "I guess I was just naïve, but I really thought that the hospital cared about the mothers.

---

[25] Hospitals are under increasing pressure from insurers, including Medicare, to discharge patients within a set given time. Transfer of patients to a physically separate "skilled nursing facility" as a transition to home is increasingly a popular means employed by hospitals to manipulate their statistics to conform to acceptable discharge criteria.

[26] Throughout this book, the terms perinatal mortality, fetal mortality and infant mortality are used. Definitions differ and various international agencies have strived to create uniform definitions for statistical purposes. In the United States, perinatal mortality encompasses the stages of fetal mortality and neonatal mortality. Fetal mortality is the death of a fetus following 20 weeks gestation but prior to live birth. Neonatal mortality is defined as the death of a live infant during the period from the day of birth through day 28 of life. Infant mortality is a death during the first year of life.

[27] The fact that there has been a proliferation of NICUs without a corresponding in maternal health care. It is one driver in childbirth related health care cost increases.

[28] Vaginal Birth After Cesarean (VBAC) rate: Number of vaginal births per 100 women with a previous cesarean delivery. The VBAC rate is calculated as the number of VBAC deliveries resulting in a live birth divided by the sum of VBAC and repeat cesarean deliveries, multiplied by 100. (marchofdimes.com)

[29] Neonatal mortality rates for 2007 were obtained from the CDC by Stapleton et al.

[30] In 2006 the American College of Obstetrics and Gynecology (ACOG) changed its position on VBAC, stating that under certain conditions a VBAC was a safe birth option. In 2010, ACOG further expanded its VBAC policy to approve with certain medical criteria to allow for VBAC after two cesareans (ACOG Practice Bulletin 115, August 2010). Despite this official change in position, many obstetricians continued to refuse to offer their patients the option of VBAC. Routine induction and cesarean birth has become an ubiquitous part of the Gleichschaltung of American birth as described in the Introduction.

Chapter Five

Care, Normalcy, and The Calling

"So much of what I do everyday is the same as the obstetricians I work with. Yet there is so much I do that is different—things that are difficult to put into words (a midwife)."

"For me, midwifery is a political thing. The spiritual piece of it is a calling but it is also a political issue. It is about reclaiming childbirth. It's about not letting medicine have control over what is a physiologic process (a midwife)."

"We live for the unmedicated births (a midwife)."

Personal and professional identities are constructed, shifting over time. As such, the words of nurse-midwives, when woven together, provide powerful insight into the profession as a whole. First person narrative also reflects the relationship of the self to the world, an interpretation of one's own history through memory and testimony. The relationship of self to work is particularly instructive for an analysis of how nurse-midwives understand what they do. As Kondo (1990) asserts, people *do* craft themselves; indeed, people *negotiate* fragments of identity, particularly through work.

> Work and personhood are inextricable from one another. As individuals transform the world around them, they themselves become transformed. ... Identity is not a state object, but a creative process, hence crafting selves is an ongoing—indeed a lifelong—occupation. ... Human beings create, construct, work on, and enact their identities, sometimes creatively challenging the limits of the cultural constraints which constitute both what we call selves and the ways those selves can be crafted (Kondo 1990, 48).

Prominent in my conversations with each midwife, was the self-awareness and views of their work and life. Some of this self-awareness has been clear in previous chapters: the self-awareness of how one goes about negotiating constraints; what can and can not be done; the self-awareness of how one negotiates between the

153

desires and needs of all players involved in social birth. This chapter goes further to discuss in more specifics the professional and cultural values of nurse-midwives.

The story of how nurse-midwifery has crafted itself, and continues to craft itself, is the story of how numerous nurse-midwives have gone about the work of crafting and negotiating their identities. The story of nurse-midwifery involves a multiplicity of voices and experiences. Narrative is not merely text (as in fiction) but is a form of data, which we as social scientists use in our quest for concrete answers. It is in the telling of stories that the shared values of nurse-midwives are unveiled.

Care, Normalcy, and The Calling

The culture of nurse-midwifery is not only about the process of delivering babies. It is so much more. For one, there exists the utter dedication to the care of mothers and babies as a mission. Coursing through the stories of nurse-midwives, is also the value placed on maintaining a place for the normality of birth. It is difficult to separate these concepts into discreet fragments. They are discreet and yet, at the same time, represent a single professional culture.

Many nurse-midwives choose to become a midwife in what they refer to as *a calling*. This calling is inexorably tied up with the value placed in the care of mothers and babies and the commitment to normal birth. It is also tied to the value placed in providing care to women who are underserved. One nurse-midwife stated to me that she defined her personal and professional identity as that of a "poverty worker".

When I asked another long-time midwife if she thought midwifery is a calling, her immediate response was absolutely categorical.

> Definitely. It has to be a calling because we're certainly not doing it for the money. We're not doing it for the easy hours. ... We're not doing it so we can punch a time card and then leave for home and forget about what you've done during the day. With midwifery, you really feel it is something that you have to do. ... Something that you are giving to society.

These three concepts—care, normalcy and the calling—are woven throughout the words of nurse-midwives. When asked to discuss what it is that they do, it would be expected that nurse-midwives speak about activities of a clinical nature. When asked what it is that they do, I expected from nurse-midwives the usual mention of clinical activities, education, and expectant counseling on a variety of issues. What surprised me was the extent to which respondents named activities that I could not easily place into clinical categories. I was also surprised by the ease with which the respondents seemed to go back and forth between listing clinical activities, along with activities that would not be found in a clinical protocol. This was true in my fieldwork interviews as well as responses to my pre-fieldwork survey. (Over six hundred nurse-midwives responded to my survey.)

The personal narratives provided in this chapter reflect a transformative period within the profession. A number of nurse-midwives have come to embrace midwifery in the sense that they see what they do in the clinical setting as "different" from that of obstetricians—they increasingly use words such as "therapeutic presence", "protecting the normalcy of birth", "empowering" the birthing mother. Their responses showed the ease with which they move between a medical/midwife care continuum. Nurse-midwives speak about placing mother and baby first and foremost in their thinking. They "listen". They "touch". They "educate". They "encourage". They "empower". Overwhelmingly, they talk about advocating for the normalcy of birth.

Nurse-midwifes place a high value on "care" and "normalcy". This has been verified in research by Kennedy (2000, 2002). In one study, Kennedy videotaped narratives of eleven nurse-midwives. They discussed their clinical practice, revealing what Kennedy cites as "alternative approaches" to care and "processes of caring for women [that] may have significant health effects (Kennedy 2002, 1759)."

"The art of doing nothing well" is also a value identified by Kennedy (2002, 1759). She describes the voices of her nurse-midwife informants speaking as if they themselves are an "instrument of care". Furthermore, she describes a "selective use of interventions"; the creation of an environment conducive to supporting the natural process of birth to the greatest extent possible; maintaining a "vigilant stance" on the part of the nurse-midwives as guardians of the birth process in the face of working within a medicalized environment. Safe care of mothers is also of high value.

The words of one long-time midwife brings to light so clearly the dedication to mothers, the value of serving women. In the case of this one nurse-midwife, the value of care and service is partially based on her own experience with birth and wanting women to have the opportunity to experience normal birth.

> MAM: You talked about how before you became a midwife you had been part of a birth activist support group. ... Could you talk more about that? How did you come to become a midwife?
>
> Midwife: I became interested during the eighties ... [It] was more of a support group. We met once or twice a year with most everybody in the group [having] a goal of becoming a midwife. ...
>
> MAM: Did you have children by that time?
>
> Midwife: Yes. It was after I had been a childbirth educator for a while. I was certified.
>
> MAM: And what made you want to become a childbirth educator?
>
> Midwife: I wanted to help other families who were going through childbirth. My [second] baby was born at home. And that is when I was looking for some way to become more involved. By that time I became interested in becoming a nurse-midwife. ...
>
> I decided I wanted to be able to deliver babies, not just talk about it. I decided to go to nursing school. We [nurse-midwives] have always had an association with nursing. Whether you consider it a compromise or a cop-out, that's where it stands. I only went to nursing school because it was a necessary route to get to midwifery. ... I never had dreams of being a nurse, that's for sure. It was a means to an end.
>
> MAM: There were so many like you.

Midwife: Some of us did see it as a cop-out, but some of us saw it as professionalizing. We tried to figure out what we wanted to do with our lives and we did nursing ... We did what we had to do.

MAM: Looking back at those times, would you have called yourself a feminist at the time?

Midwife: [She laughs] No. Was the term in use yet?

MAM: Oh yes. The first edition of the book, *Our Bodies Ourselves* was in 1971. That was the seminal work. And then there was Barbara Ehrenreich's book, *Witches, Nurses and Midwives*.

Midwife: I did have that book. ...

MAM: I'm asking how you identified yourself within the social movements of the time. You didn't think of yourself as a feminist?

Midwife: No. I saw myself as part of the counterculture. Because when I thought of feminism, I thought of Gloria Steinem and who was the other woman? Germaine Greer. Those were the feminists. ... I was a hippie. I didn't identify as a feminist.

MAM: You got turned on to the homebirth movement not as a feminist but more as part of the counterculture?

Midwife: Counterculture. Turn in. Turn off. Drop out. Or I guess it was the other way. ... Turn on. Tune in. Drop out. That was the motto. [She is laughing here.]

MAM: I'm bringing all this up because I'm trying to get a sense of where midwives, you included, place themselves in terms of women's rights, feminism and childbirth.

Midwife: ... I guess I believed that women should be able to work outside the home. And women should receive equal pay for equal work. But at that time I just wanted to be home with the children, seeing motherhood as an important job. ... In my mind, feminism was something that saw staying at home as old-fashioned. So I didn't identify myself as a feminist at the time.

MAM: Did you ever do homebirth?

Midwife: Not as a midwife. Because once I started nursing school, my orientation became hospital. So that is what I became comfortable with. I started working in labor and delivery. I didn't have the ability to be on call all the time. I realized that I wanted to work with the underserved population and that was not the women who were having homebirths. ... It wasn't that I didn't approve of homebirth. I just couldn't be on call 24/7. It takes a special person to do that. I decided I wasn't capable of it. ... I've been in practice for 18 years. Incredible. It seems like a long time.

MAM: Could you talk a little about changes you have seen over the years in the hospital?

Midwife: ... They were still separating the mother and the baby. The idea that the baby should stay with the mother was seen as quite radical. And husbands weren't allowed in the room. I would say that since the early 1980s, every hospital has given lip service to certain things. Creating a more home-like environment. Hiding equipment. Allowing the husband in the room. So that has been in place. But there are also certain underlying principles of medical management that haven't changed.

MAM: Keeping that in mind. ... The whole concept at the time was emphasis on the family and the self-care model. The whole idea was that the family would get involved in the care. In reality, perhaps that became the systemic rationale for having less nursing care during labor.

Midwife: Well she has her family with her. The husband is expected to be there and be supportive. ... Once it was accepted, the idea was that the husband would provide care. Be the coach. Hold the baby afterwards. I think that was supposed to be the focus rather than the abdication of nursing care. I don't think the idea of the family involvement was meant to give up nursing care.

MAM: I also don't think it was meant to do that. My question is whether it might have unintentionally led to less nursing care and support. One question I've had, how many husbands are really prepared to provide that kind of support?

Midwife: Well, at least they have the opportunity to be there, to be part of the experience, and to be with the newborn in a way they didn't before. They weren't just out in the waiting room, pacing, worrying about what was happening.

We go on to discuss the relationship of having the family in the labor room: the family expected to provide support, yet, sometimes unprepared for that; the lack of bedside care by nurses. This nurse-midwife had previously worked at a hospital where there was an expectation that the baby stay in the room at all times. This expectation led to a shifting back towards keeping the mother in the hospital for two days. (For a short period of time, hospitals were sending mothers home within twenty-four hours after birth; it was found that many mothers needed more time to adjust.)

Midwife: I have been thinking that the pendulum has swung back.

MAM: Swung back to...?

Midwife: Swung back as to many women believing that the doctor is right, and they don't have any choice or options regarding their choices. Especially regarding VBAC. I've talked to mothers about repeat sections for example and I may ask, "Why have you chosen this?" And a lot of reasons they give is, "Well, the doctor says the first one was so big." Or, "The baby had a cord around its neck and I don't want that to happen again." "The doctor said I should have another cesarean again this time." The attitude is, "Whatever the doctor says." And I couldn't really say, "Did you question that? Did you look at the alternatives?"

MAM: Why can't you say that?

Midwife: In most circumstances I didn't feel comfortable. ...

MAM: Do you think the women are not questioning the doctors? Or do you think perhaps this is what women want ... They would rather not give birth vaginally.

Midwife: Well. That's another discussion. But I think it's mostly due to the trending of the doctors who have never seen a normal labor and delivery. They have all seen 90% of the labors that have been epiduralized. They see a heart rate dip down and they're ready to do a C-section. So of course they think that labor has to be managed.

But in terms of what women want. That is a very pertinent question. There are women out there who want their delivery scheduled. They want their mother there. They want things organized. ...

When women think they prefer a cesarean, I don't think they realize what they are asking for. ... [But] we give informed consent and women choose. We can acknowledge that there are women who want an epidural. Not everybody wants to go through labor without pain management. So why not? If a woman chooses to have an epidural, and understands what she is getting. ...

MAM: This does bring me to one of the issues of what I'm thinking about. .... I think the idea of choice as a concept is a conundrum for midwives.

Midwife: It *is* a double edge sword. ... I don't think we're *forcing* anything on anybody. ... Women are asking for this.

MAM: I see a few women coming in refusing anything—Hispanic women, women from Africa, Jehovah Witnesses. That's their decision and I see the nurse-midwives and the nurses honoring those decisions.

Midwife: We live for the unmedicated births. This is not coming from the nurse-midwives. We had a fifteen-year old who had an unmediated birth. She did great.

MAM: How did this develop, do you think? What is going on?

Midwife: With what? The demise of midwifery? Increased use of epidurals?

MAM: Well. Let's start out with the increase in epidurals.

Midwife: ... It is a cultural phenomenon. The question is how it has passed through so many different cultures. Because on the one hand, there are the women with private insurance, educated, primarily Caucasian, who one would think would be more of the ... have more of the ability to do research, consider the pros and cons of every single intervention that can happen at birth. And yet they are opting for epidurals. And then [there are] women, like at our hospital, who are not going to read about every single procedure. And they start opting for the same things. It is an interesting phenomenon.

MAM: When did you start seeing it happen?

Midwife: When did the natural childbirth movement start to fade away? I'm not sure.

The above interview brings up so many interesting questions. This midwife, with years of experience, is dedicated to providing safe, humane care to her patients. She chose to work in-hospital so that she could bring midwifery care to underserved women. Yet her fallback position, when it comes to mothers choosing epiduralized birth, is that each mother receives informed consent and has the choice.

The question must be asked, however: is the informed consent on epidurals weighty? Are the risks described as being of consequence? What I witnessed was that during informed consent risks associated with epidural were made light of. During informed consent the distinct impression was given that the risks were fairly insignificant. At the same time, most women at Community Hospital valued vaginal birth and wanted a VBAC following a primary section. Some did not go on to have a VBAC, but the staff was dedicated to doing everything possible to make that happen safely. Only a few women opted for an elective repeat section, a decision accepted by the nurse-midwives. Women also did not want episiotomies, if possible. Their desire on these issues corresponded to nurse-midwifery care; nurse-midwives rarely performed episiotomies.

What is not revealed in the above transcription are this midwife's personal sacrifices to become a midwife: the hours of travel to nursing school; the sacrifices to attend midwifery school.

When she obtained her first midwifery job, it put an enormous strain on her marriage and her family. This is a theme that runs through many interviews of midwives.

Another midwife, also with many years of experience, spoke of becoming a midwife as a result of her own homebirth and her involvement in the alternative birth movement. I had asked what had motivated her to choose nurse-midwifery as a profession and she related to me how midwifery became her "cause" in life.

> Midwife: To answer your question as to how I became a midwife. We were living in (City X) in 1974. ... and I became pregnant. My husband immediately came up with the idea of having a homebirth because his college roommate had somehow become interested in homebirth and gave him a book, Suzanne Arms' book *Immaculate Deception*. ... [My husband gave the book to me] and he said, "Why don't we have a homebirth?" And I said, "Are you out of your mind? No." But I read the book. And we had always been political activists and so it immediately grabbed me. So we had a homebirth. And it was a transformative event. It put me on the path of midwifery and I decided that's what I wanted to do. For me it was the cause.

> MAM: How did you become a midwife?

> Midwife: [There was] a midwifery center in (City X). I went to a couple of homebirths just as an observer, a layperson ... actually I helped one homebirth as a lay attendant to confirm my feelings. I thought long and hard about it. There were a lot of lay midwives [31] in (State X) in that period at that time. I debated a long time as to whether I wanted to go the lay path ... but I knew I would be limited to out-of-hospital birth. After thinking long and hard about it, I realized I wanted to do nurse-midwifery because I wanted to be able to support my family. The people I knew who did lay midwifery, they weren't able to really practice openly. They were operating out of the radar. I wanted to have a legal, legitimate credential.

> It was so much about my own sensibilities of doing something in the world that might ... even though I had done some alternative things in my life, and I'm sure my children think we're very alternative given our age and where we have been in our lives. But we are very

traditional. ... I don't think in my twenties I was thinking about the finance piece about it as much as the credentials. I just felt that the status of the lay midwives' path was a little bit sketchy. Not really knowing what you were doing with everyone on your back or where you were going to live. I wanted to go a more traditional route. ... [My note: This midwife's comments reflect the state of the profession of midwifery at a specific time and place. Times have changed some.]

... I think for me, midwifery is a political thing. The spiritual piece of it is a calling, but it is also a political issue. It is about reclaiming childbirth. It's about not letting medicine have control over what is a physiologic process. ... I never wanted to be a staff nurse. I went to nursing school just so I could go to nurse-midwifery school.

MAM: You have said that your birth was a transformative experience.

Midwife: I remember feeling strongly after delivering that baby. We had gone to the hospital, gotten pitocin, which probably took twelve hours off my labor. ... I remember thinking how amazing it was, and "I can do anything. If I can do that, I can do anything." So I do think that natural childbirth is empowering for women. You can't do it alone from a spiritual sense, which is why you need a doula.

Later in the discussion I tried to elicit her opinions abut the epiduralized environment at Community Hospital.

Midwife: I think natural childbirth can be empowering. The population here, so many of them want epidurals, I think, because it's a way of detaching from their life. The pain process, it takes you to the other side of something. They don't like what they see or they're not prepared for it.

I think [natural childbirth] is empowering. I can speak for myself; if I can do that, I can do anything. It gave me the courage for the things that came to me in my life. But not everybody sees it that way. I've come to see in my practice that I can't impose. Even with my daughters, I can't impose my thinking on them, although I think you try as a parent.

The stories of the younger midwives were also compelling to me, as I had not expected the same themes. However, even from the younger midwives I heard the same theme of wanting to serve mothers. One midwife in her early thirties, a young woman who graduated from an Ivy League School and comes from a long line of doctors and professionals, described to me how she decided to become a midwife—to the dismay of her family. Her decision has left her in debt, with many thousands of dollars in student loans, representing an enormous sacrifice.

> Midwife: I've known since I was fifteen that I wanted to deliver babies. I went to a health-careers high school in (City X). A cousin's husband was an obstetrician. My mother felt that, because (City X) had a high teen pregnancy rate, that it would be a good idea for me to shadow this obstetrician while I was in health-careers. I got to scrub in my first C-section when I was fifteen, because I had been taught how to scrub in. And that was ... that's it. I'm going to deliver babies. ... I got home at 1:00 am and I yelled, "Mom. I'm going to deliver babies." And she said, "Yeah. Whatever. Go to bed. You're fifteen." It took ten years to get there, but I got there.
>
> MAM: How old are you now?
>
> Midwife: I'm thirty-three. It took me ten years. I was fifteen in my junior year of high school. Then I went to college and grad school. Then I went to midwifery school. I think I was twenty-five when I did my first birth during midwifery training. It was the mom's fourth baby. It was really cool.

Her narrative of having been called to deliver babies at the age of fifteen, reminded me of when I bore witness to a seven-year-old girl experiencing that same sensation. I was in training as a nurse-midwife and was delivering a mother of her second baby. A single mother, she had no one to care for her little girl. We set up a cot for her seven-year-old in the hallway, right outside the labor room. We put the little girl to bed and told her to go to sleep. I was aware that she wasn't really going to sleep. Each time I walked past her cot she would scrunch up her eyes, pretending to be asleep. As the baby was born, a nurse said to me, "We have little eyes with us." The little girl had been waiting for the birth and had quietly slipped into the room. She was standing at my side and stared as I delivered her baby brother. She gasped, her hand flew to her mouth, and then she said, "That was wonderful. I want to do that when I grow up." This seven-year-old girl witnessed what few people experience: a non-medicated, normal, physiologic birth.

But back to the above interview: this same midwife later spoke on the same theme of having been called to do what she does.

> MAM: I think I have observed you more than any other midwife here. And I've noticed that you so clearly enjoy doing what you do.
>
> Midwife: I think that it goes back to the "I want to deliver babies" thing. My mother said that when I was really young, I'm not sure where it was, and I was watching TV, and a woman was screaming and wailing and I said, "Oh my God. Is she having a baby?" And my mother thought, "What does this five-year-old know about having babies?" She brought that up a few years ago, and I thought it was very interesting. But I come from a long line of physicians. So the whole midwifery thing did *not* go over well.
>
> … My father's family is very bright. He had one sister who owns a nursing company. … Another sister was a lawyer. Then another was an engineer. These are not dumb people that I come from on both sides. So the whole midwifery thing did not go over well. It was like, "You want to be a *what*?"

The young nurse-midwife goes on to describe an existential crisis of self in walking away from her initial career choice to enter medicine.

> Midwife: It was a big choice. During college I was having a crisis of spirit. I was sitting in chemistry and thinking, "This is *crazy*. I'm not *feeling* this. And I don't think any of this is going to get any better." I learned some things. But as far as taking people down to their molecules and organs, and they become the sum of their

parts, it just didn't make sense to me. The more holistic view worked for me. Fortunately, the idea of midwifery came to me when I was having this crisis of spirit. I went to the pre-med Dean at my school. I told her it [pre-med] just wasn't for me. And she said, "You'll never make it through medical school. You should be a midwife." And I was like, "What?" And then the following year ... I met this outside person who I was talking to, to get some clarity on life. And I was telling her this story and she said, "My best friend is a midwife." ... And this person said, "It's a noble profession."

This midwife then went to nursing school, for the purpose of going on to a nurse-midwifery education.

The first two years of nursing school, I thought, "This is crap," because it was so easy. ... When I got to nursing school, it was a piece of cake. I was sick but still aced my final, even though I had barely studied. And I thought, "I hope I didn't make a mistake. Maybe I should have gone to medical school." There were portions of the program that I liked. I liked the part that used the humanities ... healing with music and healing with literature. But when I got further into the program I began to like it.

MAM: Tell me what your crisis of spirit was all about.

Midwife: It was just that I wasn't happy in the study I was in. I was a neuroscience major. I was miserable. It wasn't interesting. It made no sense to me why I should have to do linear algebra from recall. I just did not understand.

It wasn't just the memorization, because I can memorize stuff. Nobody told me that I didn't need to take two semesters of calculus. Calculus II just blew my mind. I just didn't get it. And there wasn't anyone to explain it to me well. So it was just awful. And I was thinking, "I could be learning something and I am not learning anything." And I did not appreciate that.

I had other personal things going on in my life. I wasn't happy. ... I made some very good friends, people who are still my friends today. But it was hard. I needed to find something I could work for. Something I could *believe.* And I did not *believe* in linear algebra. So I dropped neuroscience as a major.

I commented on the high degree of energy she appeared to have and her dedication to her work. She was clearly the most popular of the midwives, with very few no-shows in the prenatal clinic on the days she worked the office.

> MAM: Where do you get all of this energy? Everything that I see you do when you come on shift?
>
> Midwife: It's the drive. I figure I can do anything for twelve hours. My last position I worked twenty-fours. And it's hard being first-call for twenty-four hours in a private practice.

She spoke of putting in long shifts, and how she will often stay past her shift when asked by a patient to do so. She represented an amazing dedication to individual patients. In the following interview transcript, she is talking about one woman who needed a repeat C-section. It was her third pregnancy and she had two previous sections with a classical (vertical) scar. "She just wasn't a candidate [for VBAC]." This midwife was worried that the mother would not show up for her scheduled cesarean; the mother was just that scared of another operation. Knowing this, the midwife promised she would be there for the mother's cesarean. When the mother was admitted for her scheduled cesarean, this midwife stayed beyond her shift to stay with the mother.

> MAM: Where does that [dedication] come from?
>
> Midwife: I don't know. I'm just loyal to a fault. My mother calls me a sap. I just didn't want her [the mother] to disappear because she's the kind of person who would disappear. But it was a hard C-section. It lasted two hours. There was scar tissue everywhere. And I kept telling her, "It's almost over." She had kept cancelling her [prenatal] appointments. And I had told her, "You can't just run away. We will track you down."
>
> I can't save everybody. I don't know where this knight-in-shining armor thing comes from. But if I can help

somebody ... When I left the private practice, they made me write a letter to all the patients telling them that I was moving out-of-state. Because they were afraid that people would try to follow me.

She then went on to talk about the frustrations, particularly student debt, and the sacrifices involved in becoming a midwife.

Midwife: They [Community Hospital] haven't given us our raise. Here we are in a recession and my rent has gone up. I had to move in with my boyfriend. The thing that kills me ... I make decent money but I use to work two jobs. [But] I had to quit that job. Not having that second job has destroyed me financially. I had to finance my education. I make good money but I do not make nearly enough to offset that.

MAM: I think a lot of midwives now wind up in deep debt. It's hurting. It's hard to convince someone to be a midwife when it costs so much.

Midwife: I'm frustrated. I love what I do but I am really, really, really frustrated as far as getting ahead. ... I have to work really hard because of my loans. I have to make sure I get my overtime because if I don't, I'm in trouble.

MAM: Midwives do not make enough money.

Midwife: We do not make enough money. I'm thinking about getting a second job in January. I'm just hoping I get a refund and that I don't owe [taxes]. And with my situation ... I'm single, have no kids. I don't own [a home]. So 30% of my income is gone. And I paid eight to nine thousand dollars in interest last year [on student loans]. It annoys me.

MAM: So you're still paying off your student loans.

Midwife: Oh yeah. I'll be paying it off ... I tell people, "I have a mortgage but with no house." One of my loans is $150,000.

MAM: Wow.

Midwife: And that's with me getting nowhere. I'm not even paying on the balance. Because if I paid what I should be paying, I would be paying over $1,200 per month in loan repayment. I can't do that. On this income? Can't do it.

I asked this same midwife if she would still choose to be a midwife and she replied, "Absolutely."

MAM: So tell me. Explain it to me. This debt is weighing on you. Why do you say to me that you would still make the same decisions?

Midwife: Because I get a lot of personal satisfaction helping people. Helping a woman through the transition from pregnancy to motherhood, especially the first-time mother. Helping a woman who is in need ... makes a huge difference in my life. So I get a lot of satisfaction. Otherwise, I would be miserable right now.

I like what I do. It's fine when the baby is born. But I'm not a baby person. It's about the woman in trouble because they are forgotten in a lot of ways. Telling the woman that she has birth control options. Helping the teenage moms realize they don't have to be pregnant again. They just have to know certain things. ...

I would ask [my teenage patients], "What do you want to do when you get out of school?" [They say], "I want to go to college." "I want to be a judge." "Really? Run with that. Run with that. Don't let anyone take that away from you." You know that is a lot of school. But if I can just give someone some hope.

A little girl said to me, "I feel like I'm depressed." And I said to her, "I'd be surprised if you're *not*. You're fourteen years old and you're going to have a baby. You can't even drive a baby to the hospital, if you wanted to. You *should* be depressed." Maybe I was just meant to do this. But I don't feel that I should have to be poor to do this.

MAM: Right.

> Midwife: I did not sign up to be a nun. I really didn't. I make good money but every single cent goes away. Quickly, I might add. It's annoying. At least I'm not salaried. I can put in and get paid for every single hour I work.

Another young midwife described discovering how she wanted to be a midwife. Unlike the older midwives, she did not have a specific calling to become a midwife. She discovered midwifery during her nursing education and realized she was pulled to become a midwife.

> MAM: The first question I often ask is to have you tell me how or why you became a midwife. Some people talk about the process of becoming a midwife. Some talk about what motivated them. Whatever you feel comfortable talking about.
>
> Midwife: Well. Let's see. I first became interested in doing something health related in high school. I don't even know where the idea came from, because no one in my family is in a health field. It was one of those aptitude tests you take. It came out with, "This is a field you should look at." And it just made a lot of sense to me. I weighed out medicine vs. nursing. I was attracted to nursing being the care vs. medicine being the cure. Applied to nursing school. I wanted to focus on the care of the patient rather than the cure.
>
> MAM: That appealed to you?
>
> Midwife: It appealed to me. I think that it's part of my personality. I have a high level of connecting and interacting with people, being interested in people's lives, and also seeing it as a vehicle to another world. It's not that it was intentional. ...
>
> I wanted to have a bachelor's degree and I wanted to be a nurse. So I went to (College X). Loved the school. Loved the city. Loved my first job. I started out in orthopedics and urology.
>
> I first started thinking about midwifery in college. I didn't know what kind of nursing I wanted to do. But I thought it would be something with mothers and/or babies. I was looking forward to my maternity rotation. It was actually the negative experiences that led me to

midwifery. I saw routine episiotomies. Shouting at women to push. And I thought, "There's got to be a better way."

... And so I was discouraged, but I had a belief that there has got to be a better way out there. ... But the thing that really influenced me in midwifery, besides having this negative experience and thinking that there had to be something better that coincided ... I guess it was the same year. It was a course ... here are the basic kinds of nursing. Here are the different kinds of advanced practice nursing. Nurses in those different areas would come in and lecture.

MAM: So it was a professional issues course.

Midwife: Yeah. It was nursing as a profession. A nurse-midwife came to the class. I don't even remember her name. I sat there listening to her talk about what she did, and something just clicked and I thought, "That's me."

And then around the same time, my sister went to a used book sale in our hometown. The library would purge these books out and have a book sale. And she was rummaging through and found the book, Ina May Gaskin's *Spiritual Midwifery*, and gave it to me. She wrote in there, "This is so you." And I don't even know if I had told her that I was interested in being a midwife at that point. And so I picked up that book from cover to cover with all the birth stories. And I thought, "This *is* me. That is what I'm going to do."

... I think a story connects. Like this lecturer, giving you a vision. This book just spoke to me. I really felt it was meant to be. Something had gotten that book into my sister's hands, which then put into mine. It was meant to be. ... So that's when I decided, "Okay. That's what I'm going to do."

I have chosen these narratives as they reveal the common themes articulated so often by the nurse-midwives that I have interviewed over the years. These narratives, with the description of professional values, are reinforced by my observations. A genuine caring and compassion for mothers shines through in their words and actions, as well as in the words of all the nurse-midwives at Community Hospital, some of which I have not included here. There is also the common, articulated experience of what I would call very simply, a calling. Yet a part of this story is that care and compassion can only go so far when these midwives are forced to negotiate, from a subordinate position, how they carry out their profession.

---

[31] The term *lay midwife* has become archaic and within midwifery circles is considered by some to be pejorative, as non-nurse-midwives have developed their own professional certification.. Its use by this nurse-midwife reflects the fact that she has been a nurse-midwife for decades and began practice when the term was widely used. It was originally used to distinguish between nurse-midwives and midwives who practiced outside the legalities of professional certification.

Birth Ecology and Epiduralized Birth:
An Examination of the Evidence

"One has only to read the manufacturer's information leaflet of any of the drugs commonly given to women during labor to realize that all of these drugs enter the blood and brain of the baby within seconds or minutes and place the mother and her baby at significant risk (Doris Haire 1994)."

"I don't think there has ever been a consensus task force on the use of epidurals [in labor] (A midwife)."

I've written earlier in this book about my unease at what I perceived as the indistinguishable nature of births that I witnessed. However, there was something else that continued to bother me—something I couldn't quite put my finger on. Then, in the middle of one night, I woke up, sat straight up in bed, and the thought came: "It's the babies. There is something not quite right with the babies."

As I contemplated this impression, I realized a number of things. The behavior of babies I had seen born at Community Hospital tended to be different than those I myself had delivered, most of whom had been unmedicated births. Of course, all the babies I saw born at my field site were not precisely the same; there were common characteristics, and Apgar scores were generally good. However, the newborns appeared as if in a haze. They tended to be unattached and unaware. They tended not to make eye contact with the mother. They tended to be uninterested in the nipple. This was in the immediate period following birth when it is normal for babies to be alert. My unease grew at what I was observing. I continued to observe the newborns from a distance, as physical assessment of the newborn was not in my IRB protocols. I turned to the scientific literature regarding the epidural and in the medications used with epiduralized birth in order to better understand what I had observed.

****

There is no consensus regarding the impact of the epidural on a mother and baby. Does the epidural prolong overall labor? Does the local anesthetic in an epidural, usually bupivacaine, negatively impact maternal/newborn behavior? What is the impact of administering bupivacaine and pitocin together, both powerful medications? What is the impact of a steady administration of exogenous, synthetic oxytocin (pitocin) on the secretion of maternal endogenous oxytocin? These are merely a few of the questions involved in the debate regarding the safety of epiduralized birth. Developing research suggests that the medications used in epiduralized birth are not benign. The debate now is to what extent the drugs used in epiduralized birth are harmful to the mother and the fetus.

To place this discussion in perspective, it is important to place as a central concept that there is no placental barrier. Every drug given to the mother during labor and delivery passes directly into the fetal blood stream. These drugs are received by the fetus in larger doses relative to the dose received by the mother due both to the relatively small size of the fetus, as well as the immaturity of the fetal neurological and metabolic systems (Haire 1994).

A second central concept is that of medicine's embrace of the risk/benefit analysis in determining the appropriate application of medical procedures and medications. Risk/benefit analysis is a central tenant of modern medicine and always has an element of clinical judgment. However, that judgment must be grounded on evidence. In the case of epiduralized birth, any risk/benefit analysis must take into consideration possible harm to mother and baby with the use of bupivacaine and pitocin, administered either alone or in combination. This is often ignored in the risk/benefit analysis within the modern labor and delivery unit. For that purpose, this chapter offers an alternative balance in its presentation of evidence of negative impacts of epiduralized birth, evidence that is often ignored by modern obstetrics.

Obstetrics: Is it Evidence-Based?

An essential foundation of modern medicine is the application of evidence-based research to clinical practice. The gold standard for clinical evidence remains randomized, double-blind studies. However, these studies are difficult to carry out on pregnant women due to ethical issues. Two opposing approaches to maternity care exist. The approach held by many obstetricians is to carry out technological interventions *unless* they have been *proven* to be *unsafe*. This enables obstetricians and anesthesiologists to continue to carry out interventions inherent to epiduralized birth, despite research that suggests major risks. There is an opposite approach: the onus is on obstetrical providers to *prove*, to a high degree of certainty, that unnecessary technological interventions are in fact *safe* before implemented during pregnancy for no clear medical indication.

In modern obstetrics, this second approach has not been the norm. Interventions are all too often implemented and become routine when, in fact, *they have not been proven to be safe*. Additionally, in some cases interventions are actually known, or suspected, to be unsafe. Yet, the risks are shrugged off as minor. In too many cases, convenience and tradition trumps science.

A case in point is urinary catheterization, an intervention inherent to epiduralized birth. Most obstetrical providers view urinary catheterization as a minor intervention. However, the incidence of hospital-acquired urinary tract infection (UTI) is not a minor problem. There is an approximate 3–5% daily risk for acquiring a UTI in a hospital when a patient is catheterized (Lo et al. 2008). During routine consent, prior to epidural administration, I did not witness a single provider emphasize the fact that urinary catheterization, an inevitable intervention in epiduralized birth, is not benign and can result in infection. The incidence of antibiotic resistant infection in hospitals has become a serious risk with any intervention but particularly in the case of urinary catheterization. The growth of antibiotic resistance should make any unnecessary intervention a concern.

Doris Haire (1994) emphasized the fact that virtually everything a mother takes into her body rapidly passes to the baby from the placenta via the maternal blood supply. We all know this. Women are admonished during pregnancy to take no medications of any kind unless found to be necessary by their provider. Even the occasional glass of wine is frowned upon on the grounds that there is no known safe limit of alcohol during pregnancy. And yet during labor we think nothing of administering medications to the mother that rapidly disperse to the fetus. Again, to quote Haire:

> During the hours that surround an infant's birth the brain is particularly vulnerable to drug-induced trauma and permanent injury. ... It is the nerve circuitry of the brain and central nervous system of the fetus that is rapidly developing as labor begins, making these awesomely complex structures vulnerable to permanent damage from the drugs and procedures administered to the mother during this time (Haire 1994).

The amount of medication dispersed to the fetus through the mother is not "minuscule", as characterized to me by one anesthesiologist. Because of the relative small size of the fetus in relation to the mother, a drug that is provided to the mother in a "minuscule" amount is dispersed to the fetus in relatively larger doses. In pediatrics, medication dosage is carefully adjusted to account for infant size. Why is this principle ignored during labor?

There is also a relationship between time in labor and the total dosage of medications received by the fetus. "If a drug is frequently or continuously administered to the mother during labor, there is a tendency for the drug to accumulate in the maternal and fetal blood and brain." In addition, the drugs administered during labor are "trapped" in the infant's tissue. The newborn's "immature metabolic and endocrine systems cannot readily break down and excrete the drugs." As a result, drugs and their metabolites may continue to circulate in the newborn for days (Haire 1994).

It is truly stunning that the obstetrical community has known for decades the potential toxicity of drugs commonly used during labor. Yet that knowledge is ignored. Obstetricians (and sadly many nurse-midwives) fail to provide full evidence to mothers.

Doris Haire sounded the alarm in the early 1990s. Yet since that time, toxic drugs are now routinely administered during epiduralized births.

Rachel Carson, in her book Silent *Spring*, provided an understanding of the dangers of indiscriminant use of DDT. She was the mother of ecology. A careful consideration of Carson's writing shows that she wanted the use of DDT to be carefully considered for its benefits vs. its risk. Haire testified to a similar consideration with regards to birth interventions, including the routine medications used in epiduralized birth.

Throughout this chapter I will present the scientific evidence regarding the toxicity of labor drugs, particularly bupivacaine and pitocin. The evidence is overwhelming. I do not pretend to be unbiased in this matter. I adhere to the clinical position that these medications must be *proven to be safe* before administered on a routine basis. Given their risks, there is no basis for use on a routine basis. Sources that I reviewed include four editions of the medical text *Anesthesia for Obstetrics* ranging from 1979 to 2013, along with over one hundred medical journal articles.

How Pain Came To Be A Medical Indication

The experience of pain in childbirth is subjective and variable. All social cultures rely on various customs and interventions to help laboring mothers cope with the pain of childbirth, i.e. through the use of supportive care and social support (Catton et al. 2002). Numerous academics have identified the use of ether gas, during the labor of privileged women, as a turning point in Western culture's belief system regarding pain in childbirth. Prior to the modern era, many physicians refused to use pharmaceutical pain relief. Many were of the philosophical belief that pain in labor represented a woman's lot in life. Some physicians were also hesitant to use ether because of its potentially negative impact on the newborn (respiratory depression). It was difficult to control the dosage of ether and the impact of a given dosage was highly variable. On a positive note, most physicians continued to hold the traditional belief that labor was a physiologic process that should be interfered with only when medically necessary.

Until the modern era, most physicians maintained this traditional philosophy of birth (Catton et al. 2002).

During the Progressive Era of the early twentieth century, a change occurred in cultural attitudes regarding pain management. Women's rights activists played a pivotal role in demanding that physicians use pharmaceuticals to provide pain relief during childbirth. This in turn advanced the movement of birth into hospitals, where pain medication could be administered in a safer, controlled environment. The demand for pain medication also provided impetus to the developing medical specialty of obstetrics, which "criticized the philosophy of 'watchful expectancy' that had dominated obstetric practice throughout most of the nineteenth century (Canton et al. 2002, S25)."

This fundamental change in the U.S. cultural belief system regarding pain in labor helps to explain how opioids and the epidural, both known to have possible negative side effects, have so rapidly come to be incorporated into obstetrical care. Pain came to be seen as serving no useful purpose and to be inhumane in any circumstance. Many women and obstetricians saw the alleviation of pain as a humanistic ideal. Also, a belief within obstetrical ideology is that pain itself is a stressor that puts the fetus at risk. As a result, physicians were motivated to use "increasing doses of various drugs administered by a variety of new techniques (Catton et al. 2002, S25)." This change in cultural attitudes justified the growing technological interventions in childbirth.

Associated with this spirit of reform was an unbounded faith that human reason, through science and technology, could identify and overcome all causes of suffering and pain. This social reform milieu accounts in part for both the intensity of demands of early feminists and the subsequent response of modern obstetricians to emphasize pain management during labor. It also helps to explain the feckless pursuit and use of new drugs and techniques by obstetrics to alleviate pain (Catton et al. 2002, S26).

Following the use of ether, narcotics (i.e. morphine, Demerol and, more recently, Fentanyl) began to be used for pain relief in labor. However, narcotics create difficulties: timing of administration is critical to avoid neonatal respiratory depression at birth. The use of twilight sleep (a combination of morphine and scopolamine, an amnesiac), while popular from the 1950s through the 1970s, also presented problems for obstetrical staff. Some women during twilight sleep, unaware of their surroundings and behavior, were at times difficult to manage.

Epidural anesthesia, prior to its use during labor and delivery, was developed as an alternative to general anesthesia in surgery. When first introduced as a means of pain relief during labor, the absence of glaring, obvious side effects such as neonatal respiratory depression, as well as the complete elimination of pain, made it appear to be the perfect alternative for pain relief.

In the early years of the use of the epidural in obstetrics, the implications of using a local anesthetic via epidural throughout the entirety of labor were not understood. Early advocates for the use of epidural during labor did not recommend its use throughout the entirety of labor. Initially, it was used as pain relief only when labor was well-established (Wester and Krumperman 1958). Nor did physicians consider the possibility that there may be adverse impacts on the mother or fetus. What was considered important was that the epidural did not cause respiratory depression of the newborn and usually provided excellent pain relief.

Epidural was also seen as an alternative to other more difficult forms of analgesia. For example, epidural during labor became an alternative to pudendal anesthesia, [32] which was traditionally administered for relief of extreme pain experienced by some women as the fetus proceeds through the birth canal past the ischial spines. The pudendal block is a difficult procedure to master and occurs at a time in delivery when the mother has difficulty remaining still. However, epidural anesthesia requires the services of an anesthesiologist, bringing a new specialist into maternity care. As cesarean sections became more common, it became an advantage to have an epidural in place, "just in case".

As the use of the epidural became routine, the timing of administration became a subject of debate. At first, studies regarding the impact of epidural analgesia on the length of first stage of labor were inconsistent and inconclusive. Epidurals progressively came to be administered earlier during labor. Relief of pain, even in early labor, became an indication for epidural administration, particularly as "pitocin augmentation appears to readily correct any observed decrease in uterine activity [as a result of the epidural] (Shnider and Levinson 1987, 45)." As epidurals became more commonplace, there was growing empirical recognition of the disruption and lengthening of labor; and so augmentation of labor with pitocin came to be a routine intervention associated with epidural analgesia.

Labor as a Mechanical Process

The modern obstetrical profession holds a philosophical framework of labor that is essentially different from that of earlier physicians. While early physicians had no scientific understanding of the neurohormonal system involved in labor, they empirically understood that the laboring mother responded to various environmental factors, factors that influenced the process of labor. For modern obstetricians, labor is seen as fundamentally a mechanical process that can be manipulated. This viewpoint was congruent with the adaptation of epidural anesthesia for use in labor.

For decades, students of obstetrics have been taught a philosophy of normal labor referred to as "the three Ps."—passage, power, and passenger. Labor was reduced to a mechanical process resembling plumbing. Labor was as simple as a combination of the *passage* (the size and shape of the pelvis); the *power* of contractions; and the *passenger* (the position and size of the fetus) (Simkin and Ancheta 2011). This viewpoint became institutionalized with the wide acceptance of Friedman's mechanistic analysis of normal labor, widely referred to as the Friedman's Curve.

Birth is an event that is, in reality, highly variable and resistant to standardization. This fact has not stopped modern obstetrics from doing just that—standardize birth. Friedman's Curve, and external fetal monitoring (EFM), became a routine part of the management of labor—a major turning point for modern childbirth in the United States. Friedman (1972) was an early proponent of the concept of the laboring mother as a machine, a metaphor that has been analyzed in critiques of modern obstetrics (Martin 2001[1987]). The significance of the adaptation of Friedman's curve to the management of labor in the American hospital can hardly be overemphasized. It was the beginning of the industrialization of birth through routinization and standardization of birth: an endeavor to standardize a physiologic event—birth—so that it could be more conveniently managed.

The standardization of human labor was fundamental to the industrialization of birth. Friedman's 1972 journal article, *An Objective Approach to the Diagnosis and Management of Abnormal Labor*, became *the* authoritative treatise establishing the rationale for a reorganization of obstetrical care. In order to "simplify" the clinical observation of progress of labor, Friedman presented a framework dividing labor and delivery into three stages. The first stage, labor, was then divided into three phases—latent, active and transition. A standard time frame, a "progression of time in labor", was established for "normal" cervical dilation and fetal descent. "Ongoing measures" were obtained on a routine basis through frequent examination of the cervix, with findings plotted on a Cartesian coordinate graph. A standard graph of the expected parameters of "normal" labor was seen as a "simple, practical, and objective tool for the study of individual labors in progress (Friedman 1972, 843)."

By the end of the 1970s, Friedman's Curve was an established, essential, and fundamental part of every labor room in the United States. It existed as an actual object; a large, rectangular shaped graphing paper that lay on, and took up the space of, the rolling bedside table of the type found in every hospital room. (After all, as the mother was not permitted to eat or drink, she had no personal use for the table.) Friedman's curve was printed on this graph. Findings for the laboring mother were plotted by nurses alongside the "normal curve" The x-axis represented time and the y-axis represented cervical effacement and dilation along with fetal descent. The graph was designed to plot the mother's progress of labor in comparison to a "normal" progression of labor as determined by Friedman. The ideal progress of labor took on the form of a type of sigmoid curve—thus the term "Friedman's Curve".

An acceptable curve reflected progress in active labor of at least 1.2 centimeters cervical dilation per hour for nulliparas (first time mothers) and 1.5 centimeters per hour for multiparas. A mother's progress of labor, based on frequent cervical examinations, was plotted on the graph and juxtaposed over Friedman's Curve. When progress of labor fell "off the curve", it was considered "aberrant". "Graphic analysis" of labor "made possible the study of abnormal patterns... (Friedman 1972, 850)."

The concept of the laboring mother as functioning like a machine, a fundamental concept for industrialized birth, was clearly expressed by Friedman (1972, 844) and was visually represented by the ubiquitous labor graph. When the laboring mother is simplistically looked upon as a machine, it is not necessary to consider other possible factors involved in progress of labor. With a mechanistic viewpoint, the tasks demanded of the gravid patient consist of simple elements: cervical dilatation and effacement along with fetal descent. The sources of energy for accomplishing both are uterine contractions and expulsive efforts. Labor is reduced to these quantifiable measurements.

The role of hormones in the process of human labor (the neurotransmission of those hormones, as well as the impact of the environment in that transmission) was poorly understood in 1972; nor was there appreciation of the mind-body connection. Elements involving the role of the environment in the progress of human labor (elements such as a woman's sense of safety, the need for quiet and privacy, and the presence of a trusted attendant) did not fit into a mechanized framework of birth.

Friedman's mechanized view of human labor served as a theoretical premise for the industrialization of childbirth. Under this schema of industrialized labor, time came to be every laboring mother's nemesis, particularly first-time mothers. Obstetrics did not consider that the constant observation of the laboring mother, an elemental aspect of industrialized birth, might itself be a cause of the disrupted, abnormal labors that were increasingly seen in labor units. By placing limits on what was considered normal progress of labor over time, obstetrics denied the wide variation that in fact exists in physiologic birth.

Standardization, and disruption, of labor created the need for more frequent augmentation of labor with pitocin, increasing the pain of labor. This set up a cycle of interventions. The neonatal respiratory depression seen so frequently with the administration of opioids for pain relief was problematic, and so there was a need for a new form of pain relief during labor. The epidural came to be seen as a benefit precisely due to the fact that it does not lead to neonatal respiratory depression of the neonate. Pitocin administration then became even more routine in order to promote a more effective labor pattern, as the epidural brings its own disruption of normal labor.

Fetal distress, at times, is a direct result of pitocin augmentation itself. Therefore, the use of pitocin requires continuous external fetal monitoring (EFM). With EFM came the phenomenon that was called the cascade of interventions, all of which served to bring about the increased incidence of cesarean sections. The standardization of all of these interventions together resulted in the system of epiduralized birth described earlier in this book.

Possible Negative Impact of the Epidural

Scientific literature regarding the use of epidural during labor shows that the epidural may have a number of side effects. First, it is now recognized to disrupt and prolong labor. The epidural is also known to reduce the strength of contractions as well as decrease the frequency of contractions, particularly when given in early labor: thus the need to augment labor with pitocin (Suresh et al. 2013). Other known side effects include: hypotension requiring fluid infusion; relaxation of the bladder resulting in urinary retention and thus requiring a urinary catheter; and maternal fever, which then requires that the newborn be evaluated for sepsis. Additionally, there is some evidence that regional anesthesia (epidural) has a negative impact on newborn behavior. Decreased blood levels of maternal endogenous oxytocin are shown to occur during epidural and pitocin administration.

Disruption of the oxytocin feedback system between mother and fetus may be a result, thereby disrupting maternal-infant bonding.

A possible negative impact of the epidural on newborn behavior and disruption of maternal-infant bonding has been debated for decades and remains controversial. As mentioned previously, it is difficult to carry out experimental studies with pregnant women as subjects. Most medical studies on the use of bupivacaine in labor recognize the difficulty of carrying out robust experimental studies on laboring women. The FDA has labeled Bupivacaine a Category C medication in pregnancy[33] precisely because animal studies have shown adverse effects in mammalian newborns with administration of bupivacaine. Animal studies remain some of the most reliable research available to obstetrical clinical practice. Despite this fact, mainstream obstetrics discounts such research when conclusions are inconvenient for everyday clinical practice.

Studies using animals as subjects can be extremely helpful in understanding the physiology of birth. However, human birth, as with other mammals, is more than a physiological process. Cultural norms and values are involved in forming culturally specific birth practices. As humans, our social and cultural natures interact with physiology, in turn impacting physiology in ways that we are only beginning to understand. Odent (2001, S43), a birth physiologist, makes this point:

> [There] is a reason to clarify what we can learn from non-human mammals and also the limits of what we can learn from them. Let us take as an example the experiment by Krehbiel and Poindron, who studied the link between the birth process and maternal behavior. They found that after giving birth with epidural anesthesia, ewes do not take care of their lambs. It is obvious that the effects of an epidural anesthesia during labor among humans are much more complex than among sheep. It is easy to interpret such differences. Human beings use elaborated forms of communication and create cultures; this implies that our behaviors are less directly under the effects of the hormonal balances and more directly under the effects of the cultural milieu. This does not mean that we have nothing to learn from the sheep. *Animal experiments indicate which*

> *question we should raise where human beings are concerned.*
> *If ewes do not take care of their lambs after giving birth with*
> *an epidural anesthesia, this implies that where human beings*
> *are concerned the right question is: what is the future of a*
> *civilization born under epidural anesthesia?* [Emphasis
> mine]

It is now widely accepted that the second stage of labor, the stage of pushing, is prolonged with the epidural resulting in a significant increase in instrumental vaginal deliveries. This is associated with increased use of forceps or vacuum extraction during delivery and an increase in perineal lacerations. Other side effects that are widely recognized include:

- Hypotension (resulting in the need for administration of intravenous fluids);
- Bladder atony and maternal unawareness of a full bladder (resulting in urinary retention and the need for a urine catheter) and;
- Maternal fever, with an incidence of up to 33% of newborns evaluated for possible sepsis.

Two issues related to epidural administration, the possible impact on newborn behavior and a relationship to increased cesareans, continues to be debated. Research is contradictory for both issues (Suresh et al. 2013; Cunningham et al. 2001).

The Safety of Bupivacaine

Bupivacaine is a local anesthetic. It is most commonly administered via local infiltration to block pain. In this function, as a local anesthetic, bupivacaine is safe unless mistakenly given intravenously. It is the medication used most frequently in the administration of epidural anesthesia and in this function is not a benign medication. It is a cardiotoxin and a neurotoxin. In an epidural, bupivacaine is administered to the mother via the epidural space of the spinal cord. However, as the medication makes its way to the fetus, via the placental circulation, we are in

185

fact administering this toxic medication intravenously to the fetus, something that is contraindicated in an adult. This is an obvious fact that maternity providers choose to ignore.

The FDA has categorized bupivacaine as a Category C medication in pregnancy, to be used sparingly and only when the benefits clearly outweigh risks. Many obstetricians and anesthesiologists claim that pain itself is a medical risk and in this way justify the routine use of bupivacaine, despite the FDA's warning. During informed consent, women are told that an epidural may result in a longer labor, the need for pitocin, and maternal fever. These are presented as minor aggravations when compared to the promise of a pain-free labor.

Women believe that pitocin and bupivacaine are safe when, in fact, research calls into question the safety of both medications. In my observations at Community Hospital, mothers were not given this information and were not informed that, according to the FDA, bupivacaine should be limited in use during pregnancy. Doris Haire (2005), in a statement provided to the American Foundation for Maternal and Child Health, described this state of affairs.

> Obstetricians, midwives and nurses who care for women during childbirth need to know that there is no obstetric related drug that has been proven safe for the neurologic development of the fetus. There have been no adequate and well-controlled studies to determine the delayed, long-term effects of bupivacaine or any other epidural drug on pregnant women, or on the neurologic, as well as general, development of children exposed to the drug in utero or during lactation.

Haire (2000, 2001 2005) goes on to state that the FDA warns in the approved label for bupivacaine that it readily crosses the placenta into the fetal circulation, can cause damage to the fetal central nervous system, and should be used only in exceptional circumstances. Despite these warnings, epidural and pitocin administration, given alone or simultaneously, have become routine during labor without clear evidence as to the safety of using these medications and with little debate within the obstetrical community.

This situation has been partially created by the FDA itself. Despite classifying bupivacaine as a Category C medication during pregnancy, the FDA has inconsistently stated that its use is acceptable during labor, giving a pass for its routine use, perhaps in fear of disrupting institutional obstetrical practice.

The Epidural and Prolonged Labor

Thirty years ago, common clinical practice was to administer an epidural only after labor was well-established because the epidural was observed to prolong labor. In 1987, the textbook *Anesthesia for Obstetrics, 2nd Edition* stated that timing of epidural administration for nulliparas was preferable at cervical dilation of 6–8 cm, and with strong, regular contractions 3–5 minutes apart (Shnider and Levinson 1987). Administration for multiparous mothers was recommended no sooner than 4–6 cm. By 2002, *Anesthesia for Obstetrics* stated that epidural administration was appropriate in early labor. "There is no reason to avoid epidural analgesia during the latent phase of the first stage," stated the authors, who then went on to justify their position. "It is more important to provide pain relief on request than to deny it until an arbitrary cervical dilation has been attained (Hughes et al. 2002, 2054)."

Women should receive epidural analgesia in early labor, stated Sng et al. (2014), in a Cochrane Review meta-analysis of the clinical significance of early vs. late administration of labor, agreeing with Huges et al. (2002). Unfortunately, the study does not provide a clear justification for such a recommendation. The Sng et al. study measured two variables—Apgar scores[34] and neonatal umbilical blood pH. Sng et al. claimed that no adverse outcomes were observed but then prevaricated. "It is hard to assess the outcomes clearly (Sng et al. 2014, 2)." Despite coming to no clear conclusion, the researchers still recommended that a mother should be given an epidural upon request at any time in labor, including early labor.

There is a limitation to using Apgar scores as a measurement when assessing the safety of the epidural. The Apgar score is a rudimentary measurement of the status of the neonate. In reality, the Apgar score does nothing but provide a simple, easily quantifiable and replicable measure of the viability of the newborn at the time of birth. It does not measure the subtleties of newborn behavior nor maternal/newborn interaction.

The Sng et al. study is an example of poor research used to provide justification for an obstetrical practice (in this case early administration of epidural) without providing proof that it is without complications. The researchers failed to provide clarity on the impact of epidural administration on cesarean rates and second stage instrumental delivery. The authors do not reflect on the implications of prolonged exposure to both bupivacaine and pitocin, as inevitably occurs with early administration of epidural.

Whether epidural anesthesia prolongs first stage of labor continues to be debated. However, according to *Williams Obstetrics 21st Edition,* "Epidural analgesia usually prolongs the first stage of labor, and increases the need for labor stimulation with oxytocin (Cunningham et al. 2001, 376)." The text *Snider and Levinson's Anesthesia for Obstetrics Fifth Edition* (Suresh et al. 2013) also describes the prolongation of labor that occurs with epidural administration. During my observations at Community Hospital, labor augmentation with pitocin was routine when a mother received an epidural. This alone suggests that empirical knowledge has shown what some research studies have not been able to definitively conclude—epidural anesthesia does in fact prolong both first and second stage of labor, making augmentation of labor (pitocin) a necessity. This reality of prolonged labor has led the obstetrical profession to redefine the parameters of normal labor, a development I will discuss later in this chapter.

The Epidural and Augmentation of Labor

As mentioned previously, augmentation of labor has become a routine, concomitant intervention with the epidural. Augmentation of labor presents obstetrical providers with a no-win cycle that results in increased cesareans (Rooks 2009). The knotty situation created by the disordered thinking behind epiduralized birth goes like this:

- Epidural analgesia often stalls or prolongs labor.

- Pitocin is then, almost always, incorporated with the epidural to augment labor, in order to establish a more productive labor pattern.

- If a low-dose protocol of pitocin administration is followed, the risk of cesarean section is increased.

- If a high-dose protocol of pitocin administration is followed, the risk of uterine hyperstimulation with resulting fetal hypoxia is increased, often leading to emergency cesarean.

As is the case with bupivacaine, pitocin is not a benign medication. The risks of pitocin are so great that in 2012 the Institute for Safe Medication Practices (ISMP) added the medication to its list of high-risk medications, one of only twelve medications to be given this distinction (ISMP 2012, 2014). The significance of the designation of pitocin as a high-alert medication is made clear by the ISMP (2012):

> High-alert medications can be defined as those medications that bear a heightened risk of causing significant patient harm when they are used in error. Although mistakes may or may not be more common with these drugs, the consequences of errors are often harmful, sometimes fatal, to patients.

Pitocin is the cause of many adverse outcomes during birth, particularly fetal distress (Clark et al. 2009). At the level of clinical decision-making, there is a lack of clear protocol; decision-making is vague and ambiguous, creating a "clinical anarchy" (Clark et al. 2008, 2009). There is a need for clear protocols for the safe use of pitocin (Diven et al. 2012). Clark et al. (2009) acknowledge that the ubiquitous use of pitocin is driven by the desire to control the timing of delivery. These obstetrical researchers, however, declare that this is merely the reality of modern obstetrics: something that cannot be changed.

As of today, there are no clear, nationally accepted protocols regarding the administration of pitocin. Initial dosage, as well as the timing and amount to be given during incremental titration, are decisions made by individual obstetricians based on empirical knowledge and tradition. There is no upward limit on how much pitocin can be administered. There remains a wide variation in regimens for pitocin administration (Cunningham et al. 2001). At Community Hospital, when I asked if protocols existed for the administration of pitocin, I was told, "If there are protocols, I haven't seen them."[35]

At Community Hospital, given that most mothers received epidurals, the administration of pitocin was commonplace. Most of the midwives I observed began pitocin at a starting dose of 0.5–1mU/minute, a conservative, low dosage. Following this low starting dose, each midwife seemed to have her own preference for how quickly to increase the dosage and the maximum levels at which the pitocin would be administered.

A conservative, nonaggressive regimen of pitocin administration is recommended by Simpson (2011), one that includes a halt to administration once regular contractions are observed, rather than a prolonged infusion of pitocin. Simpson argues that there exists a limited number of oxytocin receptor sites for oxytocin uptake and that "continued rate increases over a prolonged period causes oxytocin receptor desensitization or downregulation, making continuous pitocin infusion less effective in producing normal uterine contractions (2011, 218)." On the other hand, Cunningham et al. (2001) advocate a more aggressive protocol for pitocin administration.

Few obstetricians seem to consider that oxytocin is a complicated hormone that functions in a variety of ways beyond its role in maintaining labor contractions during labor. So important is the use of pitocin to epiduralized birth, so routine has its use become, that most obstetricians seem unable to think outside of the box and ask a fundamental question: is synthetic/exogenous oxytocin (pitocin) safe for the fetus? Prasad and Funai (2012) do raise the issue as to whether the lack of research on safe parameters of pitocin administration should perhaps be considered when using it indiscriminately. "The use of oxytocin for labor induction and augmentation has been understudied, and safety issues beg for more objective data to support practice patterns (Prasad and Funai 2012)."

Changes in the Management of Labor: The Epidural and Friedman's Curve

The routine use of the epidural for pain relief during labor was once limited for financial reasons. Until perhaps twenty years ago, many women had to pay out-of-pocket for an epidural, as Medicaid and many insurance policies did not cover routine, elective epidural during labor. Social and institutional influences changed this. Regionalization and centralization of maternity care brought about on-site availability of anesthesia in a growing number of maternity units. Furthermore, physicians and nurses came to realize the advantage of giving epidurals early in labor for the routinized management of laboring women. Demand for the use of epidurals by both mothers and providers forced insurance companies and Medicaid in most states to provide coverage of the procedure.

In the 1990s, advocates for the administration of epidurals early in labor stated that pain alone justified early administration, even though there was still no consensus on whether the epidural prolonged labor. As epidurals began to be routinely given ever earlier in the labor process, it became obvious to providers that epidural anesthesia does, in fact, prolong labor (Zimmer et al. 2000; Kukulu and Demirok 2008; King 1997; Lieberman and O'Donoghue 2002; Leighton and Halpern 2002). This negative side effect was thought to be easily dealt with—routinely administer pitocin with the epidural. However, it has been found that even with pitocin administration, active labor is often prolonged and second stage is significantly prolonged with the epidural (Alexander et al. 2002).

Concerns for the safety of epidural administration during labor, and the impact on the length of labor, led to the practice of combining the local anesthetic, usually bupivacaine, with a narcotic (i.e. morphine or Fentanyl). The two medications (bupivacaine and narcotic) act synergistically[36] allowing for a lower concentration of the local anesthetic. Anesthesiologists have worked with this mix to find the "regimen that will maximize the sensory block and minimize the most common complications (King 1997, 379)." Most obstetrical providers, however, do not recognize as significant the potential toxicity of bupivacaine on the fetal central nervous system.

The reality of the prolongation of labor as a side effect of the epidural, has forced obstetricians to take a new look at Friedman's Curve. This is an irony of large proportions. I have discussed earlier how the standardization of labor was advanced with the adoption of Friedman's Curve in the modern labor and delivery unit. Beginning in the 1970s, the labors of many thousands of women were carefully observed with hourly cervical checks and augmented with pitocin because their labor had fallen "off the curve". At the same time, the cesarean rate in the United States began to climb. The routine use of the epidural only exacerbated the disruption of labor that resulted from the constant interruptions and observations in the modern labor and delivery environment.

Obstetricians are now in a proverbial bind: how to balance the practice of upholding the validity of Friedman's Curve with the need to give women more time in labor when they have been given an epidural. The solution that has been settled on, in an intellectual sleight of hand, is to "reevaluate" Friedman's Curve: simply declaring that it is no longer relevant in the context of "contemporary" clinical practice. It has become necessary to "expand" the concept of normal progress in labor (Cesario 2004; Zhang et al. 2002). There is no acknowledgement, in this readjustment of Friedman's Curve, that the fundamental assumptions behind Friedman's Curve were erroneous from the beginning of its use in labor and delivery. The call to reform the Curve is not a recognition of the variation of normal, spontaneous labor. Rather, because the original Friedman's Curve is no longer helpful in the realty of clinical practice, the Curve has been conveniently modified.

Analysis of thousands of vaginal births from nineteen hospitals shows that contemporary labor patterns look different today than when Friedman first developed his curve of normal labor (Zhang et al. 2010). Active labor, according to Zhang et al. does not seem to begin until 6 centimeters dilation and it is common to see no appreciable cervical change at various times in labor for up to four hours. Various factors are suggested to explain this observed change in the labor patterns of obstetrical patients—obesity, age of the mother, and contemporary "obstetrical practice" (a euphemism for the combined use of the epidural and pitocin administration.) Zhang et al. (2010) did not focus on the obvious: that epiduralized birth itself is quite possibly the fundamental element in the observed changes in labor patterns. They instead proposed an expansion of the Friedman's Curve, as a result of these findings.

The obstetrical community has conveniently accepted the Zhang et al. studies (2002, 2010) and the expansion of Friedman's Curve. It relieves obstetricians from an existential conundrum created by epiduralized birth—on the one hand, the need to avoid admitting the reality of the pharmaceutical disruption that prolongs labor, while not having to outright reject Friedman's Curve for what it was all along: an invalid basis for obstetrical clinical practice.

Zhang et al. (2010), in their study, included only one-third of their original study group (a total of 62,413 laboring women) because inductions and cesareans, both of which involve an interruption of normal labor, disqualified most study subjects. Among the remaining subjects, which included only primiparous women who began labor spontaneously and went on to have a vaginal delivery with a healthy newborn, half of the study group had labor augmented with pitocin and 80% received epidural anesthesia. With this study group, the authors still found a pattern of prolonged labor. "Defining 'normal labor'," state the authors, "remains a challenge (Zhang et al. 2010, 128)." Modern obstetrics seems unable to define the parameters of normal in a process that they so frequently observe—birth.

The obstetrical profession has adjusted Friedman's Curve, despite the fact that the profession has been wedded to the curve for decades, and despite the fact that application of the Curve resulted in uncountable unnecessary cesareans. Friedman's Curve, when applied under the realities of epiduralized birth, has proven to be inconvenient. And so modern obstetrics is now ready to "revise" Friedman's Curve in order to "meet the needs of current patient populations, technological advances, and nursing responsibilities (Cesario 2004, 13)." It is easier to modify Friedman's Curve than to change contemporary obstetrical practices that are the underlying causes in the disruption of physiologic labor.

"Labor appears to progress more slowly now than before, even though more labors are being treated with oxytocin for augmentation," state Zhang et al. (2010, 1286). However, the authors give no suggestions as to what is causing this counterintuitive situation, except to state that "frequent obstetric interventions, (induction, epidural analgesia, and oxytocin use) *may* [emphasis mine] have altered the natural labor process (Zhang et al. 2010, 1282)."

Zhang et al. (2010) go on to state the obvious: given the realities of epiduralized birth, more time and patience is called for when all is well with both the mother and baby. They also suggest that expanding the curve of normality can help decrease cesareans, particularly in the first time mother, by providing the laboring mother more time for labor. However, time and patience is precisely what the model of industrialized birth, with its emphasis on moving things along, does not allow for.

One midwife was frank about the overwhelming use of epidurals and the subsequent conflict over time within labor and delivery.

> Midwife: It's true that the epidural was first used in surgery on adults. And in the 1990s the epidural was only given once the mother was quite far along in labor and so the exposure to the anesthetic was much less. Now we are giving it when the mother is 2 or 3 centimeters and that's unproven technology for sure. The mother is receiving the epidural for ten, twelve

hours. We really don't know what it does to the baby.

MAM: It is interesting that this technology has been transferred over to obstetrics with so little research on the safety.

Midwife: I don't think there has ever been a consensus task force on the use of epidurals. There has been research as to whether epidurals slow labor down, but you're right. I don't think there has been research on the impact on the baby.

MAM: This takes us back to the issue of Community Hospital's low cesarean rate. You have about an 80% epidural rate and yet have a 23% cesarean rate.

Midwife: I think it is much lower. 20%. 18%. I think the big reason for the low cesarean rate is patience. It's just patience that distinguishes us. And we are less quick to react to occasional variables in the baby's heart rate. At some of the hospitals, there is a philosophy, "Oh. The baby's heart rate has changed. Let's crash her." They call it intrauterine resuscitation. Rather than looking more carefully and critically at the rhythm.

I also think we allow for more variation in length of labor and length of gestation. So that's what I think it is. And we primarily have a younger, healthier population. So that's in their favor. And our favor.

MAM: I think with the epidural, we are able to titrate the pitocin higher.

Midwife: Yeah. It's true. And in some other hospitals they are more concerned about how long the patient has been in the hospital. Or, "Oh my God. The baby's heart rate just went down. Let's crash her." So I think it's lack of patience that contributes to the difference. And then there are the high rates of repeat cesareans. When you have three or four repeat cesareans scheduled every single day, Monday through Friday, that impacts on the cesarean rate. [My note: She is talking here in general about common practice in other hospitals, not Community Hospital.]

MAM: I also think that routine induction has something to do with it.

> Midwife: Yes. People who don't deliver by dinnertime—
> that becomes a failed induction.

The Fallacy of External Fetal Monitoring

The validity and reliability of external fetal monitoring (EFM) in the diagnosis of fetal distress is questionable. This complicates the clinical situation in epiduralized birth. Even before epiduralized birth became the norm in our obstetrical units, the frequent use of pitocin for augmentation of labor (to keep the laboring mother "on Curve") required a means for fetal evaluation. Continuous fetal monitoring with the external fetal monitor (EFM) appeared to be the perfect tool. The addition of the epidural to the clinical mix of interventions made continuous fetal monitoring even more significant clinically. Epiduralized birth also made tracings from external fetal monitoring seemingly more reliable with fewer artifacts due to less movement by the mother.

We are learning that EFM has always been, and remains, an inexact assessment tool. Interpretations of fetal heart patterns are exceedingly inconsistent and false diagnosis of fetal distress is common. EFM has low specificity, with a high number of false positives: reportedly as high as 99% (Sartwelle 2012). The interpretation of EFM data by individuals remains extremely subjective. An analysis of the reliability of EFM as a diagnostic tool has shown it to be of scant clinical value.

> Tested under controlled circumstances, experts frequently disagreed with each other and themselves. Inter-observation/intra-observer variability was the rule, not the exception. ... Harmless fetal heart rate changes were interpreted as fetal distress. Ominous tracings were seen as reassuring. ...
>
> In one study, experienced obstetricians agreed in only 20% of cases. Two months later, the same tracings were presented to the same interpreters. Twenty percent were interpreted differently. In another study 12 national EFM experts interpreted 14 abnormal tracings. On average, two experts disagreed one-third of the time when asked to classify the patterns as innocuous, non-

reassuring, or ominous, and they disagreed with almost the same frequency over the issue of continuing the labor or delivery immediately. In a British study, the experts classified 32% of the normal tracings, the controls, as having ominous tracings in the second stage of labor (Sartwelle 2012, 327).

The external fetal monitor has been shown, in controlled testing conditions, to be a highly subjective assessment tool. When shown the same EFM tracing, experts frequently disagree among each other as to interpretation. When individual obstetricians are shown the same tracing at a later time, they often change their interpretation. Inter-observation variability, as well as intra-observer variability, is not unusual. Harmless fetal heart rate changes are interpreted as fetal distress. Ominous tracings are equally misinterpreted. Yet even with this knowledge as to its lack of validity and reliability, EFM has remained the standard of care in industrialized childbirth. The result has been the rise of unnecessary cesarean sections (Sartwelle 2012).

In the meantime, intermittent fetal monitoring through auscultation has been shown to be as sensitive, if not more so, compared to EFM, in detecting fetal distress (Albers 2007; Prentice and Lind 1987). However, industrialized maternity care continues to hold tightly to external fetal monitoring despite clear scientific evidence that it is of limited value in predicting fetal distress. As such, AFM is itself the cause of clinical iatrogenesis[37] in the form of unnecessary cesareans due to false positive diagnosis of fetal distress . [38]

External fetal monitoring is perhaps one of the best examples of how modern obstetrics continues a traditional practice that is shown to be nothing more than a clinical ritual. How else do we explain that EFM continues to be a standard of care despite clear scientific evidence that as a routine clinical intervention it has no scientific basis? It is a "too frequent intervention" with "too little benefit" (Prentice and Lind, 1987). What makes this all the more tragic is that this has been known for several decades, yet the obstetrical community continues to hang on to external fetal monitoring as a nation-wide standard of care.

The Epidural and Maternal Fever

Maternal fever, a temperature greater than 100.4°F, is widely recognized as a side effect of epidural anesthesia. Estimates of maternal fever as a result of epidural vary from 14.5% to 34.0% (Lieberman et al. 1997; Cohen et al. 1997). Elevated maternal temperature is directly related to length of labor with an epidural (a fact that would argue against early administration of an epidural.) It is hypothesized that this rise in temperature is due to thermoregulatory changes that are a direct result of the epidural. Infection is a rare, but serious, occurrence with the epidural. However, maternal sepsis is difficult to rule out in the case of maternal fever, as a fever can mask sepsis.

Differential diagnosis of fever in the mother receiving an epidural is difficult. The mother's white blood cell count is normally elevated in pregnancy. Palpation cannot be used to assess for abdominal pain because the laboring mother who has received an epidural has little tactile sensation in the abdominal area. The result is that the neonate born to a mother with elevated temperature is usually evaluated for neonatal sepsis. This involves frequent blood draws and often prophylactic administration of antibiotics. In many hospitals, the newborn is subsequently admitted to the neonatal ICU for a 48-hour evaluation. These newborns are therefore separated from their mothers during hours that are critical for bonding and initiation of breastfeeding.

Newborns appear to be directly impacted when the laboring mother has fever. These newborns are more likely to have a one-minute Apgar score of less than seven. They are more likely to be hypotonic. They are more likely to require resuscitation (Lieberman et al. 2000). It is unclear why maternal fever has this impact on the fetus. However, it is known that "even modest temperature elevation during labor is associated with an increased risk of cesarean section and operative vaginal delivery." It is also "associated with a number of adverse outcomes in the newborn (Lieberman et al. 2000, 12)." While most adverse outcomes are "transient," more research is needed to determine if there are any lasting adverse effects (Lieberman et al. 2000). Women are informed that they may have a temperature during labor.

However, in my observations, they were not given precise information as to the potential consequences to the newborn if they develop a fever during epidural administration.

The Epidural, Newborn Behavior and Maternal-Infant Bonding

Bupivacaine is not given intravenously due to its toxicity. Yet that is exactly what we are giving the fetus when we administer an epidural during labor, a point of time in fetal development when the brain is not yet fully developed. Low concentrations of bupivacaine are found in the maternal bloodstream following epidural administration. However, bupivacaine readily passes through the micro-blood vessels of the maternal epidural space into the blood stream, crosses the placenta barrier, and enters directly into the fetal blood stream where it is found in larger concentrations relative to maternal blood levels (Lieberman and O'Donoghue 2002). The fetus is also unable to metabolize the drug as efficiently as the mother.

> Drugs administered by epidural enter the mother's bloodstream immediately and go straight to the baby at equal, and sometimes effectively greater, levels than in the mother (Fernando & Bonello 1995; Brinsmead 1987). Some drugs will be preferentially taken up into the baby's brain (Hale 1998), and almost all will take longer to be eliminated from the baby's immature system after the cord is cut. For example, the half-life of bupivacaine (i.e. time for blood levels to fall by half) is 2.7 hours in the adult, but around 8 hours in the neonate (Hale 1997). Studies using the Brazelton Neonatal Assessment Scale (NBAS) have found deficits in newborn abilities consistent with toxicity from these drugs [administration of local anesthetics via epidural] (Lieberman and O'Donoghue 2002; Buckley 2003, 276).

Some anesthesiologists claim that bupivacaine administered to the mother via the epidural does not reach the fetus, and if it does so, it is only in "miniscule" amounts. Unfortunately for the obstetric community, most medications do freely pass through the placenta.

> Virtually all drugs administered to the mother, including oxytocin, rapidly filter across the placental membranes and enter the blood, brain and other major organs of the fetus within minutes of administration to the mother during pregnancy, labor and birth (Haire 2001).

The medical specialties of obstetrics and anesthesiology have promoted the idea that drugs, along with other substances, are harmful to the fetus only during the period of organogenesis. This ignores the physiology of the immature fetal brain, which at birth has a high concentration of blood vessels and cerebral blood flow, greater than that of the adult brain. This makes for efficient transfer of drugs to the fetal circulation and central nervous system. Furthermore, the fetal brain has yet to fully develop the myelin that protects brain nerve fibers, making the fetal brain even more vulnerable to toxins (Haire 2001).

Adding to the above negative side effects, epidural anesthesia and pitocin both result in a decrease of endogenous oxytocin in the maternal blood level. The release of oxytocin by the mother is an essential hormone involved in maternal/infant bonding (Rooks 2007).

One robust human study shows the problems associated with epidural administration. Murray et al. (1981) was a controlled study comparing three groups—non-medicated mothers, mothers receiving epidural anesthesia and mothers receiving both pitocin and epidural. The focus of the study was to study the possible impact of epidural analgesia on the maternal-fetal unit. The study found a significantly prolonged second stage in the two medicated groups, a phenomenon that is now well-recognized by birth attendants. There was a greater incidence of malpresentation of the fetus in the medicated mothers resulting in a significant increase of instrumental delivery. Separation of the mother from the newborn occurred more frequently with medicated mothers, making it difficult to determine if abnormal newborn behaviors were a direct result of medication or a result of the maternal/newborn separation.

All babies were assessed in the first twenty-four hours using the Neonatal Behavioral Assessment Scale (NBAS). [39] The researchers found that:

> Compared with the nonmedicated babies, babies in the two epidural groups performed poorly on the motor, state control, and physiological response clusters as well as their total score on the NBAS. ... The percentage of babies with deficient or near-deficient scores (scores of 5 or 4, respectively) was markedly higher in the medicated groups. ... These findings parallel reports by Standley et al. (1974) that 1-3 day-old babies exposed to a variety of local and regional anesthetic techniques were tremulous, irritable and motorically immature (Murray et al. 1981, 76).

Bupivacaine is typically eliminated from the fetal system only after five to six half-lives (48 hours). The continued presence of bupivacaine in the fetal system led the researchers (Murray et al. 1981) to suspect that there was, in fact, a direct relationship between epidural administration and abnormal newborn behaviors. Furthermore, babies exposed to both pitocin and bupivacaine showed an even more pronounced abnormal motor function. These babies were more "tense and hypertonic". Reflex responses and integrated motor actions were even more depressed as compared to the epidural-only group.

The researchers postulate a possible "added effect" when the two medications are administered together, as is routine in our maternity units today. It is unclear if this is a result of a synergistic effect between the two medications, or whether it is a result of the stronger, more frequent contractions so commonly seen when pitocin augmentation is given along with epidural analgesia. One of the advantages of epidural anesthesia, from a practical clinical standpoint, is that the mother is able to tolerate pitocin titration to higher levels. This reality has complicated the ability to separate the possible effects of these two medications on the well-being of the fetus.

At one month postpartum there were no differences in NBAS scores suggesting "direct drug effects had worn off by 1 month (Murray et al. 1981, 78)." Other abnormalities, however, were found at one month. "Mothers of medicated babies reported that their baby was less adaptable, more intense, and more bothersome in their behavior. These mothers also rated their babies "... as having poorer interactive ability and state control[40] and poor overall performance." Mothers of non-medicated babies were significantly more likely to rate their baby's state control as "exceptional". The medicated babies were fed less often, "a finding consistent with reports that they [the mothers] did not respond as promptly to their babies' cries (Murray et al. 1981, 78)."

These findings could be a result of maternal characteristics, but the researchers state that they controlled for socio-economic factors. The mothers had also been carefully screened for any differences in "belief in reciprocity" using the Cobler's Maternal Attitude Scale.[41] The researchers, however, could not rule out that the findings of newborn behavior among medication-exposed babies were a direct, ongoing result of one or both of the medications as opposed to initial interruption of maternal/newborn interaction among the medicated groups. (Perhaps we need to consider all of the above as reasons for abnormal newborn behavior.)

Self-reports by mothers were given a high-value by the researcher who stated that such reports were possibly more valid than the NBAS assessments.

> The differences between the examiners' and mothers' assessments at 1 month raise the issue of the veridicality of the mothers' perceptions. The discrepancy may be more apparent than real, however, because the NBAS is designed to elicit and score best behavior, whereas mothers are likely to have based their judgments on characteristic or typical performance. Neonatal assessments that score modal rather than best performance may be more sensitive to drugs effects (Brackbill, 1979) and may provide more stable predictions of later functioning (Horowitz, Sullivan, & Linn, 1978). (Murray et al. 1981, 80)

In other words: No one knows a baby better than the mother. Murray et al. (1981, 81) end with this unambiguous recommendation: "Although it is at times necessary and appropriate for some mothers to receive medications during childbirth, the implications of this study are that the elective use of medication should be minimized."

A research review by Liebermann and O'Donoghue (2002) had similar findings. It found that babies exposed to epidural were 50% more likely to have "poor state control" from birth to day five; this difference continued through at least the first month of life. "The epidural-exposed infants," they found, "showed less alertness and ability to orient during the first month of life and were less mature in motor function (2002, s59)." They also point out that, due to the common side effect of fever in the mother who receives an epidural, the epidural-exposed newborn is more likely to be admitted to a neonatal unit for a work-up to rule out newborn sepsis.

Epidural anesthesia may inhibit all the hormones involved in the normal process of birth (Buckley 2003): oxytocin (which is important for functional labor contractions, maternal/infant bonding, and the let down of breast milk); beta-endorphins (excreted by the pituitary gland during labor in response to pain); estrogen and progesterone (known to increase the number of uterine oxytocin receptor sites); catecholamines (thought to activate the fetal ejection reflex, stimulate release of surfactant and aid in the newborn metabolism) and finally, prolactin—along with oxytocin known to be involved in maternal behavioral changes and production of breast milk. Buckley also cites animal studies showing profound disturbance of normal maternal/infant bonding behaviors when an epidural is given during labor.

Not all studies show a relationship between epidural administration and abnormal newborn behavior. Lieberman and O'Donoghue (2002) acknowledge studies that have not found these changes in newborn behavior in epidural-exposed newborns. However, the studies that failed to associate abnormal newborn behavior with epidural exposure used several assessment tools considered unreliable (Lieberman and O'Donoghue 2002). The authors conclude that more research on the potential effects of epidurals on mothers and babies is needed. However, in their conclusion they point to areas where the evidence is clear.

In addition to demonstrating where further research is needed, this review also reveals that there are some unintended effects that consistently accompany epidural use. These unintended effects are present in randomized trials as well as observational studies. We are obligated to inform women about these side effects so they can make truly informed decisions about the use of pain relief during labor. Information about choices for pain relief during labor needs to be conveyed during pregnancy; once women are in labor, it is too late. This obligation is particularly pressing because use of epidural for pain relief during labor is an elective procedure.

Nulliparous women should be told that they are less likely to have a spontaneous vaginal delivery, that they are more likely to have an instrumental vaginal delivery, and that their labor is likely to be longer. They should also be informed of the implications of the higher rate of instrumental vaginal delivery, specifically the increased rate of serious perineal lacerations that accompany its use. Women should also be informed of the higher rate of intrapartum fever. They should be informed that if they develop a fever their infant may be more likely to be evaluated for sepsis and treated with antibiotics for suspected sepsis but that there is no evidence that epidural increases infection in mothers or infants. Issues addressed in informed consent will need to be modified as we learn more.

Epidural analgesia represents one of a spectrum of options for pain relief during labor that should be available to women. In addition to continuing research related to epidural, research into other pharmacologic and nonpharmacologic methods of pain relief should also continue (Lieberman and O'Donoghue 2002, S64).

Other researchers agree. A controlled clinical study (Rahm et al. 2002) showed that endogenous oxytocin levels were significantly higher in non-medicated birthing mothers than mothers who had received epidural anesthesia. The authors believed so strongly in their conclusion, that epidural anesthesia is associated with a decrease in endogenous oxytocin and prolonged labor, that they presented this recommendation.

Most studies of the EDA [epidural anesthesia] during labor have focused on its effects on labor outcome but only few of those studies have considered the role of possible alteration of the endogenous oxytocin. In our prospective study, we saw a decrease in plasma oxytocin levels, prolonged labor, and an increased use of exogenous oxytocin in women with EDA. Even though this study cannot determine the extent to which the decrease in endogenous oxytocin contributed to the results, it seems to be important to further investigate the role of endogenous oxytocin during labor. Because EDA is an important method for pain relief during labor, it is necessary to make objective information available to medical staff as well as patients about the disadvantages and advantages of EDA (Rahm et al. 2002, 1038).

Oxytocin: The Disregarded Neurohormone

I refer to oxytocin as "disregarded" because maternity providers have chosen to disregard the evidence surrounding its use. Odent (2001, 2002) has discussed what he calls an epidemic of abnormal labor patterns in the Western world, that of prolonged labor and labor arrest—or what obstetrics calls dysfunctional labor. This interruption of normal labor, according to Odent (2002), is most often a result of a birth environment that interferes with physiologic birth. Normal labor contractions depend on oxytocin attaching to receptor sites in the uterus. Hormones associated with the fight or flight syndrome, specifically epinephrine and norepinephrine, compete with oxytocin at these receptor sites. During labor, environmental stimulators (such as noise, activity, fear and anxiety) can interfere with the uptake of oxytocin at receptor sites by stimulating the secretion of the fight or flight hormones.

Odent owes much of his work to Niles Newton (1966a, 1966b, 1987), one of the first scientists to describe the significance of environment on the progress of labor and successful delivery. In a controlled experiment, pregnant mice exhibited prolonged labor and higher levels of stillbirth when placed in stressful environments (Newton 1966a). Newton's initial and subsequent work continues to be seen as the impetus in the study of environmental impact on successful labor and delivery, as well as the impact on mother/infant attachment. Newton's findings, as well as Odent's subsequent work, have paved the way for a theoretical understanding of a physiological approach to birth, an approach that involves providing a birth environment that is undisturbed with limited stimulation—an environment of quiet, calm, and safety.

Childbirth and lactation are physiologic processes that rely on oxytocin. However, the hormone plays a significant physiologic role at other times throughout our life experiences. Moberg (2003) refers to oxytocin as the "calm and connection" hormone—a key neurohormone of the parasympathetic system that mediates the ability to interact socially and provides a sense of calm and relaxation.

To understand the role that oxytocin plays in birth, it is necessary to understand how, as a key hormone in the parasympathetic system, it normally interacts with neurohormones that are a part of the sympathetic system. Moberg (2003, 24) provides an explanation of this relationship.

> It is important to emphasize that both the fight or flight reaction and the condition of calm and connection are essential to life. Precisely like other animals, we humans must have the ability to meet challenges and mobilize all our powers to take whatever action is needed at a given time. Likewise, we also need the opposite. The body needs to digest food, replenish its stores, and heal itself. We must be able to take in information, express feelings, be open and curious, and establish contact with other people. It is this ability that enables us to recover after more or less challenging incidents or periods. ...
>
> The two conditions of fight or flight and calm and connection tend to operate in balance, as if on a seesaw. When we contentedly digest food, we seldom experience agitation, anger or stress. When we are wound up, angry, or hurried, digestion slows down and we feel less sociable. *One mechanism does not exclude the other, but either one of them can temporarily dominate.* [emphasis mine]

Oxytocin serves to balance the well-known flight or flight system, a part of the sympathetic nervous system that has been well researched. The fight or flight system involves the rapid secretion of stress hormones, including epinephrine and norepinephrine, that have a multi-system impact on the human body. These two systems, the fight or flight system and the calm and connection system are usually in balance. During labor, however, stress hormones create an alertness and hormonal tension that interfere with oxytocin at the cellular receptor sites associated with labor. The stress hormones (particularly epinephrine), as part of the sympathetic nervous system, interfere with the parasympathetic nervous system during labor, of which oxytocin is a key element (Moberg 2003).

Few obstetrical providers consider that the process of normal labor is a parasympathetic mediated, physiologic experience dependent on endogenous oxytocin, and to a lesser extent other hormones. As such, labor is easily thrown out of balance by any surge of sympathetic mediated neurotransmitters. For undisturbed labor to proceed, the birthing mother requires an environment that prevents stimulation of the neo-cortex in order that the parasympathetic system can dominate, allowing for adequate oxytocin secretion.

The Fetal Ejection Reflex and Maternal-Fetal Oxytocin Feedback

The fetal ejection reflex is a well-recognized event in undisturbed birth, indicating the beginning of what Western obstetrics calls second stage of labor (pushing). Providers experienced in non-epiduralized birth easily recognize this reflex where powerful expulsive contractions, uncontrollable by the mother, result in the birth of the fetus. The altered state of consciousness seen in the mother during non-medicated birth is a part of the ejection reflex. This reflex is eliminated by the epidural and there are many providers, both nurse-midwives and obstetricians, who rarely see this phenomenon and do not recognize its significance. Without the fetal ejection reflex, second stage becomes a mechanical event with the mother coached through pushing, given directions on how to bear down in order to bring the baby to the introitus (the opening of the vagina).

The fetal ejection reflex is part of a neurohormonal feedback system important to physiologic birth and maternal/newborn attachment. Summerlee (1981) discusses the numerous tests on laboring animals showing the elevation of endogenous oxytocin throughout undisturbed birth, stating how important this hormone is to physiologic labor. Laboratory studies show that oxytocin levels dramatically increase "with the appearance of the head of the fetus at the vulva... (Summerlee 1981, 2)."

A decade after the Summerlee (1981) research, another laboratory study examined the pattern of endogenous oxytocin release during the parturition of pigs. The authors reported that oxytocin release "is very sensitive to environmental disturbance. ... Environmental disturbance will result in a cessation of parturition and fall in circulating oxytocin." Their measurements of oxytocin release during parturition showed that "oxytocin secretion during parturition in the pig is complex and pulsatile, with one clear component being a postpartum oxytocin pulse. This pulse is closely linked to the passage of material (either fetuses or placentae) down the birth canal (Gilbert et al. 1994, 13)." Oxytocin secretion seems to occur in a pulse-like pattern, rather than the continuous infusion of exogenous oxytocin (pitocin) that is a central feature of epiduralized birth.

A rapid increase of endogenous oxytocin during the period of fetal expulsion was also found by Gilbert et al. (1994) but to a lesser extent than observed by Summerlee. This pulse like secretion of endogenous oxytocin is important for successful breastfeeding in humans. However, the release of endogenous oxytocin is interfered with by the administration of exogenous oxytocin (pitocin). According to Jonas et al. (2009), the mother's endogenous oxytocin levels are decreased the greater the dose of pitocin administration. When epidural analgesia and oxytocin are administered together, endogenous oxytocin levels are even less.

Animal studies suggest that the fetal ejection reflex is significant for the maternal-infant bonding that is promoted through the secretion of endogenous oxytocin. As mentioned previously, the fetal ejection reflex appears to be absent in epiduralized birth. Odent (1987, 2006) has observed that in non-medicated births, even in hospital settings, it is common to see the fetus ejection reflex as a point of no return where maternal contractions result in birth. There is no need for directed pushing as the baby is born with little voluntary effort by the mother. Her contractions are involuntary and beyond her control.

Odent (2006) questions the entire obstetrical framework where human labor is divided into three stages. In epiduralized birth, providers often disagree as to when a woman is actually in labor. With early epidural administration, pitocin is automatically initiated and so the designation of "in labor" is actually a moot point. In physiologic birth, it is also not uncommon for a woman to be completely dilated, a moment when Friedman's framework would state that labor has progressed to second stage, and yet there is no urge to push for one or two hours. At what point would we say that the mother has reached second stage: when she is fully dilated or when she experiences the urge to push? Friedman's entire framework ignores the significance, and the very existence, of the fetal ejection reflex.

The conception of a second stage associated with full dilation has led to the routine practice of directing the mother to begin actively pushing at full dilation rather than waiting for the fetal ejection reflex to takeover. It is common to hear the words, "You are fully dilated. You should start pushing now," in the labor room. Numerous birth advocates, as well as midwives (Roberts and Hanson 2007), have questioned this practice of active pushing—a "bearing down" by the mother—stating that it is associated with a series of adverse outcomes: malpresentation of the fetus, decreased fetal oxygenation, pelvic floor damage, future urinary and/or fecal incontinence, and sexual dysfunction due to pelvic floor damage.

Prior to Friedman's writings, birth attendants often relied on observation of the mother to determine if birth was imminent. Prior to the mechanized viewpoint of birth, and later epiduralized birth, the fetus ejection reflex was recognized as the point when the birth attendant knew to get ready to assist with the delivery of the baby. Of course, this assumes that there is a birth attendant watching, or as it once was called, "labor-sitting". This is no longer feasible in the context of the modern obstetrical unit. In the old days of obstetrics, when a mother was feeling a powerful urge to push, it was common to tell her not to push until the doctor had arrived: an admonition impossible for the mother to obey, as many old time labor nurses will attest to. There were many babies born into the hands of nurses while all were awaiting the presence of the obstetrician.

In his critique of the concept of second stage, Odent (2006, 1) emphasizes the importance of recognizing the fetus ejection reflex as a key part of physiologic birth.

> Today I consider this 'reflex' as the necessary physiological reference from which one should try not to deviate too much. During the powerful and irresistible contractions of an authentic ejection reflex there is no room for voluntary movements. A *cultural misunderstanding* (my emphasis) of birth physiology is the main reason why the birth of the baby is usually preceded by a second stage, which may be presented as *a disruption of the fetus ejection reflex*. [Again, my emphasis.] All events that are dependent on the release of oxytocin (particularly childbirth, intercourse and lactation) are highly influenced by environmental factors. ...
>
> These considerations about ejection reflex versus second stage are opportunities to suggest that the true role of the midwife is to protect an environment that makes the ejection reflex possible. The point is to keep in mind the basic needs of labouring women. The point is to reconcile the need for privacy and the need to feel secure. This means the importance of the midwife as a mother figure. A mother is first a protective person.

Odent and Newton wrote of the significance of environment to the normal progress of birth, and to the fetal ejection reflex, before birth became widely industrialized. They both emphasize privacy, quiet, and a feeling of security and safety as key environmental elements for successful birth in humans. One could expect improved neonatal outcomes when birth is undisturbed, given the extent to which decreased endogenous oxytocin levels are shown to interfere with labor.

Newton (1987, 107) pointed to neonatal outcomes of the North Central Bronx Hospital (what was once a midwife-led service serving a high-risk population) where emphasis was placed on non-medicated births. This maternity service had significantly better neonatal outcomes compared to "institutions where less attention is paid to minimizing environmental and psychologic disturbances." Newton goes on to state that, "The endocrine research on human labor is complex and sometimes contradictory. ... Much better controlled research is needed on the environmental regulation of labor. It may be especially important to know which environmental factors inhibit or promote normal human labor (1987, 108)."

A growing body of research now shows that exposure to pitocin during labor disrupts and alters the maternal-fetal oxytocin feedback system (Buckley 2003). Not surprising (given his ecological emphasis) Odent has spoken to the dangers of pitocin and the growing evidence among researchers that there is a relationship between exposure to pitocin during labor and neurological disorders. Odent (2007) claims that human birth involves a rearrangement of central oxytocin binding. Induction of labor interferes with this central oxytocin binding in the mother. Wahl (2004) also points to the fact that neurohormones of the oxytocin family have been shown in many studies to influence social behavior in both animals and humans. What is still unknown is the precise mechanism that causes the disruption in oxytocin regulation.

It is possible that decreased maternal endogenous oxytocin levels following birth, as occurs with pitocin administration, interfere with maternal/infant bonding. Studies have shown that mothers who have been given pitocin during labor have decreased blood oxytocin levels two days after birth as compared to mothers who have had births without pitocin (Rissenberg 2010). In light of this research, Wahl (2004, 458) calls for obstetrical providers to "reexamine administration of OT [oxytocin] at childbirth, and to conceive and administer alternative labor inducing analogues that are proven not to have neurobiological effects."

The complexity of neurohormonal interactions between the maternal-fetal unit is not completely understood. Rissenberg (2010, 12-13), however, sketches a probable scenario:

Exogenous postpartum OT [pitocin] in the infant could, by influencing feedback mechanisms, interfere with the endogenous release of OT [oxytocin] in response to the mother's touch, along with its stress-reducing effects. Both OT release and stress reduction increase with positive physical contact (Ditzen et al. 2009), and OT increases the stress-protective effects of touch (Heinrichs et al. 2003). The soothing effect on a baby of being touched and held likely operates by stimulating the release of OT in the infant's brain, reducing anxiety, distress and crying. This early sensory activation of the OT system may be necessary for its subsequent development, as is true for other sensory neural systems. A reduction in the OT-mediated reward value of touch may help explain the hypersensitivity to touch associated with ASD [Autism Spectrum Disorder] (American Psychiatric Association, 1994). OT may also mediate the reward value for the baby of other social emotional stimuli and responsive behaviors, such as making eye contact and exchanging smiles with the mother and babbling in response to her voice, which are likely necessary for the development of visual and auditory processing of emotion and communication, processes that are characteristically deficient in ASD.

At the same time, reducing distress in the baby is highly rewarding for the mother, whereas failure to do so increases her distress and anxiety. This in turn can interfere with maternal care, including breastfeeding (Zanardo, 2009), depriving both mother and baby of the stress-reducing effects of nursing and the regular close physical contact it ensures (Heinrichs et al. 2001; Uvnäs-Moberg 1996). The OT-mediated calming effects on mother and baby are thus mutually reinforcing, and disruption of postpartum OT function in either the infant or the mother at this critical time is likely to interfere with mother-infant bonding and the subsequent development of the baby's OT system and social emotional processing later in life.

It is quite possible that a complex feedback system involving oxytocin occurs between the mother and fetus throughout pregnancy and birth, one that is critical for mediating the interaction between mother and newborn. Feldman et al. (2007) show a correlation of maternal-infant attachment with increasing maternal oxytocin levels from early to late pregnancy. Oxytocin is not the only neurohormone responsible for social bonding but is considered to be one of the most important. Human survival depends on a complex set of behaviors that occur between mother and infant—touch, eye contact, vocalizations, and breastfeeding. The presence of endogenous oxytocin in both the mother and infant is key to this complex of bonding behaviors (Feldman et al. 2007).

Oxytocin and Human Behavior

Beyond oxytocin's importance in childbirth, there is growing interest in the role of oxytocin in human behavior. A thorough discussion of the complicated physiology of oxytocin is beyond the scope of this chapter. For the reader interested in this key hormone, I refer to the 2014 article, Beyond Labor, The Role of Natural and Synthetic Oxytocin in the Transition to Motherhood by Aleeca Bell, Elise Erickson, and Sue Carter (2014).

Researchers have begun to recognize the significance and the precise role of the hormone oxytocin in human social cognition and behavior. This interest includes the role of endogenous oxytocin vs. that of synthetic, exogenous oxytocin (pitocin) during childbirth.

> Given the predominance of synthetic oxytocin in clinical practice, research is needed on how synthetic oxytocin may affect the intrinsic regulation of endogenous oxytocin and subsequent oxytocin-related outcomes.
>
> ... With the ubiquitous use of synthetic oxytocin in modern birth care, research questions abound regarding the long-term implications of manipulating the oxytocin system during labor—a complex transitional window of development for both mother and infant (Bell et al. 2014:35-36).

Beyond the role of oxytocin during childbirth, researchers have begun to study the influence of oxytocin in humans, although such research is still sparse. With the research that does exist, there are provocative implications of post-childbirth outcomes following perinatal exposure to pitocin. Oxytocin appears to play a mediating role in social behavior (Bartz et al. 2011; Bell et al. 2014; Hollander et al. 2007; Guastella 2010). It is hypothesized that a disruption of oxytocin pathways is involved in disorders where essential social skills are disturbed. For example, researchers have replicated animal studies in human studies showing that the nasal administration of synthetic oxytocin can improve on aspects of social behavior in autistic individuals. This research has included controlled double-blind, cross-over studies (Hollander et al. 2007; Guastella 2010).

A recent large-scale epidemiological study, the first study of its kind in the United States, has shown that autistic individuals are significantly more likely to have experienced induction and/or augmentation during birth. The power of this study lies in its use of two large data sets, the North Carolina Detailed Birth Record 1990-1998 (NCDBR) and the North Carolina Education Research Data Center of 1997-2007 (NCERDC). According to the authors, both data sets have been found to be highly valid. The two data sets were compared for matches. In the end, after limiting for various co-founding variables, 625,042 children were matched from both data sets. A group of 5,500 children diagnosed with exceptional autism was identified.

The number of children diagnosed with autism among the larger matched set was consistent with nationwide statistics. It also showed a 4:1 difference between boys and girls, also consistent with nationwide statistics. Among the study group, children induced and/or augmented during labor with pitocin were significantly more likely to be diagnosed with autism (Gregory 2013). The researchers could not conclude what precisely might underlie this association: was the association due to the drug pitocin vs. the act of induction or augmentation; maternal medical conditions; or acute incidences occurring during labor. The study certainly raises suspicion regarding the routine use of pitocin during labor. The study did not account for epidural during labor. But a significant number of mothers who receive synthetic oxytocin during labor also have received an epidural. This study did not account for this confounding factor.

The precise means of the pathways of both oxytocin and pitocin are not entirely known. However, as described earlier in this chapter, it is known that pitocin appears to result in lower oxytocin blood plasma levels in breastfeeding mothers who have been administered pitocin during labor; these mother and babies have more difficulty establishing breastfeeding. "A growing body of evidence suggests a link between oxytocin and optimal mothering behaviors in humans... (Bell et al. 2014:42)."

It is possible that some newborns are more sensitive to the effects of the medications common to epiduralized birth. One reason may be hereditary. Others may involve environmental factors inutero and during birth. There is much we still do not know. However, it behooves maternity providers to take notice of recent research suggesting that pitocin is not a benign medication to be used routinely.

Summary

The question must be asked: How safe is the use of bupivacaine and pitocin during labor? There are, of course, situations where the use of both medications is warranted. But what can be said, unequivocally, is that epiduralized birth has become normative for American births with no thought as to its implications: the exposure of the fetus to neurotoxins during labor, prolonged labor, the interference of the mother's secretion of endogenous oxytocin and other hormones, the interruption of breastfeeding and maternal/infant bonding.

There is much that we still do not understand about birth. We do know, however, that birth is not the mechanical process to which it has been reduced by obstetrics. Childbirth involves a complex hormonal interaction between mother and fetus/newborn. Some of the hormones that we know are involved, and interacting, in birth include oxytocin, prolactin, catecholamines, and beta-endorphins. These are only the few that scientists have identified. How and to what extent they work together is not completely understood.

Oxytocin is perhaps the most important but is only one such hormone involved. It is the hormone, in its synthetic form (pitocin) that has been used to manipulate labor. In its endogenous form, oxytocin has been shown to be significant for maternal/infant bonding as well as the development of socialization in the infant. Modern obstetrics, with its excessive environmental stimulation associated with industrialized childbirth, causes disturbed labor, thus impeding the secretion of maternal oxytocin. It then attempts to solve the very problem it has brought about through the infusion of pitocin (exogenous oxytocin) to promote labor. The addition of the epidural to the mix of medical interventions solved the problem of the increased pain that often accompanied the administration of pitocin. This has occurred with no research as to the safety of the concomitant use of these two very potent medications—bupivacaine and pitocin.

Given the extent to which epidurals have become routine in our system of childbirth, it is surprising that there is not more research on the impact of the epidural on the fetus. Furthermore, the research that has been carried out does not always take into account the combination of bupivacaine and opiate given simultaneously with pitocin. The few studies cited here that report changes in newborn behavior in babies born via epiduralized birth are significant and should give us reason to be concerned.

The impact of epidural anesthesia, along with its corresponding pitocin augmentation, on maternal endogenous oxytocin both during and after birth is an area that is only beginning to be of interest to researchers. To the extent that both pitocin and epidural administration interfere with natural levels of endogenous oxytocin in the mother and the newborn, the safety of the epiduralized birth of our modern childbirth system needs to be questioned.

How can so many providers and researchers believe that epiduralized birth is safe? To understand this phenomenon we have to go back to the observation by Kloosterman (DeVries 2004a), the Dutch physician. Kloosterman expounded on his observation that American obstetrical practice is often based on tradition rather than on science. Evidence-based research, states DeVries (2004b, 595) often "becomes a rhetorical justification for whatever particular groups [are] going to do anyway." This is particularly true for obstetrics. What is considered to be evidence-based practice in obstetrics is often biased and influenced by cultural and structural factors (DeVries and Lemmens 2006). Clinical decision-making is influenced too often on convenience and tradition rather than what is known to be safe.

The reformulation of Friedman's curve, in order to normalize the prolonged labor of epiduralized birth, is a prime example of clinical practice based on convenience rather than science. The health and safety of a mother and baby depends on clinical protocols that are truly evidence-based; evidence that *proves* a routine intervention to be safe based on science; protocols that are not led by convenience or the desire to justify a practice that has already become so routine that no one wants to face the possibility that it may, in fact, pose risks to the mother and/or baby.

The failure of providers to carry out safe practice too often comes down to the Gleichschaltung of birth described throughout this book. In our epiduralized system of birth, various obstetrical interventions work together in a way that reinforce the totality of interventions, making industrialized birth possible. Epiduralized birth serves the interests of providers, mothers, and hospitals to such an extent that it is difficult for any individual to have the intellectual and moral strength to take a step backwards, to take an objective look, and to question the safety of the various interventions that make up the entirety of epiduralized birth.

The impact of the epidural (bupivacaine) on the fetal brain is still not known definitively. The administration of bupivacaine together with pitocin has not been adequately studied to declare it to be clinically safe. The Murray et al. (1981) study stands out and is unequivocal in its recommendation. I quote it once again. "Although it is at times necessary and appropriate for some mothers to receive medications during childbirth, the implications of this study are that the elective use of medication should be minimized (Murray et al. 1981, 81)"

At the time when the administration of the epidural and pitocin became routine, the research into maternal-fetal attachment had gone out of vogue. Bupivacaine and pitocin, whether given singularly or concomitantly, possibly have a significant impact on the maternal-fetal unit during birth and afterwards. When used together, is that impact a synergistic one? There is still much ambiguity in the present research.

There is also the need for alternative forms of pain relief to be considered. Nitrous oxide is a method of pain relief used widely throughout Europe. This method of pain relief is used in many dental offices in the United States. With new technology in its administration, it does not pose a danger to medical personnel. While nitrous oxide does not completely block pain during labor, it has an advantage in that the laboring mother controls its administration. Its use does not require the presence of an anesthesiologist. It has been widely studied, is shown to have a low toxicity level, and is rapidly excreted in the mother and the newborn. It does not cause respiratory depression in the newborn (Reynolds 2009). There have been recommendations that hospitals consider its use as a safe alternative to the epidural (Rooks 2007).

Nurse-midwives are challenged by Rooks (2009, 348) to be more proactive in providing assertive, informed consent needed by women to make safe decisions. "Women who request epidural analgesia need to be told that because it reduces the release of oxytocin from their own brains that loss will probably have to be replaced with synthetic oxytocin administered through an intravenous drip." Women also need to be informed of the difficulty inherent in pitocin administration. A low-dose regimen increases the probability of cesarean section due to prolonged labor. A high-dose regimen increases the possibility of uterine hyperstimulation and resulting fetal hypoxia, a situation that also increases the probability of a cesarean.

Mothers deserve to know that epiduralized birth places their baby at risk. Not all children exposed to the medications of epiduralized birth will go on to have developmental deficits. The human newborn is resilient. However, it is unknown which newborns will suffer deficits as a result of exposure to toxic medications during birth. Mothers at Community Hospital were often not clearly provided this information.

32   Pudendal anesthesia involves injection of a local anesthetic into the pudendal canal, into which the pudendal nerve if positioned near the ischial spines of the pelvis. This in a lack of sensation in the area of the perineum, vagina and vulva. It requires careful detection by the obstetrician and involves the use of a long needle. By contrast, the epidural is a much easier procedure to carry out..

33   A medication that has been the designation of "Category C in Pregnancy" is a medication that has been shown in animal studies to be harmful to the fetus while human studies are inconclusive. A Category C medication should only be given in pregnancy when the benefits clearly outweigh the risks.

34   The Apgar Score is a ten point measurement of fundamental physiologic mechanisms in the newborn. As such it is a gross estimate of fetal well-being with scoring taking place at one minute and five minutes after birth. Measurement elements include respiration, heart rate, muscle tone, reflexes, and skin color.

35   The Northern New England Perinatal Quality Improvement Network has published a guideline for the use of pitocin. It calls for an initial infusion of 2m/U per minute with incremental increases of 2m/U every thirty minutes. The guideline gives no recommendation as to a maximum dose, stating that pitocin should be incrementally increased until regular contractions are observed.

36   Synergy in the combination of medications reflects the fact that when several medications are combined , at times the effect of the combination can be greater than the sum of the parts—in other words, at the clinical level , the same effect can be obtained by combining smaller doses of each medication.

37   Iatrogenesis: An illness or injury caused by medical treatment.

38   As a student nurse in 1981, I had a rotation at Jefferson Davis Hospital, a public maternity hospital in Houston, Texas. Most mothers were assigned to a ward. In the morning, obstetricians carried out rounds in the old-fashioned manner—an obstetrician followed by interns and residents surrounded a mother's bed and discussed her case. One interchange has never left my mind. External fetal monitoring was a fairly new intervention. The obstetrician was quizzing his students as to their interpretation of the strip. One intern spoke up. "Isn't there controversy regarding the reliability of EFM?" The obstetrician's response: "No one gets sued for an unnecessary cesarean."

39   The Neonatal Behavioral Assessment Scale (NBAS) was developed in 1971 by Dr. T. Berry Brazelton. It has come to be widely used as a means of assessment of infant behavior. The assessment tool consists of twenty-eight behavioral characteristics and eighteen reflexes. The assessment analyzes if a newborn and infant are reaching normal developmental goals.

40   State control in the infant is the observed type and degree of response to stimulation. State control is the ability of the newborn to be calmed, to cuddle, self-soothe, and to show hand to mouth activity.

41   A mother's disbelief in the importance of reciprocity with her infant has been shown to be a strong predictor of abuse and neglect on the part of mothers.

Chapter Seven

Doing More But Accomplishing Less

"Birth keeps the lights on in hospitals (Dr. Jeff Thompson 2012)."

A childbirth system is more than the reflection of a country's cultural beliefs and practices. Systems of childbirth are dynamic processes influenced by and also transformed by macro factors, including the overall organization of health care and the social history of a people.

Most health care policy experts agree that the American system of childbirth is in need of extensive reform. Poor maternal and infant outcomes can be partially explained by the organization of our childbirth system. In Western Europe, 75% of normal deliveries are attended by midwives (Wagner 2006). In contrast, most deliveries in the United States utilize the care of a physician (or resident) for normal deliveries, a characteristic of a childbirth system unique to the United States.

At the same time, the United States has seen a slow but steady trend towards increased midwife attended births (DeClercq 2009, 2012). Nurse-midwives now attend from 11–12% of U.S. births (DeClercq 2014), although with wide geographical variation. The high cost of obstetrical care, along with relatively poor outcomes, is also a characteristic that sets the United States apart from other wealthy countries.

A fundamental element of the American childbirth system is that of a profit-driven health care system. Perkins (2004) refers to overall poor perinatal outcomes as our "perinatal paradox," "doing more and accomplishing less (Perkins 2004, 13)." Perkins points to what she describes as a perinatal industry, a system of care that thrives on reimbursement flowing from ever more intensive uses of interventions on mothers and babies.

> Whether or not most women wanted it, intensive medical intervention remained part of the birth experience of four million American women (and babies) a year in the 1980s and 1990s. Although different procedures waxed and waned at different times, at least one was always classified as standard procedure. The annual perinatal market basket in the

mid-1990 included a million and a half episiotomies, over a million neonatal circumcisions, and close to a million cesarean sections. Put another way, for every 100 live births in the year 2000 there were 84 electronic fetal monitoring procedures, 67 ultrasounds, 26 episiotomies, 23 cesarean sections, 20 labor inductions, 18 labor accelerations, and 67 vacuum or forceps extractions. Birth intervention critics at that time claimed that the emperor was still scantily dressed and that a large gap remained between evidence of the efficacy and intervention practices in perinatal medicine.

With potential consequences for the health of every person in the nation, perinatal medicine—obstetric and pediatric services delivered to women and infants "around birth"—offers an excellent perspective on interactions between the business model of medicine and its practices. Reasonably accurate data are available concerning nearly every birth, providing an all-important population based denominator not available in other specialty areas for determining intervention and outcomes rates as well as disease incidence. Low-birth weight and mortality rates provide outcome measures across a range of population and geographic scales. While the U.S. infant mortality rate declined continuously after the mid-1930s, its international ranking fell from third in 1950 to twentieth in 1964, plateauing at that level until the 1990s, when it sank to twenty-sixth in 1996. The United State's low international ranking exposed a "perinatal paradox," which family medicine professor Roger Rosenblatt defined as "doing more and accomplishing less" (Perkins 2004, 12).

Calling perinatal medicine "an industry in its own right," Perkins (2004, 2-13) gives a striking picture of the way in which maternity care has in fact become a cash cow for our health care system. "Home with baby" is the number one discharge diagnosis for American hospitals. The growing use of unnecessary interventions on both mothers and babies accounts for an exponential rise in perinatal expenditures. In 1980, perinatal expenditures in the United States were $30 billion dollars representing $7,000 on average per birth. This compares to $40 billion in 1993, an average of $10,000 per birth. This rise in expenditures, (along with comparatively poor outcomes) does indeed paint a picture of "doing more and accomplishing less."[42]

Perkins (2004, 13) makes the point that our childbirth system is fundamentally connected to economic organization.

> In using perinatal care to exemplify connections between medical intervention and economic organization, I am challenging feminists to take business models seriously and mainstream investigators to take the health of women and children seriously. We cannot fundamentally reform childbirth practices without changing the business model of medicine, and we may not be able to do this without women's participation.

The International Federation of Health Plans (IFHP)[43] tracks health care costs across economically developed nations. However, analysis of health care costs is complicated by structural differences in payment systems. "Comparisons across different countries are complicated by differences in sectors, fee schedules, and systems. In addition, for some countries a single plan's prices are real for that plan but may not be representative of prices paid by other plans in that market (IFHP 2012, 3)." A comparative analysis of cost is complicated in that these statistics reflect only nations that are members of the IFHP and also do not compare costs of wealthy nations to that of developing countries. To further complicate any analysis, countries have a variety of arrangements for payment of health care. Comparisons, therefore, are only estimates of actual costs based on limited information. While comparative analysis is difficult, it is clear that health care expenditures for childbirth in the United States are far greater than any other nation.

While imperfect, the comparisons do provide a general view of the wide cross-country variations in health care costs. In the United States, the average cost of a vaginal birth is estimated to be $16,530 (IFHP 2012), while the estimated average cost of a cesarean birth is $26,305. In the case of normal, vaginal deliveries, physician fees in the United States account for approximately one-third of total cost of birth ($5,400). For cesarean births, physician fees account for approximately one-fourth of total cost ($10,500).[44]

In a cost comparison, the U.S. compares unfavorably to the next most expensive childbirth system—Australia. The average cost of a vaginal birth in Australia is $6,800 (American dollars), approximately one-third that of the United States. The average cost of a cesarean birth is $10,500 (also slightly less than a third of the U.S.) The physician fees for vaginal and cesarean births in Australia are even more dramatically different than that of the United States—$1,800 and $2,100 respectively.

The picture of an expensive U.S. maternity care system becomes more clear when costs are factored by type of insurance. For women who have commercial insurance (usually employer-based), the total cost of a vaginal birth in 2012 was $32,093 and for cesarean birth the cost was $51,125. With Medicaid, the costs for a vaginal birth was $9,131 and for cesarean $13,590. There are also wide geographic variations in costs. What remains consistent throughout the United States is that both commercial insurers and Medicaid, in general, pay 50% more for cesarean births than for vaginal births. These figures do not capture costs involved in neonatal care, an important factor given the high rate of low-birth weight and preterm birth in the United States (Truven Health Analytics 2013).

The high cost of commercially insured birth, as compared to average cost of Medicaid births, possibly reflects the cost-shifting (an industry misnomer which actually means payment shifting) that occurs in the U.S. health care system. Cost-shifting occurs because Medicaid does not pay the true costs of care, in general contracting with providers to pay 50% less than commercial payers. Because of the uninsured as well as underinsured, which includes Medicaid and self-insured individuals, there is wide variation in expenditures—or in others words payments for services.

For births covered by commercial insurance plans, 59% of costs are associated with the birth facility and 25% of costs are accounted for by payment to the maternity care provider. The IFHP (2012) documents a wide disparity in U.S. physician payment for vaginal and cesarean birth as compared to other countries. These figures reflect the high cost to our health care system that results from of our rising cesarean rate.

According to Childbirth Connections (2011), the type of facility and provider can have a significant impact on the charges for birth. The average U.S. charge for a vaginal birth in a freestanding birth center, with a midwife attendant, is five times less than an uncomplicated vaginal birth occurring in a hospital with a physician attendant. If midwives attended most normal births, the cost savings to our health care system as a result of decreased cesareans and unnecessary interventions would be significant (Rosenblatt et al. 1997; Gabay and Wolfe 1987).

Despite our expensive childbirth system, the quality of our maternity care lags behind other wealthy nations. The World Health Organization (WHO) has set a cesarean rate benchmark of 10–15% as an indication of optimum maternal and infant care (Wagner 2006). The American cesarean rate continues to rise annually, although 2010 statistics do show a slight decrease from 2009. The cesarean rate increased 60% between the years 1996 and 2009. There does appear to be a slowing in the trend of rising cesareans, with a reported cesarean rate of 32.8% in 2012 (Childbirth Connection 2012). The CDC (Hamilton, Brady 2016) reported the 2015 overall cesarean rate in the U.S. to be 32.0%—a slight decrease that has been the trend for the previous three years. Nonetheless, the cesarean rate in the U.S. remains stubbornly high.

The abnormally high cesarean rate in the U.S. imposes an enormous economic cost onto its health care system. Cesareans have become the most frequently performed operation in American hospitals (Childbirth Connection 2009). In 2008, cesareans accounted for 46% ($7.3 billion) of total costs for deliveries in the United States (Podulka et al. 2011). However, economic costs do not take into consideration the issues of maternal and infant morbidity and mortality associated with cesarean section.

A dramatic rise in cesarean births in the hospital has also been seen in some less developed countries among the privileged classes (Khawaja et al. 2004). However, it is more meaningful to compare the United States to Western countries with wide access to health care technology. When compared in this way, the

United States cesarean rate is higher than other industrialized nations (Wagner 2006, 244).

The World Health Organization tracks trends in cesarean utilization, as well as determinants of that utilization among wealthy countries. Laurer (2010) shows that the capacity of a health care system to provide surgical obstetric care is a significant factor contributing to differences in cesarean rates and the utilization of cesareans in each country. Other determinants of cesarean utilization include the variable of health care system financing. The greater the government contribution to the financing of a country's health care system, the lower the cesarean rate. Furthermore, an increase in the number of hospitals and hospital beds per capita results in a significant increase in cesarean rates. Income levels have a very small statistical impact on cesarean rates. In other words, rising cesarean rates in the developed world have to do with systemic factors, particularly those involving financial incentives, within each country's health care system.

In the industrialized world, a cesarean rate above the WHO recommendation of 10–15% culminates in unsafe births. A cesarean section is major surgery resulting in unnecessary risks to both mother and baby when carried out without clinical justification. Increased maternal risks include:

- A threefold increase in maternal death.
- Abdominal adhesions.
- Hemorrhage due to blood vessel laceration.
- Bladder damage.
- Infection, sometimes leading to infertility.
- A twofold increase of stillbirth in subsequent pregnancies.
- Increased incidence of detached placenta in subsequent labors.

Risks to the newborn include a 2–6% probability that the baby will be cut during the operation, prematurity due to poor dating of the pregnancy, and increased possibility of respiratory distress (Wagner 2006).

Infant, Perinatal, and Neonatal Mortality as Health care Measures

Neonatal mortality rates[45] are measured as deaths per 1,000 births in the first 28 days of life. Early neonatal mortality is death in the first seven days of life. Both have become more reliable as a means for cross-comparison of the health of newborns, the overall health of a country, as well as the state of a country's maternity care. Throughout the world, perinatal mortality rates have some variation in reliability between wealthy vs. developing countries. However, the measure of early neonatal deaths [46] is overall reliable.

Early neonatal mortality accounts for three out of four neonatal deaths. Neonatal mortality overall worldwide represents more than half of overall infant mortality[47] and over one-third of under-five deaths. There are, however, considerable differences between wealthy and developing countries (WHO 2006, 24).

Cross-comparison based on the two measures of perinatal and neonatal mortality tends to be limited due to issues of consistent reporting based on uniform definitions. The WHO (2006) describes the inherent difficulty in obtaining consistent reporting because of the variations in culture and maternity care systems of each country. For example, my discussions with midwives in the Netherlands reveal that a fetal death at 22–23 weeks gestation would not necessarily be considered a perinatal death but rather a miscarriage (also referred to as spontaneous abortion).

> Evaluation of reporting of early deaths has shown that we may be underestimating perinatal deaths in many countries. It is likely that the decision whether to classify a delivery long before term as a spontaneous abortion or as a birth, which must be registered, may be affected by the circumstances in which the birth occurred and by the cultural and religious backgrounds of the people making the decision. ... For example, a stillbirth at 22 weeks of

gestation must be registered as such: at 21 weeks and six days, registration is not required (WHO 2006, 6).

As the World Health Organization becomes more confident on the reliability of newborn statistics, they are placing a greater value on these statistics.

> Mortality and morbidity in the perinatal and neonatal period are mainly caused by preventable and treatable conditions. Interventions that benefit mothers by reducing maternal deaths and complications, as well as special attention to the physiological needs of the newborn baby—resuscitation when necessary, immediate breast-feeding, warmth, hygiene (especially for delivery and cord care) and the prevention, early detection and management of major diseases—will help ensure the survival and health of newborn infants. Safe and clean delivery, early detection and management of sexually transmitted diseases, infections and complications during pregnancy and delivery and taking into account the physiological needs of the newborn baby, are all interventions that should be available, attainable and cost-effective. They all have an immediate beneficial impact on the mother and the unborn and newborn infant. Good maternal nutrition, the prevention and management of anaemia and high-quality antenatal care will reduce the incidence of complications and thereby improve the chances of survival of the mother, the fetus and the newborn infant. The incidence of low birth weight—an important determinant of perinatal survival—may take time to change substantially. Universal access for women to care in pregnancy and childbirth and care of the newborn is required to improve the chances for both mother and baby (WHO 2006, 25).

Both the perinatal and neonatal death rates are sensitive to aspects of obstetrical care and factors related to low-birth weight. In wealthy countries, however, both measures are skewed by the availability of high-tech interventions that result in decreasing the perinatal death rate, albeit at increased neonatal morbidity. In health care systems of developing countries, unreliable reporting can skew measures. Health care researchers and policy analysts, therefore, consistently refer to infant mortality rate (IMR)—the number of infant deaths per 1,000 live births within the first year of life—as a significant measure for the overall health and living conditions of communities. The IMR for the United States was 6.05 in 2011, the last available data from the CDC (MacDorman et al. 2013).

While this latest IMR rate for the United States represents a slight improvement from the IMR of 7.0 in 2006 (Mishel et al. 2007), the US IMR continues to compare poorly to that of other wealthy nations. A 2013 report by the Organization for Economic Co-Operation and Development (OECD) points to the fact that the United States remains an outlier when compared to other countries.

> All OECD countries have achieved remarkable progress in reducing infant mortality rates from the levels of 1970, when the average was approaching 30 deaths per 1,000 live births, to the current average of just over four. Besides Mexico, Chile and Turkey where the rates have converged rapidly towards the OECD average. ... Portugal and Korea have also achieved large reductions in infant mortality rates, moving from countries that were well above the OECD average in 1970 to being well below the OECD average in 2011.
>
> By contrast, in the United States, the reduction in infant mortality has been slower than in most other OECD countries. In 1970, the US rate was well below the OECD average, but it is now well above ... . Part of the explanation for the relatively high infant mortality rates in the United States is due to a more complete registration of very premature or low birth weight babies than in other countries... However, this cannot explain why the post-neonatal mortality rate (deaths after one month) is also greater in the United States than in most other OECD countries. There are large differences in infant mortality rates among racial groups in the United States, with black (or African-American) women more likely to give birth to low birth weight infants, and with an infant mortality rate more than double that for white women (11.6 vs. 5.2 in 2010) (NCHS, 2013). [OECD 2013, 36]

The incidence of low-birth weight at birth and preterm birth is greater in the United States as compared to European countries. When infant mortality rates are adjusted to exclude early neonatal births, which can often be the result of complications unrelated to maternal health or living conditions, the United States continues to rate poorly in comparison to other wealthy nations (Heisler 2012). Countries with lower infant mortality rates include those of Western Europe and East Asia. Many of these countries have a GNP well below that of the United States. The 2011 United States IMR rate of 6.05 was higher than the overall IMR average of 4.0 reported by other members of the OECD. Furthermore, the international comparative ranking of the U.S. IMR has continued to fall (OECD 2013). The primary cause of infant mortality in the United States is congenital malformation (20.1%) but is closely followed by low-birth weight and preterm birth (16.9%). Both low-birth weight and preterm birth are directly related to issues of poverty—i.e. income and access to care (Heisler 2012).

International comparisons of infant mortality rates remain controversial. Some critics of the use of the IMR for comparative purposes point to national discrepancies in how live birth statistics are gathered.[48] However, influential health analysts disagree with those who criticize the use of IMR as a means of comparing national health.

> Differences in how live births are recorded may affect international IMR comparisons; however, it is unlikely that these recording differences would entirely explain the high U.S. IMR or the variation between the U.S. IMR and those of some European countries... Researchers at the National Center for Health Statistics (NCHS) conclude that for recording differences to completely explain the high U.S. IMR, European countries would have to misreport one-third of their infant deaths... a possibility considered to be improbable by the NCHS (Heisler 2012, 7).

To a large extent, racial disparities continue to account for the high infant mortality rate of the U.S. Heisler (2012) provides statistical evidence of these racial disparities and the role these disparities play in raising the overall U.S. IMR.

> In 2008, the IMR for infants born to black mothers was 12.7, more than double the white IMR of 5.5. This difference has the effect of increasing the U.S. IMR, as births to black mothers make up 16% of U.S. births, but

30.4% of U.S. infant deaths in 2008. In contrast, the U.S. IMR for white infants was 5.53. This rate is closer to the Canadian IMR of 5.6; however, it is still higher than the OECD average of 4.6 and the IMRs of other English-speaking countries. ... Eliminating these disparities would likely lower the U.S. IMR, but would not likely lower it below the OECD average, or below those countries with the lowest IMRs (those in Scandinavia). (Heisler 2012, 8-9)

A greater incidence of multiple births due to reproductive technologies can account to some extent for our increased trend in preterm and low-birth weight births. However, the CDC notes that shorter gestations have also increased among singleton births (Hamilton et al. 2009).

Figure Eight compares Infant Mortality Rates in relation to GDP per capita and expenditures as a percentage of GDP.[49] (IMR rates are from MacDorman et al. 2014) The first six countries listed in Figure Eight report the lowest IMR in 2014. As can be seen, the United States in 2014 had an IMR of 6.1, while spending 17.9% of GDP on health care. This compares to Japan with health care expenditures at 9.5% of GDP and an IMR of 2.3.

Figure Nine
IMR Related to GDP: Selected Countries

	IMR	GDP (%) Per Capita	Health care As % GDP
Japan	2.3	36,200	9.5
Sweden	2.5	41,700	9.6
Spain	3.2	30,400	9.5
Italy	3.4	30,100	9.5
France	3.6	35,500	11.9
Switzerland	3.8	54,600	11.9
United States	6.1	49,800	17.9

The infant mortality rate of each country is a robust estimate and is generally accepted by international policy experts as reflecting "the effect of economic and social conditions on the health of mothers and newborns, the social environment, individual lifestyles as well as the characteristics and effectiveness of health systems (OECD 2013, 36)."

Health care expenditures as a percentage of GDP do not reflect how much a country focuses its expenditures onto primary care, including maternal and child health care, as opposed to large expenditures on health care processes involving extensive technology. Figure Eight does clearly show, however, that the United States, with regards to infant mortality, receives poor results for its heath care dollars.

Aggregate infant mortality rates do not tell the entire story of the health of a nation's people in countries like the United States, with known wide disparities in wealth and infant mortality. At the aggregate level, infant mortality within the United States is similar to that of other wealthy countries. However, infant mortality in the United States is known to be highly variable, with high infant mortality associated with specific racial and geographical areas, all related to wealth, health care access, and living conditions. Likewise, GDP per capita does not capture the overall wealth and well-being in countries with a wide disparity of wealth. Again, the United States is the best example.

The OECD (2013) points out that among wealthy countries, there is generally a relationship between per capita health care spending and infant mortality (which includes perinatal mortality rates). However, we can see from Figure Nine that the United States is an exception. A number of countries spend much less on health care while obtaining good results in terms of infant mortality.

We can take Spain as an example. Spain has a GDP per capita of €30,400 (approximately $32,000), compared to a GDP per capita of $49,800 in the United States. Spain has an infant mortality rate of 3.2, which places it among the countries with a comparatively low infant mortality rate. Spain, with its IMR of 3.2, obtains excellent outcomes as compared to the United States, with its IMR of 6.1. Yet Spain's health care expenditures are 9.5% of GDP while the United States spends 17.9% of GDP on its health care system. It appears that in the United States, increased health care spending does not result in improved overall perinatal outcomes.

The underlying causes behind infant mortality rates are different for wealthy and emerging/developing countries. According to the OECD (2013, 36), "around two-thirds of the deaths that occur during the first year of life are neonatal deaths (i.e., during the first four weeks). Birth defects, prematurity and other conditions arising during pregnancy are the principal factors contributing to neonatal mortality in developed countries." Among all countries followed statistically by the OECD, there has been a significant decrease in infant mortality rates but this has been particularly true in developed/wealthy countries where infant mortality rates have reached a point of leveling off in recent years. In Figure Eight we can see that the IMR of developed countries hover around 2–4/1,000. The United States stands out as the exception to this trend.

> At one time the infant mortality rates in the United States was well below the OECD average, but it is now above average. … Significant differences are evident among ethnic groups in the United States with Black or African-American women more likely to give birth to high-risk, low birth weight infants, and with an infant mortality rate more than double that for white women (12.9 versus 5.6 in 2006) [OECD 2011, 36].

Maternal mortality in the United States, the number of pregnancy related deaths per 100,000 live births, is another health indicator where the need for improved maternity care is apparent. The Centers for Disease Control began its Pregnancy Mortality Surveillance System in 1986. From the year 1987 to 2008, maternal deaths in the United States increased from 7.2–15.5/100,000 (CDC 2013). The factors involved in this trend of increased maternal mortality in the United States are not entirely clear. The CDC speculates that this trend in maternal deaths can to some extent be explained by computerized data collection and increased awareness by hospitals and providers as to the criteria for identification of pregnancy related deaths.

In developing countries, hemorrhage accounts for the vast majority of maternal deaths. By contrast, hemorrhage accounts for only 11% of maternal deaths in the U.S. Chronic health conditions (i.e. hypertension, cardiovascular disease, cardiomyopathy, and diabetes) account for the bulk of maternal mortality in the U.S.

> As with infant mortality, we see a racial discrepancy with regards to maternal mortality. Although the overall risk of dying from pregnancy complications is low, some women are at a higher risk than others. Variability in the risk of death by race, ethnicity, and age indicates that more can be done to understand and reduce pregnancy-related deaths. ... Considerable racial disparities in pregnancy-related mortality exist. During the 2006–2008 period, the pregnancy-related mortality ratios were 11.3 deaths per 100,000 live births for white women. 34.8 deaths per 100,000 live births for black women. 14.5 deaths per 100,000 live births for women of other races (CDC 2013, 3).

These statistics raise significant questions as to the quality, and the inherent inequality, of the American system of childbirth. Health care disparities, and deficient social support for many pregnant women, particularly for women of color, are routinely cited as causes of inferior outcomes—our increasingly poor comparative rates of preterm labor, low-birth weight, infant mortality, and maternal mortality. This is despite the large health care expenditure output by the United States.

The American obstetric practice of routine, planned induction at 37–38 weeks has contributed to our high cesarean rate. Cesareans in turn account, to some extent, to the poor outcomes listed above. Numerous studies have shown adverse impacts on the newborn with this practice of early induction (Rodgers and Cox 2013; Robinson et al. 2010). In response to these studies, ACOG (2013a) has now taken on an official position against medically unnecessary induction prior to 39 weeks gestation. We must wait to see if this new policy has a positive impact on our infant and maternal outcomes, as well as our cesarean rate.

The impact of our cesarean rate on American women and infants cannot be overly emphasized. Too many American obstetricians still refuse to offer the procedure vaginal birth after cesarean (VBAC). This remains the case despite the fact that VBAC has been shown, through clear evidence, to be safe when carried out judiciously, as well as to be safer than repeat cesarean in many situations. Vaginal birth after cesarean offers the possibility of decreasing the cesarean rate in the U.S. As the rate of VBAC increases, there is a corresponding decrease in overall cesarean rates. The reverse is also true: as the rate of VBACs decrease, the overall cesarean rate increases. The primary cesarean rate, a mother's first cesarean, is a fundamental component of the cesarean problem in the U.S. given that subsequent pregnancies will often result in scheduled cesareans (NIH 2010).

In the early 1990s, as obstetricians began to carry out VBAC in response to strong childbirth activist demand, there occurred a corresponding temporary dip in the cesarean rate. A decreased VBAC rate in the mid to late 1990s reflected a return to rising cesareans rates. The unreliability of state-by-state statistics regarding primary cesarean and VBAC rates make if difficult to chart these variables beyond 2005. NIH statistics, however, do clearly show a relationship between rising cesarean rates and an increase in primary cesareans along with a decreased VBAC rate. This corresponds with anecdotal evidence.

Nurse-midwifery has shown its ability to provide improved outcomes for mothers and babies at less cost to society. Public policy analysts have noted these outcomes and point to nurse-midwifery as an important element in successful reform of our childbirth system. Poor clinical maternal-child outcomes in the United State are associated with a childbirth system where pregnancy is considered a medical condition that comes under the professional purview of an obstetrical specialty, unlike many European countries where midwives are the attendants at most normal births. Another factor noted by policy experts is the lack of an independent midwifery in the United States (Pew Health Professions Commission 1999; Gabay and Wolf 1995a, 1995b). The World Health Organization has long called for the promotion and integration of trained midwives into a maternity care system as a key component for safe pregnancy care in both industrialized and emerging nations.

I make the statement that American nurse-midwifery is not a truly independent profession in this sense: American obstetrics is usually in a position to control the clinical practice of nurse-midwives. In the U.S., the clinical practice of nurse-midwives is controlled by physicians through a variety of mechanisms: through direct supervision, through statutory requirements for nurse-midwives to obtain a physician signed practice agreement, or through informal rules in the work place. The obstetrical committees in most hospitals block attempts by nurse-midwives to obtain admitting privileges. Admitting privileges are key for nurse-midwives to practice independently in hospitals. Even in states where practice agreements are not legally mandated, some third party payers require practice agreements for reimbursement of midwifery services. The ACNM has made progress on fighting these barriers. Still, these factors continue to effectively place many nurse-midwives under the control of their competition.

Health care policy experts need to look seriously at the factors that continue to marginalize nurse-midwifery as a profession. Nurse-midwives, when practicing in a hospital maternity service that is not truly midwifery-led, are impeded from practicing the midwifery model of care that has been shown by numerous studies to improve maternal and child outcomes (Johantgen et al. 2012; Goodman 2007; Waldenstrom and Turnball 1998; Haire 1991; Blanchette 1995; Sharp and Lewis 1984; Mann 1981).

---

[42] These figures provided by Perkins (2004) are from the mid-1990s and are not indexed for inflation. As cesareans and routine inductions have increased since her research, these figure are likely conservative. There value her in this document is to reinforce the critique of maternity care as a business.

[43] The International Federal of Health Plans is a voluntary association representing a variety of health care insurers in thirty countries.

[44] The "costs" presented here represent dollar amount paid, not the actual total charge.

[45] Neonatal and perinatal mortality rates: The neonatal mortality rate is the number of deaths in the first month of life per 1,000 births. Early neonatal death is a death in the first week of birth. Perinatal deaths are the sum of fetal deaths (in the US after 22 weeks gestation) plus neonatal deaths in the first week following birth.. There are several standard definitions for the perinatal mortality rate. It is therefore important to know which definition is used.

46   Early neonatal death: death occurring between birth to day seven.

47   Infant Mortality Rate (IMR): The number of infant deaths from live birth to one year. Represented by # of infant deaths per 1,000 live births.

48   There is no uniform definition for statistical purposes of what constitutes a live birth. The World Health Organization is attempting, with increasing success, to establish a uniform definition based on gestational age. There remains, however, some variation among countries.

49   2010 IMR rates are from McDorman et al. (2014). GDP per capita and health care as a percentage of GDP are form the CIA Factbook.

Conclusion

We seek to promote healthy interprofessional cultures through midwifery leadership. We will continue to strengthen partnerships with physicians, nurses, and other midwives to promote physiologic birth and other evidence-based, women- and family-centered care (ACNM 2015, 24).

To build a bridge ... you need pylons at each end of equal height to suspend the bridge upon and equal strength to support it. Until we are equals the bridge will not be built. The stronger we become as midwives the better we will collaborate with our medical colleagues. Strength invites respect and respect gives strength. ... We need to do some serious work...on the notion that we are not a second rate option, we are a first rate choice (Dahlen 2006, 6-7).

The historical roots of the nurse-midwifery profession lies in the Progressive Movement of the early twentieth century. In accordance with its history, the long-standing mission to serve mothers and children remains fundamental to the nurse-midwifery profession. Throughout a year of ethnographic research, I observed nurse-midwives who are dedicated to their patients: midwives who work tirelessly to bring humane, personalized, safe, quality care to mothers and babies. Based on my observations and interviews over the years, I believe that this mission has become ingrained within the inner-core of the professional identity and culture of nurse-midwives. Exceptional clinical outcomes, as well as dedication, have been documented in this book

Even as the nurse-midwives I observed impressed me, it was unsettling to realize the extent to which the American system of childbirth, including care by nurse-midwives, has come to be defined by the intensive use of technology. Nurse-midwives face powerful forces antagonistic to physiologic birth. Our epiduralized birth system has taken medicalization to an entirely new level. Epiduralized birth is contrary to the reality that, in most cases, birth is physiologic and does not require such intensive technology. Intensive birth technology is contrary to ecological birth.

Birth technology has been life-saving. However, technological interventions are routinely implemented without clear evidence that intensive technology is safe for mothers and babies. This intensification of birth technology as routine has brought about a threat to the ecology of birth. With epiduralized birth, we are not merely intervening in a benign manner. We are potentially changing the very physiology of childbirth. Epiduralized birth promotes unnecessary fear, "fear beyond reason". In a system of epiduralized birth, "birth is not revered, rather it is feared and with that fear it is devalued (Dahlen 2006, 5)."

A variety of factors have brought about high-tech birth in the United States. Market forces are significant: the drive to manage labor in order to expedite the assembly-line of the hospital maternity unit; the application of efficient production prototypes to maternity care in order to maximize labor-saving staffing and bed utilization. In sum, epiduralized birth is fundamentally about the need to control the inherently ungovernable nature of birth to fit the modern assembly-line. It is *not* about meeting the needs of the mother and baby, despite its appeal to convenience. As a routine, epiduralized birth is not about saving babies. It is an inappropriate use of technology.

Mothers desire an epiduralized birth with its promise of a painless birth, and the promise of control over when a baby comes—a value to many families in our modern society. However, mothers are often lacking the entirety of information that shows the extent to which much of the technology they seek is possibly unsafe. ACOG formally supports elective cesareans (including primary cesareans with no medical indication), all in the name of choice (ACOG 2013b). To what extent does the convenience of cesareans, both for the physician and mother, play into this position?

Nurse-midwifery has broken out of its marginalization over the past four decades, expanding and maturing as a profession despite immense obstacles. As CNMs have made inroads into hospital births, the position they hold within the health care system has continued to expand (Schuiling et al. 2013). Deliveries by CNMs have steadily increased from 4% of vaginal births in 1989 to 11.9% in 2012 (Declerq 2015).[50] It is likely that the true number of CNM births is actually greater due to underreporting (Declercq 2012). Homebirths continue to represent a small but slowly expanding portion of births nationwide. Notably, an increasing number of CNMs attend these homebirths. In 2004, 15.5% of homebirths were attended by a CNM vs. 22.0% in 2012 (Declercq 2015).

An increase in CNM deliveries has occurred despite a national cesarean rate that remains approximately 33%—the national cesarean rate has shown a slight decrease in the past several years (Martin et al. 2013). It is realistic to project that births attended by nurse-midwives will likely continue to increase in numbers.

This growth has been impressive, although there is a need for still more nurse-midwives in order to reach the critical mass necessary for midwifery to become the default profession in normal birth. At the same time, the profession has come a long way in positioning itself as an integral part of maternity care in the U.S. It has come to this point in time by keeping its eye on its mission and its strategic goals. (A growth in the annual number of graduate nurse-midwives is a strategic goal for the ACNM (Germano 2014.)

A look at both the historical record, as well as the individual words of nurse-midwives, shows the crafting of a modern profession steeped in ambiguity and paradoxes from its onset. Through the decades since its inception, nurse-midwives have shifted, negotiated and re-crafted their identities. Helen Varney Burst illustrates this point. Her words are from a presidential address, *Our Three-Ring Circus*, given in 1978 at the 23rd annual meeting of the ACNM in Phoenix, Arizona.

> In order to be able to function as best we can in whatever system we're in, we find ourselves in the constant, and tiring, position of having to negotiate, balance, and compromise; be skilled politically and in interpersonal relations; and take put-down with a smile, coolness of response, and outward negation of pride. ...
>
> Maternity care is a political issue and our purpose [is] one of identifying recommendations, which would address the redistribution of power pertaining to

> maternity care. ... Now I, like most of you, am for progress and against impotence; but I do not believe in annihilation. There must be a way. When I was a student nurse I frequently heard a great deal of pride given to an attribute, which was presented as characteristic of nurses. This attribute was ingenuity, i.e. figuring out how to create necessary items out of materials not before considered for that purpose. As we are nurse- midwives I call upon us, individually and collectively to create the modes of practice that will take us out of our binds and conflicts without destroying ourselves in the process (Varney Burst 1978, 13-14).

This description of the "binds" and "conflicts" in which nurse-midwives find themselves holds true as much today as in 1978. Nurse-midwives face a daily conflict between their professional values and the realities of clinical practice. They face an existential paradox: their belief in physiologic birth runs counter to epiduralized birth and the demands of the various players within the US system of childbirth. In facing this professional paradox, the instilled values of negotiation, balance, and compromise are both strengths and weaknesses.

For thirty years now, nurse-midwives have debated about what is, in one way or another, referred to as "collaborative practice". Other words used to describe the relationship between nurse-midwifery and obstetrics have included "a network of mutual dependence" (Ernst 1984), "cooperation" (Thompson 1984), and "interdependency" (Rooks 1984). These various terms imply the need to establish nurse-midwifery as a respected and integral part of the maternity care team—one equal profession among other essential health care providers.

Nurse-midwifery's overall professional survival strategy has involved an incremental approach to change, maintaining a long-term view towards carving out a place as experts in normal birth. Strategic elements that have been a foundation for the profession include: (1) Never loose sight of the historic mission to serve mothers and children, particularly the underserved. (2) Institutionalize support for nurse-midwifery through the building of coalitions with other maternity and health care providers, government, and policy makers. (3) Establish credibility through an emphasis on education and training in institutions of higher

242

education. (4) Expand the number of nurse-midwives and the profession's market share in the maternity care system. (5) Expand nurse-midwifery's scope of practice beyond maternity care. (6) Avoid direct confrontation with ACOG. In recent years, a seventh element has become a significant strategic element: professional self-control and autonomy. Nurse-midwifery leaders often avoid the use of the term, but what they are speaking about is an independent profession.[51]

In light of these strategic principles, the emphasis on negotiation, balance, and compromise, as expressed by Varney Burst (1978), makes sense. However, for various issues, and at any given time, these strategic principles can be in conflict. Finding a balance can be problematic. Ernst (1984) criticizes a dependence-independence dichotomy as a sign of professional immaturity. However, the true dichotomy facing nurse-midwives in their daily clinical practice is not dependence vs. independence. In the drive to establish independence, the day-to-day dichotomy faced by nurse-midwives in the clinical arena lies in finding a balance between cooperation and subordination.

Defining independence for nurse-midwifery, let alone earning independence, is a knotty proposition. In our complex, modern society, no profession has absolute independence. All health care professionals engage in mutuality. The ability to consult and refer, in short to collaborate as part of a team, is an essential part of providing quality care. Even among physicians this does not always occur smoothly. I have observed physicians as they negotiate clinical decision-making among themselves. It is not unusual to see conflict and competition in these negotiations. Medicine has its subtle, and at times not so subtle, internal hierarchies. However, physicians usually manage to arrive at consensus as one equal to another. When needed, all teams rely on formal and/or informal rules when negotiating.

Within medicine, various specialties carve out territory. When territory overlaps, there can be conflict, but ultimately everyone comes to agree on who has the final say, even with shared responsibility. When it comes to birth, nurse-midwives must insist that normal birth falls within its area of expertise, its provenance. To be truly independent in normal birth (and to have the ability to provide quality care), the opinion of the primary nurse-midwife must ultimately carry the most weight in decision-making. It is only in this way that nurse-midwives can guarantee that mothers and babies under the responsibility of the nurse-midwife receive the quality care that they deserve.

An independent midwifery does not imply functioning alone or without consultation and collaboration. However, an independent midwifery must have autonomy to the extent that the midwife has the right to final decision-making within its professional scope of practice. Within the context of collaboration, a truly independent midwife is not trumped by an obstetrician, is not subject to the whims of an individual obstetrician, with regards to normal birth. But most nurse-midwifes do not, in reality, have that mutuality with obstetricians. How many nurse-midwives can honestly claim otherwise? Very few.

Nurse-midwifery cannot separate its mission to serve mothers and babies from the issue of autonomy and independence. The two are inseparable. In the face of obstetrical intransigence, can nurse-midwives adequately promote physiologic birth without having the autonomy to do so? Without true autonomy, can nurse-midwives provide honest, robust informed consent? Another example is that of nurse-midwifery's professional code of ethics. An element of any independent, modern profession is not only *having* a code of ethics but the *ability* to *apply* that code of ethics in practice.

The American system of epiduralized birth will not change without a truly independent midwifery. Only an independent midwifery will have the power and influence to carry out accurate, evidence-based, informed consent: informed consent where women are told the unvarnished truth about the potential dangers of epidurals and pitocin, two interventions so central to our epiduralized birth. This will not be easy. Modern obstetrics has convinced mothers, and themselves, that this dream of totally painless childbirth through epiduralized birth is benign. Women will now be loath to hear otherwise.

But if we are to truly stand with women, we need one more strategic goal. We need to heed the call by Judith Rooks (2007) to push for alternative means of pain relief other than opioids and bupivacaine. A strategic goal should be that every maternity unit offer nitrous oxide for pain—a means of pain relief proven to be safe and used throughout developed countries other than the United States.

If we are to stand with women, we need to fight: fight for undisturbed birth; fight for individualized bedside care rather than abdicating responsibility for bedside care. We need to gently but firmly advise mothers as to the dangers of epiduralized birth.

The reality of any situation can be difficult to navigate when that reality goes against the grain of deeply held beliefs and values. There can be a disconnect between what we wish to believe to be true and the reality of what happens. Constraints are a part of life. Every profession, including medicine, must reconcile the fact that there is always a degree of disconnect between theory and practice, between inclinations and reality. However, the constraints placed on nurse-midwives are too often untenable and go beyond the constraints faced by physicians.

Nurse-midwifery is easily subsumed into a culture of medicalization. Its ideal is a belief in physiologic birth, but the promotion of physiologic birth is difficult in the context of a subordinated midwifery. Collaboration in the context of a hierarchical relationship with obstetrics is an illusion. There can be no genuine collaborative relationship when an obstetrician has the right to ultimate decision-making. In the absence of authentic professional independence, genuine collaborative care is a myth, mere window-dressing. Reliance on a beneficent, friendly obstetrician is not true independence.

I hear voices from young midwives demanding professional independence. At a recent ACNM annual meeting, I heard young midwives speak of their frustration. "We are not empowered to practice midwifery." "Our inability to practice independently is the greatest barrier to our providing normal birth." One young student midwife criticized her educational program: "Many of us graduate without ever seeing a normal birth." The theory-practice gap in nurse-midwifery has been documented, with 50% of respondents in one study identifying an incongruity between what they are taught and the reality of clinical practice (Kennedy 2006, 2010). Nurse-midwives *believe* in physiologic birth, but in many clinical settings are unable to put into *practice* the values and beliefs they hold dear.

The American College of Nurse-Midwives states that it supports an independent midwifery (ACNM 2012b). A stated strategic goal for the ACNM is to dispose of statutory requirements for a written practice agreement in all states. The good news for nurse-midwifery is that this is happening. ACNM leadership is also working with a legal strategy for removing barriers to obtaining hospital admitting privileges. These are all significant steps forward. As important as these legal reforms are, however, they alone will not bring about an independent midwifery. For an independent midwifery to come about, there must be fundamental changes in the professional culture within nurse-midwifery.

With regards to physiologic birth, words will not be enough to give nurse-midwives the authority to promote normal birth. The ACNM sees itself as making progress in the promotion of physiologic birth. However, guidance by the ACNM to its membership remains inadequate. It is not enough to inform mothers that much of our birth technology has not been proven to be safe. The inconvenient truth is we do have evidence that many common birth interventions may be quite harmful to the mother and baby. We owe it to mothers to strongly put forth that evidence during informed consent.

Disruption of physiologic birth is harmful. As this book has shown, medications used in the epidural and in induction/augmentation of labor have been shown, in all probability, to have a variety of dangerous side effects. Nurse-midwives who work in hospitals need to see it as their responsibility to tell mothers the truth about the evidence regarding epidurals and pitocin—neither of which are benign interventions. Standing for the autonomy of the childbearing woman and the right of mothers to make choices is a positive attribute of the nurse-midwifery profession. However, there is no true autonomy without thorough informed consent (Whitney et al. 2003; Cahill et al. 2010).

For years I believed that there was no realistic place for freestanding birth centers in the United States: that realistically there was only room for homebirth or hospital birth in our maternity care system. I have made a 180-degree turn on this issue, coming to believe that freestanding birth centers, or maternity centers in hospitals that are truly midwifery-led, are the incubators of independent midwifery in the United States. Sandall et al. (2010) define midwife-led care as an institution where "the midwife is the woman's lead professional",—as opposed to obstetrical-led care or "shared models of care", that we call collaborative care in the U.S. Sandall et al. (2009, 2010) shows the superiority of midwifery-led care in normal birth by a wide range of measures: decreased fetal loss, fewer interventions for pain relief, greater satisfaction by mothers of their care, increased continuity-of-care, and cost savings. Yet freestanding birth centers, where maternity care is truly midwifery-led, struggle to survive both financially and often exist in the face of opposition by the obstetrical profession.

Unnecessary interventions are so embedded in obstetrical culture and practice that I believe it will only be in genuine midwifery-led maternity units that physiologic birth can become the norm. With genuine midwifery-led units, whether in-hospital or freestanding, there can be the possibility of a midwife-physician collaboration that is mutual, collaboration that truly respects the professional authority of midwifery in normal birth. In this type of collaborative relationship, there can be the continuity-of-care that is so necessary for safe birth. It will be in such units that women can have undisturbed birth—the calm, privacy and sense of safety so necessary for successful birth. More ethnographic studies of these midwife-led maternity centers are sorely needed, particularly those few that exist in the United States, to document outcomes.

For the aspiring or young midwife who is reading this: you must take heart. Nurse-midwives have come so very far and at great personal sacrifice; nurse-midwifery is a righteous, honorable profession. The profession has endured. We are anything but redundant. However, it is time, once again, for a historic leap. The profession belongs to the young. Grab it. Run with it. As Hanna Dahlen (2006, 9) says so eloquently in her writing, *At the Edge of History:*

> Are you brave enough for this future? For it is true we
> get in life what we have the courage to ask for. What do
> we as midwives have the courage to ask for? Nelson
> Mandela said, 'our deepest fear is not that we are
> inadequate. Our deepest fear is that we are powerful
> beyond measure. It is our light not our darkness that
> most frightens us. ... And yet when we let our light
> shine, we unconsciously give people permission to do
> the same. As we are liberated from our own fears, our
> presence automatically liberates others. As we stand at
> the edge of history with the future blowing wildly in our
> faces. As we see the air brightening at times and
> blinding us at others let us remember that we are
> powerful beyond measure and our greatest power is we
> are midwives: we are with women!

There is the need for a new paradigm. It may come about out of necessity. Institutions may come to recognize the dangers inherent in epiduralized birth. It may come about as insurance companies and the government come to realize that we can no longer afford the unnecessary costs of the technology upon which epiduralized birth depends. We can also hope for a new generation of women's health care activists who recognize the need for change.

---

[50] 1989 is the first year when statistics on birth attendants began to be gathered by the CDC.

[51] I have identified these strategic goals based on my observations and interviews, particularly my observations and notes at professional meetings.

Glossary

AABC   American Association of Birth Centers

ACNM   American College of Nurse-Midwives

ACOG   American Congress of Obstetricians & Gynecologists

AFI   Amniotic Fluid Index

AMCB   American Midwifery Certification Board

Augmentation of Labor   Interventions to strengthen/increase labor contractions.

Biophysical Profile   An ultrasound assessment of the fetal well-being utilizing a set of pre-determined measures.

Bupivacaine   A local anesthetic used in an epidural for pain relief during labor by injection into the epidural space of the spine, near nerves innervating the abdominal area.

CDC   Centers for Disease Control

CNM   Certified Nurse-Midwife

Cesarean Section   Surgery with incisions to the abdomen and uterus to remove the fetus.

EDA   Epidural anesthesia/analgesia

EDC   Estimated Date of Confinement, commonly referred to as Estimated Due Date.

EFM   External Fetal Monitoring

Epidural   A method of pain relief. A local anesthetic, often bupivacaine is injected into the epidural space of the spine.

Episiotomy   Cut made to the vaginal opening during a vaginal delivery.

FDA   Food and Drug Administration

Forceps   An obstetrical instrument, resembling two large spoons. Used to facilitate delivery of a baby's head.

Friedman's Curve   A graph that has been used in modern obstetrics to define and measure "normal" progress of labor.

GBS   A bacteria, Group B Streptococcus, that can potentially cause serious neonatal infection.

HHC   New York Health & Hospital Corporation

IFHP   International Federation of Health Plans

Induction of Labor   Interventions used to initiate labor.

Infant Mortality Rate   Number of infant deaths per 1,000 live births in the first year of life.

IRB   Institutional Review Board

ISMP   Institute for Safe Medication Practices

L&D   Labor and Delivery

m/U   Milliunit

NBAS   Brazelton Neonatal Assessment Scale

NCHS   National Center for Health Statistics

Neonatal Mortality Rate   # of infant deaths per 1,000 life births in the first 28 days of birth.

NICU   Neonatal Intensive Care Unit

OECD   Organization for Economic Co-operation and Development

Oligohydramnios   Insufficient amniotic fluid.

Oxytocin   Pituitary hormone that regulates contractions and ejection of mother's milk.

Perinatal Mortality Rate   The number of perinatal deaths per 1,000 births. The World Health Organization defines perinatal mortality as the sum of fetal deaths (starting at 20 weeks gestation to birth) plus neonatal deaths from birth to the first week of life. Some countries define perinatal death as fetal death from 28 weeks gestation plus neonatal death up to 28 weeks following birth.

Pitocin   Synthetic form of oxytocin.

PROM   Premature Rupture of Membranes

Pudendal Anesthesia   Also referred to as a pudendal block. A local anesthetic is injected into the pudendal canal, where the pudendal nerve is located, providing pain relief in the perineal area during the pushing stage of labor.

Pulse Oximeter   A device to measure blood oxygen saturation.

ROM   Rupture of Membranes

SDP   Single Deepest Vertical Pocket. A measurement of the overall amount of amniotic fluid by measuring the largest single vertical pocket seen on ultrasound.

Tertiary-Care   Specialized, consultative hospital health care.

24/7 Coverage   Full time staff coverage: seven days a week, twenty-four hours daily.

UTI   Urinary Tract Infection

Vacuum Extraction   Obstetrical procedure. A device is applied to the fetal head; suction facilitates delivery.

VBAC   Vaginal Birth After Cesarean

WHO   World Health Organization

Bibliography

Albers, Leah. 2007. "The Evidence for Physiologic Management of The Active Phase of the First Stage of Labor." *Journal of* Midwifery and *Women's Health* 52(3): 207-215.

———.2001. "Monitoring the Fetus in Labor: Evidence to Support the Methods." *Journal of Midwifery and Women's Health* 46(6): 366-373.

Alexander, James M., Shiv K. Sharma, Donald D. McIntire, and Kenneth Leveno. 2002. "Epidural Analgesia Lengthens the Friedman Active Phase of Labor." *Obstetrics & Gynecology* 100(1): 46-50.

American College of Nurse-Midwives. 1967. *What is a Nurse-Midwife?* Washington D.C.: American College of Nurse-Midwives.

———.2010. " Induction of Labor." Approved October 2010. Accessed 12.15.2013. www.midwife.org.

———.2011a. *Collaborative Agreement Between Physicians and Certified Nurse-Midwives and Certified Midwives.* Approved December, 2011. Accessed 2.15.2013. www.midwife.org

———.2011b. *Reproductive Health Services.* Approved August 2011. Accessed 12.16.2013. www.midwife.org.

———.2012. *Fact Sheet: CNM/CM-Attended Birth Statistics in the United States.* Accessed 12.16.2013 www.midwife.org.

———.2012a. "Supporting Healthy and Normal Physiologic Childbirth: A Consensus Statement By ACNM, MANA, and NACPM." *Journal of Midwifery & Women's Health* 57(5): 529-532.

————2012b. *Independent Midwifery Practice.* Approved February, 2012. Accessed on 1.3.14. www.midwife.org.

————2013a. *Fact Sheet: Essential Facts About Midwives.* Accessed 1.3.14. www.midwife.org.

————2013b. *ACNM 2013 Annual Report.* Washington D.C.: American College of Nurse-Midwives.

————2014a. *Fact Sheet: Essential Facts About Midwives.* Accessed 3.2.2014. www.midwife.org.

————2014b. Harrod, Kate. "ACNM Future Focus: Go Out and Be Bold: A Report from the March ACNM Board Meeting." *Quickening: Official Newsletter of the American College of Nurse-Midwives* 45(2): 8.

————2015. "Setting the Future in Motion: The New ACNM 5-Year Strategic Plan Will Guide Our Actions for US Midwifery." *Quickening: Official Newsletter of the American College of Nurse-Midwives* 46(3): 24.

American Congress of Obstetricians and Gynecologists. 2010. "Vaginal Birth After Previous Cesarean Delivery. Practice Bulletin Number 115." *Obstetrics and Gynecology* 116(2): 450-463.

————2013a. "Nonmedically Indicated Early-Term Deliveries. Committee Opinion No. 561." *Obstetrics and Gynecology* 121(4): 911-5.

————2013b. Cesarean Delivery On Maternal Request." Committee Opinion No. 559. *Obstetrics & Gynecology* 121(4): 904-907.

————2014. "Safe Prevention of the Primary Cesarean Delivery." Obstetric Care Consensus No. 1. *Obstetrics & Gynecology* 123(3): 693-671.

Arms, Suzanne. 1981[1975]. *Immaculate Deception.* New York: Bantom Books.

Belizán, Jose M., Fernando Althabe, and Maria Luisa Cafferata. 2007. "Health Consequences of the Increasing Caesarean Section Rates." *Epidem*iology 18(4): 485-486.

Bartz, Jennifer, Jamil Zaki, Niall Balger, Kevin Ochsner. 2011. "Social Effects of Oxytocin in Humans: Context and Person Matter." Trends *in Cognitive Sciences* 15(7): 301-309.

Bell, Aleeca, Elise Erickson and C. Sue Carter (2014) "Beyond Labor: The Role of Natural and Synthetic Oxytocin in the Transition to Motherhood." *Journal of Midwifery & Women's Health* 59(1): 35-42.

Blanchette, Howard. 1995. "Comparison of Obstetric Outcome of a Primary-Care Access Clinic Staffed by Certified Nurse-Midwives and a Private Practice Group of Obstetricians in the Same Community." *American Journal of Obstetrics and Gynecol*ogy 172(6): 1864-1871.

Boston Women's Area Health Book Collective. 1971. *Our Bodies Ourselves.* Boston: New England Free Press.

Bridges, Khiara M. 2011. *Reproducing Race. An Ethnography of Pregnancy as a Site of Racialization.* Berkeley: University of California Press.

Buckley, Sarah J. 2003. "Undisturbed Birth: Nature's Blueprint for Ease and Ecstasy." *Journal of Prenatal and Perinatal Psychology and Health* 7(4): 261-288.

Burst, Helen Varney. 1978. "Our Three-Ring Circus." *Journal of Nurse-Midwifery* Fall, 23: 13-14.

————.2010. "Nurse-Midwifery Self-Identification and Autonomy." *Journal of Midwifery & Women's Health* 55(5): 406-410.

Cahill, Alison G., Molly J. Stout and Aaron B. Caughey. 2010. "Intrapartum Magnesium for Prevention of Cerebral Palsy: Continuing Controversy?" *Current Opinion in Obstetrics and Gynecology* 22(2): 122-127.

Carson, Rachel. 2002[1962]. *Silent Spring.* New York: Houghton Mifflin.

Caton, Donald, Michael Frölich and Tammy Eullano. 2002. "Anesthesia for Childbirth: Controversy and Change." *American Journal of Obstetrics and Gynecology* 186(5): S25-S30.

Caughey, Aaron B. 2012. "Obstetric Ultrasound For Estimated Fetal Weight: Is the Information More Harm Than Benefit?" *American Journal of Obstetrics and Gynecology* 207(4): 239-240.

Center for Disease Control. 2012. "Births: Final Date for 2010." *National Vital Statistics Reports* 61(1).

————2013 "Pregnancy Mortality Surveillance System" www.cdc.gov/reproductivehealth/MaternalInfantHealth /PMSS.html.

Cesario, Sandra K. 2004. "Reevaluation of Friedman's Labor Curve: A Pilot Study." *Journal of Obstetric, Gynecologic and Neonatal Nursing* 33(6): 713-722.

Childbirth Connection. 2009. *Cesarean Section. Relentless Rise in Cesarean Section Rate.* Accessed 4.7.2009. childbirthconnection.org.

————.2011. *Facility Labor and Birth Charges by Site and Mode of Birth, United States, 2008-2010.* Accessed 4.16.201. childbirthconnection.org.

————.2012. *United States Maternity Care Facts and Figures."* December 2012. Accessed 1.3.2013. childbirthconnection.org.

Clark, Steven L., Michael A. Belfort, Spencer L. Byrum, Janet A. Meyers, and Jonathan B. Perlin. 2008. "Improved Outcomes, Fewer Cesarean Deliveries, and Reduced Litigation: Results Of A New Paradigm in Patient Safety." *American Journal of Obstetrics and Gynecology* 199(105): e1-7.

Clark, Steven, Kathleen Rice Simpson, Eric Knox and Thomas J. Garite. 2009. "Oxytocin: New Perspectives On An Old Drug." *American Journal of Obstetrics and Gynecology* 200(35): e1-6.

Cohen, Amy, Frederic Frigoletto, Janet Lang, Ellice Lieberman, Douglas Richardson and Steven Ringer. 1997. "Epidural Analgesia, Intrapartum Fever, and Neonatal Sepsis Evaluation." *Pediatrics* 99(3): 415-419.

Cohen, Nancy Wainer and Lois J. Esner. 1983. *Silent Knife: Cesarean Prevention and Vaginal Birth After Cesarean.* Massachusetts: Bergin & Garvey Publishers.

Comaroff, Jean and John Comaroff. 1991. *Of Revelation and Revolution, Volume 1. Christianity, Colonialism, and Consciousness in South Africa.* Chicago: University of Chicago Press.

Committee on Fetus and Newborn. 2012. "Levels of Neonatal Care." *Pediatrics* 130(3): 587-597.

Coulm, Benedicte, Camille Le Ray, Nathalie Lelong, Nicolas Drewniak, Jennifer Zeitlin and Beatric Blondel. 2012. "Obstetric Interventions for Low-Risk Pregnant Women in France: Do Maternity Unit Characteristics Make A Difference?" *Birth. Issues in Perinatal Care* 39(3): 183-191.

Cunningham, F. Gary, Norman F. Gant, Kenneth J. Leveno, Larry C. Gilstrap III, John C. Hauth and Katherine D. Wenstrom. 2001. *Williams Obstetrics 21st Edition.* New York: McGraw-Hill.

Dahlen, Hanna. 2006 "Midwifery: "At The Edge of History". *Women and Birth* 19(1): 3-10.

Davis-Floyd, Robbie. 1992. *Birth as an American Rite of Passage.* Berkeley: University of California Press.

Davis-Floyd, Robbie and Carolyn Sargent. 1997. "Introduction" In *Childbirth and Authoritative Knowledge. Cross-Cultural Perspectives.* eds. Robbie Davis-Floyd and Carolyn Sargent, 1-54. Berkeley: University of California Press.

Declercq, Eugene. 2009. "Births Attended by Certified Nurse-Midwives in the United States Reach an All-Time High: Trends from 1989 to 2006." *Journal of Midwifery and Women's Health* 54(3): 263-265.

————.2012. "Trends in Midwife-Attended Births in the United States, 1989-2009." *Journal of Midwifery and Women's Health* 57(4): 321-325.

————.2015. "Midwife-Attended Births in the United States, 1990-2012: Results from Revised Birth Certificate Data." *Journal of Midwifery and Women's Health* 60(1): 10-15.

Declercq, Eugene, Raymond DeVries, Kirsi Visainen Helga B. Salvesen and Sirpa Wrede. 2001. "Where to Give Birth? Politics and the Place of Birth." In *Birth By Design: Pregnancy, Maternity Care and Midwifery in North America and Europe.* eds. Raymond DeVries, Cecilia Benoit, Edwin van Teijlingen and Sirpa Wrede, 28-50. New York: Routledge Press.

Descolla, Phillipe and Gísli Pálsson. 1996. "Introduction" In *Nature and Society: Anthropological Perspectives.* eds. Phillipe Descolla and Gísla Pálsson, 1-22. New York: Routledge Press.

DeVries, Raymond. 2001. "Midwifery in the Netherlands: Vestige or Vanguard?" *Medical Anthropology* 20(4): 277-311.

————.2004a. *A Pleasing Birth. Midwives and Maternity Care in the Netherlands.* Philadelphia: Temple University Press.

————.2004b. "The Warp of Evidence-Based Medicine: Lessons From Dutch Maternity Care." *International Journal of Health Services* 34(4): 595-623.

DeVries, Raymond and Trudo Lemmens . 2006. "The Social and Cultural Shaping of Medical Evidence: Case Studies from Pharmaceutical Research and Obstetric Science." *Social Science & Medicine* 62(11): 2694-2706.

Diven, Liany C., Meredith L. Rochon, Julia Gogle, Sherrine Eid, John C. Smulian, and Joanne N. Quinoñnes. 2012. "Oxytocin Discontinuation During Active Labor In Women Who Undergo Labor Induction." *American Journal of Obstetrics and Gynecology* 207(47): e1-8.

Ehrenreich, Barbara and Deirdre English. 1973. *Witches, Midwives and Nurses. A History of Women Healers.* New York: The Feminist Press.

————.1978. *For Her Own Good. 150 Years of the Experts' Advice to Women.* Garden City, NY: Anchor Book.

Engels, Friedrich. 1884. *The Origin of the Family, Private Property and the State.* First published: October 1884 in Hottingen-Zurich.

Ernst, Eunice K. M. 1984. "Pioneering Interdependence in a System of Care for Childbearing Families." *Journal of Nurse-Midwifery* 29(5): 296-299.

Evans, Richard J. 2004. *The Coming of the Third Reich.* New York: Penguin Press.

Feldman, Ruth, Aron Weller, Orna Zagoory-Sharon and Ari Levine. 2007 "Evidence for a Neuroendocrinologial Foundation of Human Affiliation. Plasma Oxytocin Levels Across Pregnancy and the Postpartum Period Predict Mother-Infant Bonding." *Psychological Science* 18(11): 965-970.

Firestone, Shulamith. 1970. *The Dialectic of Sex. The Case for Feminist Revolution.* New York: William Morrow.

Forgacs, David. 2000[1988]. *The Antonio Gramsci Reader. Selected Writings 1916-1935.* New York: New York University Press.

Frankel, Richard M. and Kelly Devers. 2000. "Qualitative Research: A Consumer's Guide." *Education for Health* 13(1): 113-123.

Fraser, Gertrude J. 1995. "Modern Bodies, Modern Minds. Midwifery and Reproductive Change in an African American Community." In *Conceiving the New World Order. The Global Politics of Reproduction.* eds. Faye D. Ginsburg and Rayna Rapp, 42-58. Berkeley: University of California Press.

————.1998. *African America Midwifery in the South. Dialogues of Birth, Race, and Memory.* Cambridge, MA: Harvard University Press.

Friedman, Emanuel A. 1972. "An Objective Approach To The Diagnosis and Management of Abnormal Labor." *Bulletin of the New York Academy of Medicine* 48(6): 842-858.

Gabay, Mary and Sidney Wolfe. 1987. "Nurse-Midwifery: The Beneficial Alternative." *Public Health Reports* 112(5): 386-395.

————.1995a. *Encouraging the Use of Nurse-Midwives. A Report for Policymakers.* Washington DC: Public Citizen's Research Group.

————.1995b. *Unnecessary Cesarean Sections. Curing a National Epidemic.* Washington, DC: Public Citizens' Research Group

Gaskin, Ina May. 1975. *Spiritual Midwifery.* Summertown, TN: The Book Publishing Company.

Geertz, Clifford. 1973. *The Interpretation of Cultures.* New York: Basic Books.

Germano, Elaine. 2014 "Report Shows Progress Toward More Midwives." *Quickening: Official Newsletter of the American College of Nurse-Midwives 45(1): 22.*

Gilbert, C.L., J.A. Goode and T.J. McGrath. 1994. "Pulsatile Secretion of Oxytocin During Parturition in the Pig: Temporal Relationship With Fetal Expulsion." *Journal of Physiology* 475(1): 129-135.

Ginsburg, Faye and Rayna Rapp. 1991. "The Politics of Reproduction." *Annual Review of Anthropology 20: 311-343.*

————1995. "Introduction" In *Conceiving the New World Order: The Global Politics of Reproduction.* eds. Faye Ginsburg and Rayna Rapp, 1-18. Berkeley: University of California Press.

Goodman, Steffie. 2007. "Piercing the Veil: The Marginalization of Midwives in the United States." *Social Science and Medicine* 65(3): 610-621.

Gramsci, Antonio. 2005[1971]. *Selections From The Prison Notebooks.* London: Lawrence and Wishart Limited.

Gregory, Simon, Rebecca G. Anthopolos, Claire E. Osgood, Chad A. Grotegut and Marie Lynn Miranda. 2013. "Association of Autism With Induced or Augmented Childbirth in North Carolina Birth Record (1990-1998) and Education Research (1997-2007)." *JAMA Pediatrics* 167(10): 959-966.

Grimm, Elaine Ruth. 1967. *Childbearing: its social and Psychological aspects.* Eds. Stephen A. Richardson, and Alan Frank Guttmacher. Baltimore: Williams & Wilkins.

Guastella, Adam J., Stephen L. Ainfeld, Kylie M. Gray, Nicole J. Rinehrat, Bruce J. Tonge, Timothy J. Lambert, and Ian B. Hickie. 2010. "Intranasal Oxytocin Improves Emotional Recognition for Youth With Autism Spectrum Disorders." *Biological Psychiatry* 67(7): 692-694.

Haire, Doris. 1991. "Maternity Care and Outcomes in a High-Risk Service: the North Central Bronx Hospital Experience." *Birth* 18(1): 33-37.

————.1994. "Caution Needed With Labor Drugs." *Chicago Tribune*, July 24, 1994. Accessed 11.20.2016.. chicago.com /articles.chicagotribune.com/1997-07 24/features/9407240086_1_infant-brain-effects.

———.2000. *Improving The Outcome of Pregnancy Through Science.* Statement Given to the FDA Science Board. November 17, 2000.

———.2001. *FDA Approved Obstetrics Drugs: Their Effects On Mother and Baby.* Statement to the Committee on Maternal And Child Health. National Women's Health Alliance.

———.2005. *The National Children's Study As A Resource For Improving Maternal and Child Health.* Statement Given to the American Foundation for Maternal and Child Health. May 4, 2005.

Hamilton, Brady E., Joyce A. Martin and Stephanie J. Ventura. 2010. "2009 Births: Preliminary Data for 2009." *National Vital Statistics Report* 59(3):1-19. Hyattsville, MD: National Center for Vital Statistics. Centers for Disease Control.

Hamilton, Brady, Joyce Martin and Michele Osterman. 2016. "Births: Preliminary Data for 2015." *National Vital Statistics Report* 65(3): 1-13. Hyattsville, MD: National Center for Health Statistics. Centers for Disease Control.

Hartcollis, Anemona. 2013. "2 Hospital Networks Agree to Merge Raising Specter of Costlier Care." New York Times, July 16, 2013: A19.

Heisler, Elayne J. 2012. *The U.S. Infant Mortality Rate: International Comparisons, Underlying Factors, and Federal Programs.* Washington D.C: Congressional Research Service.

Heller, Gunther, Douglas K Richardson, Rainer Schnell, Bjorn Misselwitz, Wolfgang Kunzel and Stephan Schmidt. 2002. "Are We Regionalized Enough? Early-Neonatal Deaths in Low-Risk Births by the Size of Delivery Units *in Hesse, Germany 1990-1999."* *International Journal of Epidemiology* 31(5): 1061-1068.

Hindley, Carol and A.M. Thomson. 2005. "The Rhetoric of Informed Choice: Perspectives From Midwives On Intrapartum Fetal Heart Rate Monitoring." *Health Expectations : An International Journal of Public Participation In Health Care and Health Policy* 8(4): 306-314.

Hollander, Eric, Jennifer Bartz, William Chaplin, Ann Phillips, Jennifer Sumner, Latha Soorya, Evdokia Anagnostou, and Stacey Wasserman. 2007. "Oxytocin Increases Retention of Social Cognition in Autism." *Biological Psychiatry* 61(4): 498-503.

Holmstrom, Scott T. and Ciaran S. Phibbs. 2009. "Regionalization and Mortality in Neonatal Intensive Care." *Pediatric Clinics of North America* 56(3): 617-630.

Horlick-Jones, Tom and Jonathan Sime. 2004. "Living on the Border: Knowledge, Risk and Transdisciplinarity." *Futures* 36(4): 441-456.

Huber, Ulli, and Jane Sandall. 2009. "A Qualitative Exploration of The Creation of Calm in a Continuity of Care Model of Maternity Care in London." *Maternity* 25(6): 613-621.

Hughes, Samuel, Gershon Levinson and Mark Rosen. 2002. *Shnider and Levinson's Anesthesia for Obstetrics. Fourth Edition.* Philadelphia: Lippincott Williams & Wilkins.

Hunter, Billie, Marie Berg, Ingela Lundgren, Ôlöf Ásta Ólafdóttir, and Mavis Kirkham. 2008. "Relationships: The Hidden Threads in the Tapestry of Maternity." *Midwifery* 24(2): 132-137.

Illich, Ivan. 1976. *Medical Nemesis. The Expropriation of Health.* New York: Pantheon Books.

Institute for Safe Medication Practices (ISMP). 2012. *Results of ISMP Survey On High-Alert Medications: Differences Between Nursing, Pharmacy, And Risk/Quality/Safety Perspectives.* February 9, 2012. Accessed at www.ismp.org.

———2014. *ISMP List of High-Alert Medications in Acute Care Settings.* Accessed at www.ismp.org.

International Federation of Health Plans (IFHP). 2012. *International Federation of Health Plans. 2012 Comparative Price Report. Variation in Medical and Hospital Prices by Country.* husp.harvard.edu. Accessed 12.13.13

Johantgen, Meg, Lily Fountain, George Zangaro, Robin Newhouse, Julie Stanik-Hutt, and Kathleen White. 2012. "Comparison of Labor and Delivery Care Provided by Certified Nurse-Midwives and Physicians: A Systematic Review, 1990 to 2008." *Women's Health Issues* 22(1): e73-e81.

Jonas, W., L.M. Johansson, E. Nissen, M. Edjebäck, A.B. Ransjö Arvidson, and K. Uvnäs-Moberg. 2009. "Effects of Intrapartum Oxytocin Administration and Epidural Analgesia on the Concentration of Plasma Oxytocin and Prolactin, in Response to Suckling During the Second Day Postpartum." *Breastfeeding Medicine* 4(2): 71-82.

Jordan, Brigitte. 1993[1978]. *Birth in Four Cultures. A Crosscultural Investigation of Childbirth in Yucatan, Holland, Sweden, and the United States. Fourth Edition.* Prospect Heights, Illinois: Waveland Press, Inc.

Keating, Annete and Valerie E. M. Fleming. 2007. "Midwives' Experiences of Facilitating Normal Birth in an Obstetric-Led Unit: A Feminist Perspective." *Midwifery* 25(5): 518-527.

Kennedy, Holly Powell. 2000. "A Model of Exemplary Midwifery Practice: Results of a Delphi Study." *Journal of Midwifery and Women's Health* 45(1): 4-19.

———2002. "The Midwife as an "Instrument" of Care." *American Journal of Public Health* 92(11): 1759-1760.

————.2006. "Student Perceptions of Ideal and Actual Midwifery Practice." *Journal of Midwifery and Women's Health* 51(2): 71-77.

————.2010. "The Problem of Normal Birth." *Journal of Midwifery and Women's Health* 55(3): 199-201.

King, Teko. 1997. "Epidural Anesthesia in Labor. Benefits Versus Risks." *Journal of Nurse-Midwifery* 42(5): 377-388.

Khawaja, Marwan, Rozzett Jurdi, and Tamar Kabakian-Khashoian. 2004. "Rising Trends in Cesarean Section Rates in Egypt." *Birth* (3)1: 12-16.

Kondo, Dorinne K. 1990. *Crafting Selves, Power, Gender, and Discourses of Identity in a Japanese Workplace.* Chicago: The University of Chicago Press.

Konner, Melvin and Marjorie Shostak. 1987. "Timing and Management of Birth Among the !Kung: Bioculture Interaction in Reproductive Adaptation." *Cultural Anthropology.* 2(1): 11-28.

Kukulu, Kamile and Hafize Demirok. 2008. "Effects of Epidural Anesthesia on Labor Progress." *Pain Management Nursing* 9(1): 10-16.

Laurer, Jeremy A., Ana P. Betrán, Mario Merialdi and Daniel Wojdyla. 2010. "Determinants of Caesarean Section Rates in Developed Countries: Supply, Demand and Opportunities for Control." *World Health Report Background Paper, No. 29.* World Health Organization.

Lawrence, H.C., J.A. Copel, D.F. O'Keeffe, W.C. Bradford, P.K. Scarrow, H.P. Kennedy and C.R. Olden. 2012. "Quality Patient Care In Labor and Delivery: A Call To Action." *American Journal of Obstetrics and Gynecology* 4(1): 147-148.

Leavitt, Judith Walzer. 1983. "Science Enters the Birthing Room: Obstetrics in America Since the Eighteenth Century." *The Journal of American History* 70(2): 281-301.

———1986. *Brought to Bed: Childbearing In America 1750 to 1950.* New York: Oxford University Press.

Leighton, Barbara L. and Stephen H. Halpern. 2002. "The Effects of Epidural Analgesia On Labor, Maternal, and Neonatal Outcomes: A Systematic Review." *American Journal of Obstetrics and Gynecology* 186(5): s69-s77.

Lieberman, Ellice, Janet Lang, Frederic Frigoletto Jr., Douglas Richardson, Steven Ringer and Amy Cohen. 1997. "Epidural Analgesia, Intrapartum Fever and Neonatal Sepsis Evaluation." *Pediatrics* 99(3): 415-419.

Lieberman, Elice, Janet Lang, Douglas Richardson, Fredric Frigoletto, Linda Heffner and Amy Cohen. 2000. "Intrapartum Maternal Fever and Neonatal Outcome." *Pediatrics* 105(8): 8-13.

Lieberman, Elice and Carol O'Donoghue. 2002. Unintended Effects of Epidural Analgesia During Labor: A Systematic Review." *American Journal of Obstetrics and Gynecology* 186: S31-68.

Liu, Shiliang, Robert M. Liston, K.S. Joseph, Maureen Haman, Reg Sauve, and Michael S. Kramer. 2007. "Maternal Mortality and Severe Morbidity Associated with Low-Risk Planned Cesarean Delivery vs. Planned Vaginal Delivery At Term." *Canadian Medical Association Journal* 176(4): 455-460.

Lo, Evelyn, Lindsay Nicolle, David Classen, Kathleen Arias, Kelly Podgorny, Deverck Anderson, Helen Burstin, David Calfee, Susan Coffin, Erik Dubberke, Victoria Fraser, Dale Gerding, Frances Griffin, Peter Gross, Keith Kaye, Michael Klompas, Jonas Marschall, Leonard Mermel, David Pegues, Tish Perl, Sanjay Saint, Cassandra Salgado, Robert Weinstein, Robert Wise, and Deborah Yokoe.

2008. "Strategies to Prevent Catheter-Associated Urinary Tract Infections in Acute Care Hospitals." *Infection Control and Hospital Epidemiology* 29(S1): S41-S50.

Low, Lisa Kane. 2016. *Recruitment for 2017 Reducing Primary Cesareans Learning Collaborative.* An email from the ACNM President. Sent to ACNM membership, dated July 29, 2016.

MacDorman, Marian F. and Gopal K. Singh. 1998. "Midwifery Care, Social and Medical Risk Factors, and Birth Outcomes in the USA." *Journal of Epidemiology and Community Health* 52(5): 310-317.

MacDorman, Marian, Donna Hoyert and T.J. Mathews. 2013. "Recent Declines in Infant Mortality in the United States, 2005-2011." *NCHS Data Brief, no 120.* Hyattsville, MD: National Center for Health Statistics.

MacDorman MF, Mathews TJ, Mohangoo AD, Zeitlin J. 2014. "International Comparisons of Infant Mortality and Related Factors: United States and Europe, 2010." *National Vital Statistics Reports*; (63)5: 1-7. Hyattsville, MD: National Center for Health Statistics.

Magann, Everett F. Suneet P. Chauhan, Dorota A. Doherty, Marcia I. Magann, and John C. Morrison. 2007. "The Evidence For Abandoning the Amniotic Fluid Index in Favor of the Single Deepest Pocket." *American Journal of Perinatology* 24(9): 549-555.

Mann, R.J. 1981. "San Francisco General Hospital Nurse-Midwifery Practice: The Fist Thousand Births." *American Journal of Obstetrics and Gynecology* 140(6): 676-682.

Marcus, George E. 2009. "Introduction: Notes Toward An Ethnographic Memoir of Supervising Graduate Research Through Anthropology's Decades of Transformation." In *Fieldwork Is Not What It Used To Be: Learning Anthropology's Method in a Time of*

Transition. eds. James D. Faubion and George E. Marcus, 2-31. Ithaca, NY: Cornell University Press.

Martin, Emily. 2001[1987]. *The Woman in the Body. A Cultural Analysis of Reproduction.* Boston: Beacon Press.

Martin JA, Hamilton BE, Osterman MJK. 2014. "Births in the United States, 2013." *NCHS Data Brief*, December (175), 1-8. Hyattsville, MD: National Center for Health Statistics.

May, Maureen. 1996. "Care and Cure: Midwifery and Obstetrics. Nurse-Midwifery on the Margins." Paper presented at the 36th Northeastern Anthropological Association Meetings. Plymouth State College. Plymouth, New Hampshire, March 27-30, 1996.

————.1998. "Midwifery and the Homebirth Movement in New York State." Paper presented at the First Annual Symposium On Midwifery Research in the Social Science and Humanities, University of Toronto. Institute for Studies in Education, April 18, 1998.

————.1999. "Midwifery in New York State: Identity, Power and Politics." Paper presented at the American Anthropological Association Annual Conference, Chicago, Illinois. Paper presented for the Panel Session, "Daughters of Time: The Shifting Identities of Postmodern Midwives." Session organizers: Robbie Davis-Floyd and Sheila Cominsky.

————.2000. "The 1992 New York Professional Midwifery Practice Act: Its Impact on Homebirth and American Midwifery." Paper presented at The Fourth International Homebirth Conference. Amsterdam, Netherlands, March 2000.

————.2007. "When Traditional Notions Encroach on Midwifery: The Paradox of American Nurse-Midwifery." Paper presented at the joint CASCA-AES Conference. May 2007, Toronto.

————.2009. "The Duality of American of Nurse-Midwifery – A Cultural Analysis." Paper presented at the joint CASCA-AES Conference. May, 2009. Vancouver, British Columbia.

————.2014. "Turning the Board Blue: America's Epiduralized System of Birth." Presented at the Society of Applied Anthropology. Albuquerque, NM. March 18, 2014.

————.2014. "Turing the Board Blue: America's Epiduralized System of Birth. A Medical Ethnography." Phd diss., Syracuse University, December 2014.

May, Maureen and Robbie Davis-Floyd. 2006. "Idealism and Pragmatism in the Creation of the Certified Midwife: The Development of Midwifery in New York and the New York Midwifery Practice Act of 1992." In *Mainstreaming Midwives. The Politics of Change.* eds. Robbie Davis-Floyd and Christine Barbara Johnson, 82-161. New York: Routledge Press.

McLachlan, Beverly K., Patricia M. Rouse, Margaret A. Baines, Peter W. Jones, Jeremy C. Wyatt and Richard B. Johanson. 2000. "A Randomised Study of Midwifery Caseload Care and Traditional 'Shared-Care'." *Midwifery* 16(4): 295-302.

McLafferty, Sara. 1982. "Neighborhood Characteristics and Hospital Closures. A Comparison of the Public, Private and Voluntary Hospital Systems." *Social Science of Medicine* 16(19): 1667-1674.

————1986. "The Geographical Restructuring of Urban Hospitals: Spatial Dimensions of Corporate Strategy." *Social Science of Medicine* 22(10): 1079-1086.

Mischel, Laurence, Jared Berstein and Sylvia Allegretto. 2007. "The State of Working America 2006/2007." Washington D.C.: The Economic Policy Institute.

Mitford, Jessica. 1992. *The American Way Of Birth*. Collingdale, PA: Diane Publishing Co.

Moberg, Kerstin Uvnäs. 2003. *The Oxytocin Factor. Tapping The Hormone of Calm, Love and Healing*. Cambridge, MA:Da Capo Press.

Morsy, Soheir A. 1995. "Deadly Reproduction Among Egyptian Women: Maternal Mortality and the Medicalization of Population Control." In *Conceiving the New World. The Global Politics of Reproduction.* eds. Faye D. Ginsburg and Rayna Rapp, 162-176. Berkeley: University of California Press.

Morton, Christine. 2009. "Where Are the Ethnographies of US Hospital Birth?" *Anthropology News* March, 2009, 10-11.

Moster, Dag, Rolv Terje Lie and Trond Markestad. 1999. "Relation Between Size of Delivery Unit and Neonatal Death in Low-Risk Deliveries: Population Based Study." *Archives of Disease in Childhood, Fetal and Neonatal Edition* 80(3): F221-F225.

————2001. "Neonatal Mortality Rates in Communities with Small Maternity Units Compared With Those Having Larger Maternity Units." *British Journal of Obstetrics an Gynaecology* 108(9): 904-909.

Murray, Ann D., Robyn M. Dolby, Roger L. Nation and David Thomas. 1981. "Effects of Epidural Anesthesia on Newborns and Their Mothers." *Child Development* 52(1): 71-82.

Namey, Emily E. and Anne Drapkin Lyerly. 2010. "The Meaning of "Control" for Childbearing Women in the U.S." *Social Science and Medicine* 71(4): 769-776.

NIH: National Institute of Health. 2010. "Vaginal Birth After Cesarean: New Insights. Final Panel Statement." NIH Consensus Development Conference on Vaginal Birth After Cesarean. Bethesda, Maryland. March 8-10, 2010.

Newton, Niles. 1966a. "Parturient Mice: Effect of Environment On Labor." *Science* 151(3717): 1560-1561.

——.1966b. "Experimental Inhibition of Labor Through Environmental Disturbance." *Obstetrics and Gynecology* 27(3): 371-377.

——.1987. "The Fetus Ejection Reflex Revisited." *Birth* 14(2): 106-108.

Oakley, Ann. 1980. *Women Confined. Towards a Sociology of Childbirth.* New York: Shocken Books.

——.1980a. "Interviewing Women: A Contradiction in Terms." In *Doing Feminist Research.* ed. Helen Roberts, 30- 61. London: Routledge Press.

——.1986[1984]. *The Captured Womb. A History of the Medical Care of Pregnant Women.* Oxford, UK: Basil Blackwell.

——.1992. *Social Support and Motherhood. The Natural History of a Research Project.* Oxford, UK: Blackwell Publishers.

Odent, Michel. 1984. *Birth Reborn.* Medford, NJ: Birth Works Press.

——.1987. "The Fetus Ejection Reflex." *Birth* 14(2): 104-105.

——.2001. "New Reasons and New Way To Study Birth Physiology." *International Journal of Gynecology & Obstetrics* 75: S39-S45.

——.2002. *The Farmer and the Obstetrician.* New York: Free Association Books.

——.2006. "Fetus Ejection Reflex and the Art of Midwifery." WombEcology.com. Accessed on 12.12.13.

———.2007. "The Autism Epidemic." *Midwifery Today E-News* 9(11) May 23, 2007.

OECD: Organization for Economic Co-Operation and Development. 2011. "Health at a Glance 2011: OECD Indicators." Paris: OECD Publishing. dx.doi.org.

———2013 "Health At a Glance 2013. OECD Indicators" Paris: OECD Publishing.

Ortner, Sherry B. 1972. "Is Female to Male as Nature is to Culture." *Feminist Studies* 1(2): 5-31.

Osterman, Michelle and Joyce A. Martin. 2011. "Epidural and Spinal Anesthesia Use During Labor: 27-State Reporting Area, 2008." *National Vital Statistics Reports* 59(5): 1-14. Hyattsville, MD: National Center for Health Statistics.

———.2014. "Recent Declines in Induction of Labor by Gestational Age." *NCHS Data Brief, no 155.* Hyattsville, MD: National Center for Health Statistics.

Papiernik, Emole and Louis G. Keith. 1995. "The Regionalization of Perinatal Care in France – Description of a Missing Policy." *European Journal of Obstetrics and Gynecology and Reproductive Biology* 61(2): 99-103.

Perkins, Barbara Bridgman. 2004. *The Medical Delivery Business: Health Reform, Childbirth, and the Economic Order.* New Brunswick, NJ: Rutgers University Press.

Pew Health Professions Commission and the University of California, San Francisco Center for the Health Professions. 1999. *Charting A Course For the Twenty-First Century: The Future of Midwifery.* San Francisco: The University of California, San Francisco.

Phibbs, Claran. 2002. "Commentary: Does Patient Volume Matter for Low-Risk Deliveries?" *International Journal of Epidemiology* 31(5): 1069-1070.

Podulka, Jennifer, Elizabeth Stranages and Claudia Steiner. 2011. "Hospitalizations Related to Childbirth, 2008. Statistical Brief #110 The Health care Cost and Utilization Project." Agency for Health care Research and Quality. U.S. Depart of Health and Human Services.

Prasad, Mona R. and Edmund Funai. 2012. "Oxytocin Use During Active Labor: Too Much Of A Good Thing? *American Journal of Obstetrics and Gynecology* 207(6): 439-440.

Prentice, A. and T. Lind. 1987. "Fetal Heart Rate Monitoring During Labour—Too Frequent Intervention, Too Little Benefit?" *The Lancet* 330(8572): 1375-1377.

Rahm, Vivi-Ann, A. Hallgren, H. Hogeberg, I. Hurtig and V. Odlind. 2002. "Plasma Oxytocin Levels in Women During Labor With or Without Epidural Analgesia: A Prospective Study." *Acta Obstet Gynecol Scand* 81(11): 1033-1039.

Rapp, Rayna. 1997. "Forward." In *Childbirth and Authoritative Knowledge.* eds. Robbie Davis-Floyd and Carolyn Sargent, xi-xii. Berkeley: University of California Press.

Reynolds, Felicity. 2009. "The Effects of Maternal Labour Analgesia On The Fetus: Best Practice & Research." *Clinical Obstetrics and Gynecology* 24(3): 289-302.

Riessman, Catherine Kohler. 1998. "The Politics of Women's Bodies." In *The Politics of Women's Bodies. Sexuality, Appearance and Behavior.* ed. Rose Weitz, 46-63. New York: Oxford University Press.

Rissenberg, Marian. 2010. "Pitocin and Autism Spectrum Disorder." (Unpublished Manuscript.)

Roberts, Joyce and Lisa Hanson. 2007. "Best Practices in Second Stage Labor Care: Maternal Bearing Down and Positioning." *Journal of Midwifery and Women's Health* 52(3): 238-245.

Rodgers, Caroline C. and Kim J. Cox. 2013. "The Case Against Early Term Elective Induction." *Journal of Midwifery and Women's Health* 58(2): 126-129.

Robinson, Christopher J., Margaret S. Villers, Donna D. Johnson and Kit N. Simpson. 2010. "Timing of Elective Repeat Cesarean Delivery at Term and Neonatal Outcomes: A Cost Analysis." *American Journal of Obstetrics and Gynecology* 202(6):632: e1-632.e6.

Rooks, Judith P. 1984. " Supporting Nurse-Midwifery in a Changing World: Institutionalizing a Support Structure and Identifying Bases of Support." *Journal of Nurse-Midwifery* 29(5): 289-295.

————.1997. *Midwifery and Childbirth in America*. Philadelphia: Temple University Press.

————.2007. "Use of Nitrous Oxide in Midwifery Practice— Complementary, Synergistic, and Needed in the United States." *Journal of Midwifery and Women's Health* 52(3): 186-189.

————2009. "Oxytocin As A "High Alert Medication": A Multilayered Challenge to the Status Quo." *Birth* 36(4): 345-348.

Rosaldo, Renato. 1993[1989]. *Culture and Truth. The Remaking of Social Analysis.* Boston, MA: Beacon Press.

Rosenblatt, Roger A., Judith Reinen and Phil Shoemack. 1985. "Is Obstetrics Safe in Small Hospitals. Evidence From New Zealand's Regionalised Perinatal System." *Lancet* 326(8452): 429-432.

Rosenblatt, Roger A., Sharon A. Dobie, L. Gary Hart, Ronald Schneeweiss, Debra Gould, Tina R. Raine, Thomas J. Benedetti, Michael J. Pirani and Edward B. Perrin. 1997. "Differences in The Obstetric Care of Low-Risk Women." *American Journal of Public Health* 87(3): 344-351.

Rothman, Barbara Katz. 1982. *In Labor: Women and Power in The Birthplace.* New York: W.W. Norton.

———.1983. "Childbirth Management and Medical Monopoly: Midwifery as (Almost) A Profession." *Journal of Nurse-Midwifery* 29(5): 300-306.

———.2000. *The Tentative Pregnancy: Prenatal Diagnosis and the Future of Motherhood.* New York: Viking Press.

Sandall, Jane. 1997. "Midwives" Burnout and Continuity of Care." *British Journal of Midwifery* 5(2): 106-111.

Sandall, Jane, Marie Haatem, Declan Devane, Hora Soltani and Simon Gates. 2009. "Discussion of Findings From A Cochrane Review of Midwife-Led Versus Other Models of Care for Childbearing Women: Continuity, Normality and Safety." *Midwifery* 25(1): 8-13.

Sandall, Jane, Declan Devane, Hora Soltani, Marie Hatem and Simon Gates. 2010. "Improving Quality and Safety in Maternity Care: The Contribution of Midwife-Led Care." *Journal of Midwifery & Women's Health* 55(3): 255-261.

Sandall, Jane, Rona McCandish and Debra Bick. 2012. "Place of Birth." *Midwifery* 28(5): 547.

Sartwelle, Thomas P. 2012. "Electronic Fetal Monitoring. A Bridge Too Far." *Journal of Legal Medicine* 33(3): 313-379.

Schuiling, Kerry, Theresa A. Sipe and Judith Fullerton. 2013. "Findings From The American College of Nurse-Midwives' Membership Surveys: 2009-2011." *Journal of Midwifery and Women's Health* 58(4): 404-415.

Scott, James C. 1985. *Weapons of the Weak. Everyday Forms of Peasant Resistance.* New Haven: Yale University Press.

————.1990. *Domination and the Arts of Resistance. Hidden Transcripts.* New Haven: Yale University Press.

Sharp, Elizabeth and Lizabeth Lewis. 1984. "A Decade of Nurse-Midwifery Practice in a Tertiary University-Affiliated Hospital." *Journal of Nurse-Midwifery* 29(6): 353-364.

Shnider, Sol and Gersho Levinson. 1979. *Anesthesia for Obstetrics.* Baltimore: Williams & Wilkins.

————.1987. *Anesthesia for Obstetrics. Second Edition.* Baltimore: Williams & Wilkins.

Shonick, William. 1979. "The Public Hospital and its Local Ecology in the United States." *International Journal of Health Services* 9(3): 359-396.

Shostak, Marjorie. 1983[1981]. *Nisa. The Life and Words of a !Kung Women.* New York: Vintage Books.

Simkin, Penny and Ruth Ancheta. 2011. *The Labor Progress Handbook. Early Interventions To Prevent and Treat Dystocia. Third Edition.* Chichester, UK: Wiley-Blackwell.

Simonds, Wendy, Barbara Katz Rothman, and Bari Meltzer Norman. 2006. *Laboring On: Birth in Transition in the United States.* New York, NY: Routledge Press.

Simpson, Kathleen Rice. 2011. "Clinicians' Guide to the Use of Oxytocin for Labor Induction and Augmentation." *Journal of Midwifery & Women's Health* 56(3): 214-221.

Sng, BL, WL Leong, Y Zeng, FJ Siddiqui, PN Assam, Y Lim, ESY Chan, AT Sia. 2014. "Early versus Late Initiation of Epidural Analgesia for Labour." *Cochrane Database of Systematic Review Issue 10*, 1-79.

Snowden, Jonathan M., Yvonne W. Cheng, Caitlin P. Kontgis, Aaron B. Caughey. 2012. "The Association Between Hospital Obstetric Volume and Perinatal Outcomes in California." *American Journal of Obstetrics and Gynecology* 207(6): 478e1-478e7.

Stapleton, Susan Rutledge, Cara Osborne, Jessica Illuzzi. 2013. "Outcomes of Care in Birth Centers: Demonstration of a Durable Model." *Journal of Midwifery and Women's Health* 58(1): 3-14.

Starr, Paul. 1982. *The Social Transformation of American Medicine: The Rise of a Sovereign Profession and the Making of a Vast Industry.* New York: Basic Books.

Summerlee, A.J. 1981. "Extracellular Recordings from Oxytocin Neurons During the Expulsive Phase of Birth in Unanaesthetized Rats." *Journal of Physiology* 321(1): 1-9.

Suresh, Maya, Scott Segal, Roanne Preston, Roshan Fernando and C. LaToya Mason. 2013. *Shnider and Levinson's Anesthesia for Obstetrics. Fifth Edition.* Philadelphia: Lippincott Wiliams &Wilkins.

Taylor, Charles. 2007. *A Secular Age.* Cambridge and London: Harvard University Press.

Teasley, Regi. 1983. *Birth and the Division of Labor: The Movement to Professionalize Nurse-Midwifery and Its Relationship To The Movement for Home Birth and Lay Midwifery. A Case Study of Vermont.* Unpublished PhD Dissertation. Michigan State University.

Tenmore, Josie L. 2003. "Methods for Cervical Ripening and Induction of Labor." *American Family Physician* 67(10): 2123-2128.

Thompson, Joyce E. 1984. "Professional Maturity or Independence." *Journal of Nurse-Midwifery* 29(5): 307-310.

Thompson, Lindsay, David Goodman and George Little. 2002. "Is More Neonatal Intensive Care Always Better? Insights From a Cross-National Comparison of Reproductive Care." *Pediatrics* 109(6): 1036-1043.

Tracy, Sally K., Elizabeth Sullivan, Hannah Dahlen Deborah Black, Yueping Alex Wang, and Mark B. Tracy. 2006. "Does Size Matter? A Population-Based Study of Birth in Lower Volume Maternity Hospitals for Low-Risk Women." *British Journal of Obstetrics and Gynecology* 113(1): 86-96.

Trevathan, Wenda. 1987. *Human Birth. An Evolutionary Perspective.* New York: Aldine De Gruyter.

———.1997. An Evolutionary Perspective on Authoritative Knowledge about Birth. In Childbirth and Authoritative Knowledge. Cross Cultural Perspectives. eds. Robbie Davis-Floyd and Carolyn Sargent, 80-88. Berkeley: University of California Press.

Truven Health Analytics. 2013. *The Cost of Having a Baby in the United States. Executive Summary.* Childbirth Connection and The Catalyst for Payment Reform Center for Health care Quality and Payment Reform.

Van Hollen, Cecilia. 2003. *Birth on the Threshold. Childbirth and Modernity in South India.* Berkeley: University of California Press.

Van Wagner, V., Epoo, B., Nastapoka, J. and Harney, E. 2007. "Reclaiming Birth, Health, and Community: Midwifery in the Inuit Villages of Nunavik, Canada." *Journal of Midwifery & Women's Health* 52(4): 384–391.

Vincent, Peggy. 2003. *Baby Catcher: Chronicles of a Modern Midwife.* New York: Scribner Press.

Visweswaran, Kamala. 1994. *Fictions of Feminist Ethnography.* Minneapolis: University of Minnesota Press.

Wahl, R. U. R. 2004. "Could Oxytocin Administration During Labor Contribute to Autism and Related Behavioral Disorders?–A Look at the Literature." *Medical Hypotheses* 63(3): 456-460.

Waldenström, Ulla and Deborah Turnball. 1998. "A Systematic Review Comparing Continuity of Midwifery Care With Standard Maternity Services." *British Journal of Obstetrics and Gynecology* 105(11): 1160-117.

Wagner, Marsden. 2006. *Born In the USA: How a Broken Maternity System Must Be Fixed to Put Women and Children First.* Berkeley: University of California Press.

Walsh, Denis. 2006a. " 'Nesting and "Matrescence' as Distinctive Features of a Freestanding Birth Centre in the UK." *Midwifery* 22(3): 228-239.

———.2006b. "Subverting the Assembly-Line: Childbirth in a Freestanding Birth Centre." *Social Science of Medicine* 62(6): 1330-1340.

———.2009. "Small Really Is Beautiful." In *Birth Models That Work.* eds. Robbie Davis-Floyd, Lesley Barclay, Betty-Anne Daviss and Jan Tritten, 159-186. Berkeley: University of California Press.

Weeks, John 2012. "Homebirth Midwives and the Hospital Goliath: Evidence Builds for Disruptive Innovation." Huffington Post. Posted March, 20 2012.

Wertz, Richard W. and Dorothy C. Wertz. 1989[1977]. *Lying In. A History of Childbirth in America.* New Haven: Yale University Press.

Wester, Mary and LeRoy Krumperman. 1958. "Anesthesia and Analgesia." *Clinical Obstetrics and Gynecology* 1(4): 977-986.

Weston, Kath. 2000. "The Virtual Anthropologist." In *Is Academic Feminism Dead? Theory in Practice.* The Social Justice Group at The Center for Advanced Feminist Studies, 137-138. New York: New York University Press.

Whitney, Simon N, Amy L. McGuire and Laurence B. McCullough. 2003. "A Typology of Shared Decision Making, Informed Consent, and Simple Consent." *Annals of Internal Medicine* 140(1): 54-59.

World Health Organization. 2006. *Neonatal and Perinatal Mortality. Country, Regional and Global Estimates.* Geneva: WHO Press.

Zhang, Jun, James Troendle and Michael K. Yancey. 2002. Reassessing the Labor Curve in Nulliparous Women. *American Journal of Obstetrics and Gynecology* 187(4): 824-828.

Zhang, Jun, Helain J. Landy, D. Ware Branch, Ronald Burkman, Shoshana Haberman, Kimberly Gregory, Christos Hatjis, Mildred Ramirez, Jennifer Bailit, Victor Gonzalez-Quintero, Judith Hibbard, Matthew Hoffman, Michelle Kominiarek, Lee Learman, Paul Van Veldhuisen, James Troendle and Uma Reddy. 2010. "Contemporary Patterns of Spontaneous Labor with Normal Neonatal Outcomes." *Obstetrics & Gynecology* 116(6):1281-1287.

Zhao, Lan. 2007. *Why Are Fewer Hospitals in the Delivery Business?* Chicago & Bethesda, Maryland: Walsh Center for Rural Health Analysis and NORC—Health Policy and Evaluation Division at University of Chicago.

Zimmer, Etan Z., Peter Jakobi, Joseph Itskovitz-Eldor, Boris Weizman, Ido Solt, Aldo Glik, and Zeev Weiner. 2000. "Adverse Effects of Epidural Analgesia in Labor." *European Journal of Obstetrics & Gynecology and Reproductive Biology* 89(2): 153-157.

Index

Made in the USA
Columbia, SC
18 May 2018